America's Best Recipes

A 1991 HOMETOWN COLLECTION

America's Best Recipes

Oxmoor House®

©1991 by Oxmoor House, Inc.
Book Division of Southern Progress Corporation
P.O. Box 2463, Birmingham, Alabama 35201

ISBN: 0-8487-1054-1
ISSN: 0898-9982

Manufactured in the United States of America
First Printing 1991

Executive Editor: Ann H. Harvey
Director of Manufacturing: Jerry R. Higdon
Production Manager: Rick Litton
Art Director: Bob Nance

America's Best Recipes: A 1991 Hometown Collection

Editor: Janice L. Krahn
Senior Foods Editor: Margaret Chason Agnew
Copy Chief: Mary Ann Laurens
Editorial Coordinator: Kay Hicks
Editorial Assistant: Kelly E. Hooper
Director, Test Kitchen: Vanessa Taylor Johnson
Assistant Director, Test Kitchen: Gayle Hays Sadler
Test Kitchen Home Economists: Caroline Alford, R.D.,
 Telia Johnson, Angie C. Neskaug, Christina A. Pieroni,
 Kathleen Royal, Jan A. Smith
Senior Photographer: Jim Bathie
Photographer: Ralph Anderson
Photo Stylist: Kay E. Clarke
Senior Designer: Cynthia Rose Cooper
Designer: Melissa Jones Clark
Associate Production Manager: Theresa L. Beste
Production Assistant: Pam Beasley Bullock

Project Consultants: Meryle Evans, Audrey P. Stehle

Cover photograph by Ralph Anderson
Illustrations by Dana Moore

Cover: *America celebrates its heritage with Pasta Primavera (page 34), Prosciutto Bread (page 77), and Almond-Anise Biscotti (page 36).*

Frontispiece: *The* Mark Twain *riverboat on the Mississippi River in Hannibal, Missouri.*

Oxmoor House, Inc., is also the publisher of *Cooking Light* books. For subscription information for *Cooking Light* magazine, write to *Cooking Light*®, P.O. Box C-549, Birmingham, Alabama 35283.

Contents

Introduction

America's Best Recipes - A 1991 Hometown Collection celebrates our country's rich culinary heritage and the hometown cooks who make America's cuisine a national treasure. By sharing the foods and traditions that are meaningful to them, these spirited volunteers from towns and cities across the country help meet the varied needs of their communities. They offer us regional American cooking at its best and, at the same time, help preserve the unique history of their communities.

Our food writers chose a blend of traditional and contemporary recipes from community cookbooks from every state in the nation. Over six hundred recipes were rigorously tested, judged, and rated by our staff of professional home economists. Only those recipes that received superlative ratings and met our high standards were included in this volume. The result is *America's Best Recipes*—a collection of over four hundred recipes that represent outstanding hometown favorites from across America.

American cookery has been shaped through the generations by the ethnic backgrounds of its citizens. To celebrate the culinary bond between the past and the present, we have focused attention on the contribution of eight ethnic groups to America's melting pot cuisine in a special chapter. Recipes were selected not just from specific ethnic group sponsored cookbooks, but from a wide variety of community cookbooks that reflect the culinary heritage of the people of their communities. Featured recipes range from appetizers to desserts so that you can enjoy a complete ethnic food experience.

We invite you to review the Acknowledgments beginning on page 324 and order other cookbooks that may be of interest to you. In this way, you will contribute to the fund-raising efforts of the organizations responsible for creating the fascinating community cookbooks featured in *America's Best Recipes - A 1991 Hometown Collection.*

The Editors

America
Celebrates
Its Heritage

A gift from the people of France to the people of the United States in 1886, the Statue of Liberty stands in the New York City Harbor as the world's symbol of freedom. The engineering for the flexible iron frame which supports the statue was created by Gustave Eiffel, designer of the Eiffel Tower in Paris.

America Celebrates Its Heritage

"Give me your tired, your poor, /Your huddled masses yearning to breathe free " reads Emma Lazarus's inspirational poem inscribed on the base of the Statue of Liberty. The impressive copper statue stands on Liberty Island in New York harbor, across from Ellis Island, as the world's symbol of freedom. Between 1892 and 1954, more than 17 million immigrants from around the world came in search of a new life for themselves, taking their first step on American soil at the processing center on Ellis Island. Coming to America seemed like a once-in-a-lifetime opportunity to escape the problems plaguing one's native country. Many arrived without employment, skills, or the ability to speak English, but they did have pride, determination, and the dream of a new and better life.

Gradually the immigrants settled in areas across the country where they were certain they could find work. New Americans of similar origins tended to live together in well-defined communities where they transplanted their culture and food traditions. As they coped with the realities of starting over in a foreign land, the common bond of language and custom offered reassurance. While eager to adapt themselves to life in America, they found that they could not find the ingredients to prepare their favorite dishes. They were forced to improvise with the unfamiliar ingredients that America had to offer and, consequently, created new recipes that slowly became part of America's cuisine.

We have chosen to explore the cooking heritage of eight immigrant groups, and invite you to try the recipes on the following pages with the same spirit of adventure with which immigrants approached a new life in America.

British Cuisine

The peak year for English immigration to America occurred in 1888. Many came to work in the copper, iron, and lead mines in Wisconsin, Illinois, and Michigan. They brought with them the Cornish pasty, a savory mixture of meat, potatoes, and vegetables wrapped in pastry, designed to give miners a warm, nourishing meal at the bottom of a mine shaft. Miners reheated the pasties on shovels held over the candles they wore on their mining hats. Other British dishes introduced to Americans included mulligatawny soup, steak and kidney pie, beef with Yorkshire pudding, fish and chips, trifle, syllabub, and lemon curd tarts.

Between 1820 and 1920, over 4 million Irish immigrated to the United States. Immigrants came to work in northeastern cities in jobs in industry, construction, politics, the priesthood, and law enforcement. The Irish gave America such dishes as Irish soda bread, Irish stew, corned beef, and Irish coffee.

From 1921 to 1931, a severe economic depression caused more than 391,000 people to leave Scotland. The immigrants turned to work in mines and textile mills. Scottish immigrants brought with them a taste for Scotch broth, cock-a-leekie soup, hearty stews, oatmeal-based breads, shortbread, and Scotch whiskey.

Syllabub

1 cup Chablis or other dry
   white wine
¼ cup brandy
1 tablespoon lemon juice

¼ cup sugar
2 cups whipping cream,
   whipped

Combine wine, brandy, lemon juice, and sugar, stirring until sugar dissolves. Add whipped cream, stirring until well blended. Spoon mixture into stemmed goblets, and serve immediately. Yield: 5½ cups.

Bound to Please
The Junior League of Boise, Idaho

Cock-a-Leekie-Soup

5 cups water
½ cup pearl barley, uncooked
6 medium leeks (3 to 4 pounds)
2 tablespoons butter or margarine, melted
6 cups canned diluted chicken broth, divided

1 cup half-and-half
1 teaspoon salt
⅛ teaspoon pepper
Garnish: chopped fresh parsley

Combine water and barley in a large saucepan. Bring to a boil; cover, reduce heat, and simmer 30 minutes. Drain and set aside.

Remove and discard root, tough outer leaves, and tops of leeks to where dark green begins to pale. Cut leeks into ¼-inch slices. Sauté leeks in butter in a large Dutch oven 3 to 4 minutes. Stir in 3 cups chicken broth. Bring to a boil; cover, reduce heat, and simmer 12 to 15 minutes or until leeks are tender. Add reserved barley and remaining 3 cups chicken broth. Cover and cook over medium-low heat 30 to 35 minutes or until barley is tender. Remove from heat.

Stir in half-and-half, salt, and pepper. Ladle into individual soup bowls. Garnish, if desired. Yield: 12 cups.   Darlene Wilde

A Rainbow of Recipes
The Education Department/Regional Treatment Center
Fergus Falls, Minnesota

Scotch Eggs

1 pound bulk pork sausage
6 hard-cooked eggs, peeled
2 eggs, beaten

1 cup Italian-seasoned breadcrumbs
Vegetable oil

Divide sausage into 6 equal portions; press each portion of sausage around 1 hard-cooked egg. Dip each sausage-coated egg into beaten egg, and roll in breadcrumbs. Deep fry in hot vegetable oil (375°) for 7 to 9 minutes or until sausage is done. Drain well. Let cool to room temperature. Cut eggs in half, and serve immediately. Yield: 6 servings.   Maedene Chase

Ex Libris, A Treasury of Recipes
The Friends of the Wellesley Free Libraries
Wellesley, Massachusetts

Pasties

2½ pounds round steak, cut
  into ½-inch cubes
2½ pounds baking potatoes,
  peeled and cubed
2½ pounds rutabaga, peeled
  and cubed
½ pound carrots, scraped and
  chopped
3 large onions, chopped
¼ teaspoon salt
¼ teaspoon pepper
8 cups all-purpose flour
1 teaspoon salt
2 tablespoons sugar
3½ cups shortening
2 eggs, lightly beaten
1 cup water
2 tablespoons vinegar
1 egg, beaten
½ cup water

Combine steak, potato, rutabaga, carrot, onion, ¼ teaspoon salt, and pepper in a large bowl; set aside.

Combine flour, 1 teaspoon salt, and sugar in a large bowl; cut in shortening with a pastry blender until mixture resembles coarse meal. Add 2 eggs, 1 cup water, and vinegar, stirring until dry ingredients are moistened.

Divide pastry into 10 equal portions; roll each portion to a 9-inch circle. Spoon about 2 cups meat mixture over half of each circle. Fold circles in half, stretching dough to fit over filling; press edges together with a fork dipped in flour to seal. Cut a slit in the top of each pasty to allow steam to escape.

Combine 1 egg and ½ cup water; lightly brush egg mixture over top of each pasty. Place on ungreased baking sheets. Bake at 400° for 45 to 60 minutes or until lightly browned. Yield: 10 servings.

Copper Country Recipes
The Copper Harbor Improvement Association
Copper Harbor, Michigan

Beef Steak and Kidney Pie

2 or 3 beef kidneys (2 to 3
  pounds)
½ cup all-purpose flour
½ teaspoon salt
¼ teaspoon pepper
2 pounds round steak, cut
  into ½-inch cubes
2 onions, chopped
2 cups canned diluted beef
  broth
1 cup Burgundy or other dry
  red wine
1 tablespoon Worcestershire
  sauce
Pastry for 9-inch pie

Trim and discard membranes and fat from kidneys; cut kidneys into ½-inch pieces. Place in a medium saucepan with water to cover. Bring to a boil; cover, reduce heat, and simmer 2 to 3 minutes. Drain kidneys, and rinse well. Repeat simmering, draining, and rinsing procedure twice.

Combine flour, salt, and pepper in a large bowl. Dredge kidney pieces and beef cubes in flour mixture; place in a lightly greased 13- x 9- x 2-inch baking pan.

Combine chopped onion, beef broth, wine, and Worcestershire sauce in a medium bowl; stir well, and add to meat and kidney pieces in baking pan. Cover and bake at 350° for 1½ to 2 hours or until meat and kidneys are tender. Remove from oven, and let cool slightly.

Roll pastry to ⅛-inch thickness on a lightly floured surface; cut pastry 1-inch larger than baking pan. Place pastry over meat mixture. Turn edges under and flute. Bake at 425° for 15 to 17 minutes or until golden brown. Let stand 10 minutes before serving. Yield: 6 to 8 servings.   George and Dorothy Graham

Capital Connoisseur
The Lawrence Center Independence House
Schenectady, New York

Yorkshire Pudding

2 eggs
1 cup milk
½ cup all-purpose flour
Salt and pepper to taste

⅛ teaspoon ground nutmeg
¼ cup plus 1 tablespoon
    clear beef drippings or
    melted shortening, divided

Beat eggs 1 minute at high speed of an electric mixer. Add milk; mix well. Gradually add flour, salt and pepper to taste, nutmeg, and 2 tablespoons beef drippings, beating until smooth. Beat 1 minute at high speed. Cover and chill 30 minutes.

Pour remaining 3 tablespoons drippings into an 8-inch cast-iron skillet. Heat at 425° for 5 minutes. Pour chilled batter into skillet; bake 30 minutes. Reduce heat to 350°, and bake 10 to 15 minutes or until top is puffed and golden brown. Serve immediately. Yield: 8 servings.   Dianne Davison Isakson

Georgia on My Menu
The Junior League of Cobb-Marietta, Georgia

English Sweet Scones

1⅓ cups all-purpose flour	½ teaspoon cream of tartar
½ teaspoon baking soda	⅓ cup butter
¼ teaspoon salt	⅓ cup milk
3 tablespoons sugar	3 tablespoons raisins

Combine flour, baking soda, salt, sugar, and cream of tartar in a medium bowl; cut in butter with a pastry blender until mixture resembles coarse meal. Gradually add milk, stirring just until dry ingredients are moistened and mixture forms a soft dough. Stir in raisins.

Turn dough out onto a lightly floured surface, and knead lightly 4 or 5 times. Roll dough to ½-inch thickness, and cut with a 2-inch biscuit cutter. Place dough rounds on a lightly greased baking sheet. Bake at 450° for 6 to 7 minutes or until scones are lightly browned. Yield: 1 dozen.

Stanford University Medical Center Auxiliary Cookbook
Stanford University Medical Center Auxiliary
Palo Alto, California

Walnut Scotch Shortbread

1 cup butter, softened	¼ cup rice flour
½ cup sugar	⅔ cup ground walnuts
2 cups all-purpose flour	

Cream butter; gradually add sugar, beating at medium speed of an electric mixer until light and fluffy. Combine flours and walnuts; add to creamed mixture, beating well.

Press mixture into an ungreased 13- x 9- x 2-inch baking pan; prick dough with a fork. Bake at 325° for 45 to 55 minutes or until golden brown. Let cool in pan on a wire rack 10 minutes; cut into squares. Let cool completely. Yield: 4 dozen.

Albertina's II
The Albertina Kerr Centers for Children
Portland, Oregon

Lemon Tarts

4 eggs
8 egg yolks
1 cup sugar
2 tablespoons grated lemon
  rind
¾ cup fresh lemon juice
¾ cup unsalted butter, cut
  into small pieces
2½ cups all-purpose flour
¼ cup plus 3 tablespoons
  unsalted butter, cut into
  small pieces

¼ cup plus 3 tablespoons
  margarine, cut into small
  pieces
¼ cup sugar
1 egg yolk
Garnishes: fresh fruit and
  fresh mint sprigs

Combine eggs, 8 egg yolks, 1 cup sugar, lemon rind, and lemon juice in a medium bowl; beat at high speed of an electric mixer until thick and lemon colored. Transfer egg mixture to top of a double boiler. Cook over simmering water, stirring constantly with a wire whisk, 10 to 15 minutes or until egg mixture is thickened.

Position knife blade in food processor bowl; add egg mixture. Drop ¾ cup unsalted butter pieces through food chute with processor running; process until butter melts and mixture is smooth. Transfer lemon filling to a medium bowl; cover and chill.

Position knife blade in food processor bowl; add flour and next 4 ingredients. Process 30 seconds or until dough leaves sides of bowl and forms a ball. Chill dough 1 hour.

Divide dough into 8 equal portions. Press each portion of dough into a greased 4-inch tart pan with removable sides; chill until firm. Prick bottom and sides of pastry with a fork. Bake at 350° for 20 to 22 minutes or until lightly browned. Let cool completely in tart pans on wire racks.

Spoon chilled lemon filling evenly into cooled tart shells. Carefully remove sides of tart pans before serving. Garnish, if desired. Yield: 8 servings.

Spokane Cooks!© Northwest
The Community Centers Foundation of Spokane, Washington

Eastern European Cuisine

During the late 1800s, many Eastern Europeans began immigrating to America to escape economic problems. Once in America, Eastern European immigrants kept their culinary arts alive. They introduced Americans to Old World favorites such as kielbasa, a sausage made with pork, caraway seeds, and garlic; pierogi, little pouches filled with cottage cheese, potatoes, meat, mushrooms, sauerkraut, or fruit; and kolaches, pastries stuffed with poppy seeds, prunes, or apricots. They taught us to cook with green peppers, tomatoes, kasha, sorrel, horseradish, dillweed, and, of course, paprika and sour cream. Borscht, chicken kiev, chicken paprika, stuffed cabbage leaves and peppers, liver dumplings, Hungarian goulash, and babka are part of their culinary legacy.

Gene's Borscht

1 fresh beet, peeled and shredded
⅓ cup water
¼ teaspoon salt
1 pound lean beef, cut into ½-inch cubes
3 cups canned diluted beef broth
2 cups water
1½ teaspoons salt
1 (16-ounce) can sliced beets, undrained
½ cup scraped, coarsely grated carrot
½ cup peeled, coarsely grated turnip
1 small onion, chopped
2 tablespoons vinegar
1 tablespoon butter or margarine
1 tablespoon tomato paste
½ teaspoon sugar
1 bay leaf
1 cup shredded cabbage
⅛ teaspoon freshly ground pepper
Garnishes: sour cream and fresh dillweed sprigs

Combine shredded fresh beet, ⅓ cup water, and ¼ teaspoon salt in a bowl; stir and set aside. Combine beef cubes, broth, 2 cups water, and 1½ teaspoons salt in a saucepan. Bring to a boil; cover, reduce heat, and simmer 1½ to 2 hours or until meat is tender.

Drain sliced beets, reserving liquid; set aside. Combine carrot and next 7 ingredients in a saucepan. Bring to a boil; cover, reduce heat, and simmer 15 minutes. Gradually stir in reserved beet liquid. Add cabbage; simmer 10 minutes or until vegetables are tender.

Add vegetable mixture, sliced beets, and pepper to meat mixture; stir well. Cook over medium heat until thoroughly heated. Stir in shredded fresh beet mixture. Remove and discard bay leaf. Garnish, if desired. Yield: 7 cups.

Scoops from the Bay
Cape Cod Academy
Osterville, Massachusetts

Csirke Paprikash (Chicken Paprika)

1 medium onion, thinly sliced
1 (4-ounce) can mushroom stems and pieces, drained
3 tablespoons butter or margarine, melted
2 tablespoons paprika
1 tablespoon vinegar
⅓ cup all-purpose flour
¼ teaspoon salt
¼ teaspoon celery salt
¼ teaspoon pepper
6 chicken breast halves, skinned and boned
1 cup water
1 teaspoon chicken-flavored bouillon granules
1 (8-ounce) carton sour cream
1 (8-ounce) package medium egg noodles
1 tablespoon butter or margarine, melted
Chopped fresh parsley

Sauté onion and mushrooms in 3 tablespoons melted butter in a large skillet until tender; stir in paprika and vinegar.

Combine flour and next 3 ingredients; stir well. Dredge chicken in flour mixture. Add chicken to vegetable mixture in skillet, and cook 3 to 4 minutes on each side or until golden brown. Add water and bouillon granules. Bring to a boil; cover, reduce heat, and simmer 1 hour. Remove from heat; stir in sour cream.

Prepare noodles according to package directions; drain well. Toss noodles with 1 tablespoon melted butter and parsley.

To serve, arrange chicken over noodles; top with sauce. Yield: 6 servings.   Richard and Bonnie Elefson

Centennial Cookbook: 100 Years of Freemasonry in North Dakota
The Masonic Grand Lodge
Fargo, North Dakota

Pierogi

6 small baking potatoes,
  peeled and cubed
1 large onion, peeled
¾ cup finely chopped onion
1 tablespoon butter
2 cups (8 ounces) shredded
  Cheddar cheese
⅛ teaspoon pepper
3 cups all-purpose flour

2 egg yolks, lightly beaten
½ teaspoon salt
¾ cup boiling water
1 tablespoon vegetable oil
1 tablespoon vegetable oil
1 tablespoon salt
4 quarts water
Melted butter or margarine
Sour cream

Cook potatoes and whole onion in boiling water to cover 20 minutes or until tender. Drain; discard onion. Mash potatoes. Add chopped onion and next 3 ingredients; stir well.

Combine flour and next 4 ingredients; stir well. Turn dough out onto a floured surface, and knead lightly 4 or 5 times. Cover; let rest 30 minutes. Roll dough to ⅛-inch thickness on a floured surface; cut with a 3-inch cutter. Divide potato mixture evenly among circles. Moisten edges of dough with water. Fold circles in half; press edges together with a fork to seal.

Combine 1 tablespoon oil, 1 tablespoon salt, and 4 quarts water in a Dutch oven; bring to a boil. Drop pierogi, a few at a time, into boiling water; cook 5 minutes or until pierogi rise to the surface. Remove with a slotted spoon. Brush with melted butter; serve with sour cream. Yield: about 3 dozen.   Kelly Colfas

Copper Country Recipes
The Copper Harbor Improvement Association
Copper Harbor, Michigan

The Copper Harbor Improvement Association of Copper Harbor, Michigan, offers Copper Country Recipes. Proceeds will go toward maintenance of the historic mining area, Fort Wilkins, and the lighthouse.

Czech-Style Kolaches

2 packages dry yeast
1 cup warm water (105° to
   115°)
1 cup milk
1½ cups butter or margarine,
   melted and cooled
¾ cup sugar
2 teaspoons salt
½ teaspoon ground nutmeg
1 egg, lightly beaten
1 teaspoon vanilla extract
7 to 8 cups all-purpose flour

1 egg white
1 tablespoon water
Apricot preserves or pitted
   prunes
2 tablespoons milk
⅓ cup sifted powdered sugar
1½ tablespoons milk
½ teaspoon vanilla extract
Additional apricot preserves
   (optional)
Honey (optional)

Dissolve yeast in warm water in a large bowl; let stand 5 minutes. Combine 1 cup milk and butter in a saucepan; heat until butter melts, stirring occasionally. Let cool to 105° to 115°. Add ¾ cup sugar, salt, nutmeg, egg, and 1 teaspoon vanilla; stir well. Gradually stir in enough flour to make a soft dough.

Turn dough out onto a floured surface, and knead until smooth and elastic (about 5 minutes). Place in a well-greased bowl, turning to grease top. Cover and let rise in a warm place (85°), free from drafts, 1½ hours or until doubled in bulk. Punch dough down. Cover and let rise in a warm place, free from drafts, 40 minutes or until doubled in bulk.

Divide dough in half. Roll each half to ¼-inch thickness; cut into 3-inch squares. Combine egg white and 1 tablespoon water in a small bowl; beat with a wire whisk until blended. Brush squares with egg mixture. Place 1 tablespoon apricot preserves or 1 prune in center of each square. Bring opposite corners together over filling, pinching ends to seal. Place 2 inches apart on lightly greased baking sheets. Brush with 2 tablespoons milk. Bake at 400° for 15 minutes or until lightly browned. Let cool on wire racks.

Combine powdered sugar, 1½ tablespoons milk, and ½ teaspoon vanilla in a small bowl, stirring well. Drizzle glaze over kolaches. If desired, serve kolaches with additional apricot preserves or honey. Yield: 3 dozen.   Richard and Bonnie Elefson

Centennial Cookbook: 100 Years of Freemasonry in North Dakota
The Masonic Grand Lodge
Fargo, North Dakota

French Cuisine

French immigrants came to America in small numbers, yet their impact and influence on American cooking was great. From regional peasant fare to elaborate dishes, the French immigrants introduced America to the "art" of cooking with classic, timeless cooking techniques. They brought their pâté, onion soup, bouillabaisse, boeuf bourguignon, Coquilles St. Jacques, French bread, croissants, brioche, ratatouille, scalloped potatoes, crêpes, cherries jubilee, and bûche de noël to the American table. Rich desserts such as chocolate mousse and flavorful sauces such as bordelaise are now a part of America's cuisine.

Potage Cressonnière (Watercress Soup)

1 clove garlic, minced
2 cups chopped onion
¼ cup butter, melted
4 cups thinly sliced baking potatoes
1 teaspoon salt
¼ teaspoon pepper
¾ cup water
1 bunch watercress
1½ cups milk
1½ cups water
2 egg yolks, lightly beaten
½ cup half-and-half

Sauté garlic and onion in melted butter in a large saucepan until tender. Stir in potato, salt, pepper, and ¾ cup water. Bring to a boil; cover, reduce heat, and simmer 15 minutes or until potato is tender.

Finely chop watercress stems; coarsely chop leaves. Add stems, half of leaves, milk, and 1½ cups water to potato mixture; cover and simmer 15 minutes. Spoon mixture into container of an electric blender; process until smooth. Return mixture to saucepan; cook until thoroughly heated. Combine egg yolks and half-and-half; gradually add to soup mixture, stirring constantly. Cook, stirring constantly, until slightly thickened. Sprinkle with remaining half of chopped watercress leaves. Yield: 7 cups.

Wild about Texas
The Cypress-Woodlands Junior Forum
Houston, Texas

Beef Bourguignon

½ pound salt pork or unsliced bacon, cubed
2 small onions, chopped
1 tablespoon butter, melted
3 pounds boneless chuck or top round roast, cut into 1½-inch cubes
2 tablespoons vegetable oil
1 small carrot, scraped and cut into ½-inch pieces
2 cups Burgundy or other dry red wine
1 cup Chablis or other dry white wine
½ cup canned beef consommé

1 tablespoon tomato paste
2 tablespoons chopped fresh parsley
1 clove garlic, minced
1 bay leaf
¼ to ½ teaspoon salt
¼ teaspoon black peppercorns
1 cup sliced fresh mushrooms
2 shallots, chopped
1 tablespoon butter, melted
1 tablespoon brandy
Buerre Manie
Additional chopped fresh parsley

Brown salt pork in a large Dutch oven; drain well, and set aside. Discard drippings. Sauté onion in 1 tablespoon melted butter in Dutch oven until tender. Remove onion, and set aside. Brown beef cubes in oil. Add reserved onion, carrot, and next 9 ingredients. Bring to a boil; cover, reduce heat, and simmer 1½ to 2 hours.

Sauté mushrooms and shallots in 1 tablespoon butter; set aside. Remove beef from Dutch oven with a slotted spoon; set beef aside. Remove and discard bay leaf and peppercorns. Add brandy to Dutch oven. Add Buerre Manie, 1 tablespoon at a time, stirring well after each addition. Return meat to Dutch oven; add reserved salt pork, and sautéed mushroom mixture. Cook over medium heat until thoroughly heated. Sprinkle with chopped parsley before serving. Yield: 4 to 6 servings.

Buerre Manie

2 tablespoons butter, softened

2 tablespoons all-purpose flour

Combine butter and flour in small bowl, stirring until combined. Yield: 3 tablespoons.

World Heritage of Cooking
Friends of the World Heritage Museum
Urbana, Illinois

Cassoulet

1½ pounds dried Great
   Northern beans
4 cups water
1 medium onion
4 whole cloves
5 medium onions, chopped
3 carrots, scraped and
   quartered
2 (10¾-ounce) cans chicken
   broth, undiluted
½ cup chopped celery leaves
3 black peppercorns
2 bay leaves
4 cloves garlic, crushed
1½ teaspoons dried whole
   thyme
1 teaspoon dried whole
   marjoram
1 teaspoon dried whole sage
1 pound Polish sausage, cut
   into 8 pieces
8 pork sausage links
1 (4- to 6-pound) roasting
   chicken, cut into 8 pieces
3 carrots, scraped and
   quartered
½ pound bacon strips, halved
   and cooked
1 (28-ounce) can chopped
   tomatoes, undrained

Sort and wash beans; place in a large Dutch oven. Cover with 4
cups water; let soak 2 hours. (Do not drain.)

Peel whole onion and stud with cloves; add to beans. Add
chopped onion and next 9 ingredients. Bring to a boil; cover, reduce
heat, and simmer 1 hour. Remove and discard bay leaves.

Cook Polish sausage pieces and pork sausage links in a large skillet
until browned on all sides. Remove with a slotted spoon, reserving
drippings in skillet; set aside. Add chicken to drippings, and cook
until browned on all sides; set aside.

Add carrot and bacon to beans. Transfer bean mixture to a
5-quart baking dish; bake, uncovered, at 350° for 30 minutes. Add
tomatoes; stir well. Arrange reserved sausages and chicken on top of
beans. Cover and bake 45 minutes; uncover, and bake an additional
10 minutes. Yield: 8 servings.   Tom Haas

Weathervane Theatre Cookbook
The Weathervane Theatre
Whitefield, New Hampshire

Mocha Pots de Crème

3 cups whipping cream
⅔ cup whole coffee beans
3 tablespoons sugar
1 (2-inch) piece vanilla bean,
   split lengthwise

6 egg yolks, lightly beaten
4 (1-ounce) squares semisweet
   chocolate, melted
2 teaspoons cognac

Combine whipping cream, coffee beans, sugar, and vanilla bean in a medium saucepan. Bring to a boil over medium heat, stirring frequently; cover, remove from heat, and let stand 30 minutes. Strain coffee mixture; discard coffee beans and vanilla bean.

Gradually pour coffee mixture into egg yolks, stirring with a wire whisk. Gradually add to melted chocolate, stirring constantly with a wire whisk. Stir in cognac.

Pour mixture evenly into 6 (4-ounce) pots de crème or soufflé cups. Place cups in a 13- x 9- x 2-inch baking pan; add hot water to pan to a depth of 1 inch. Add tops to pots de crème cups, or place a baking sheet on top of soufflé cups. Bake at 350° for 25 to 30 minutes or until a knife inserted between center and edge of custard comes out clean (custard should still look soft in center).

Uncover cups, and remove from pan. Let cool to room temperature on a wire rack. Serve at room temperature, or cover and chill. Yield: 6 servings.

Cindy Pawlcyn

A Taste of San Francisco
The Symphony of San Francisco, California

The Weathervane Theatre was founded in 1966. Housed in a renovated barn in Whitefield, New Hampshire, the repertory theatre produces seven plays during the months of July and August. Proceeds from the sale of the **Weathervane Theatre Cookbook,** *which contains recipes from former actors and technical people, will help maintain the theatre.*

German Cuisine

A strong wave of German immigration occurred in an attempt to escape a potato famine, overpopulation, and political turmoil. The German immigrants settled mainly in Illinois, Indiana, Iowa, Ohio, Missouri, Pennsylvania, Texas, and Wisconsin.

The German people contributed greatly to their new home, introducing Americans to everything from kindergarten to Santa Claus and the Christmas tree. They also founded some of the most famous wineries in California: Krug, Wente, and Beringer. German-Americans became leaders in the fields of brewing and baking. And the coffee klatch, an important aspect of life in the old country, was brought to America where it took a firm hold.

Many of the German foods were introduced to Americans through German delicatessens. There one could find sauerbraten, liverwurst, sauerkraut, pumpernickel, zwieback, and lager and bok beers. The German immigrants gave us treats such as jelly doughnuts, linzer torte, apple strudel, Sacher torte, black forest cake, cheesecakes, and stollen. They also introduced Americans to hearty fare such as sweet and sour combinations, bratwurst, frankfurters, dumplings, German potato salad, dark rye bread, and pretzels.

Bauernfruhstuck (German Omelet)

¼ cup butter or margarine	6 eggs
2 cups peeled, cubed baking potatoes	¾ teaspoon salt
	Dash of pepper
¼ cup finely chopped onion	2 tablespoons half-and-half
1 cup cubed cooked ham	½ cup (2 ounces) shredded
¼ cup chopped fresh parsley	Monterey Jack cheese

Melt butter in a 10-inch skillet; add potato and onion. Cook over medium heat, stirring occasionally, 20 minutes or until vegetables are tender and golden brown. Add ham, and cook 5 minutes, stirring frequently. Sprinkle with parsley.

Combine eggs, salt, pepper, and half-and-half in a large bowl, beating with a wire whisk until blended. Pour egg mixture over potato mixture. Cover and cook over low heat 10 minutes or until almost set. Gently lift edges of omelet with a spatula, and tilt pan so that uncooked portion flows underneath. Sprinkle with cheese; cover and cook until cheese melts. To serve, cut omelet into wedges. Yield: 4 to 6 servings.   Deborah A. Schiavone

With Great Gusto
The Junior League of Youngstown, Ohio

Sauerbraten

1 large onion, sliced
1 cup cider vinegar
1 cup water
2 tablespoons brown sugar
1 tablespoon salt
12 whole cloves
10 coriander seeds
10 mustard seeds
6 to 8 whole allspice
6 to 8 black peppercorns
6 bay leaves
1 (4-pound) chuck or rump roast
2 teaspoons vegetable oil
6 to 8 gingersnaps, crushed
¾ cup flour
1 cup water

Combine first 11 ingredients in a large Dutch oven. Add roast; cover and marinate in refrigerator 24 to 48 hours. Remove roast from marinade, reserving marinade.

Brown roast in vegetable oil in Dutch oven. Pour reserved marinade over roast; add crushed gingersnaps. Bring to a boil; cover, reduce heat, and simmer 2 to 3 hours or until meat is tender, turning once.

Place flour in a heavy skillet; cook over medium heat, stirring constantly, 15 minutes or until flour browns. Remove from heat. Gradually add water, stirring until smooth. Set aside.

Remove roast from Dutch oven; set aside, and keep warm. Strain pan juices and return to Dutch oven; bring to a boil over medium heat. Stir in enough browned flour mixture to thicken gravy. Slice roast; serve with gravy. Yield: 6 servings.   Frank Sindlinger

Aspic and Old Lace
The Northern Indiana Historical Society
South Bend, Indiana

German Potato Salad

3 pounds baking potatoes
10 slices bacon
½ cup chopped onion
2 tablespoons all-purpose
    flour
2 tablespoons sugar
1½ teaspoons salt

1 teaspoon celery seeds
Dash of pepper
1 cup water
½ cup vinegar
2 hard-cooked eggs, chopped
Garnishes: chopped fresh
    parsley and sliced pimiento

Cook potatoes in boiling water to cover 30 minutes or until tender. Drain; let cool slightly. Peel and slice potatoes; set aside.

Cook bacon in a large skillet until crisp; remove bacon, reserving ¼ cup drippings in skillet. Crumble bacon, and set aside.

Sauté onion in drippings until tender. Add flour and next 4 ingredients; stir well. Add water and vinegar; cook over medium heat, stirring constantly, until thickened and bubbly. Add potato, bacon, and chopped egg; cook until thoroughly heated. Garnish, if desired. Yield: 6 to 8 servings.   Barb Matuska

Norand 20th Anniversary Cookbook
Norand Corporation
Cedar Rapids, Iowa

Stollen

1 cup raisins
1 cup mixed candied fruit
¼ cup orange juice
2 packages dry yeast
½ cup warm water (105° to
    115°)
½ cup milk
½ cup butter
½ cup sugar
2 eggs
1 teaspoon salt
1 teaspoon grated lemon rind

¼ teaspoon ground mace
6 to 6½ cups all-purpose
    flour, divided
1 cup chopped blanched
    almonds
2 tablespoons butter, melted
2 tablespoons sugar
½ teaspoon ground cinnamon
Frosting (recipe follows)
Garnishes: slivered almonds
    and candied cherries

Combine raisins and mixed candied fruit in a small bowl; add orange juice, and toss gently. Set aside.

Dissolve yeast in warm water; let stand 5 minutes. Combine milk and ½ cup butter in a saucepan; heat until butter melts, stirring occasionally. Let cool to 120° to 130°. Add milk mixture, ½ cup sugar, and next 4 ingredients to yeast mixture; beat at medium speed of an electric mixer until well blended. Add 2 cups flour, and beat until blended. Stir in fruit mixture and almonds. Gradually stir in enough remaining 4½ cups flour to make a soft dough.

Turn dough out onto a well-floured surface, and knead until smooth and elastic (about 5 minutes). Place in a well-greased bowl, turning to grease top. Cover and let rise in a warm place (85°), free from drafts, 2 hours or until doubled in bulk.

Punch dough down; turn out onto a floured surface, and knead 4 or 5 times. Cover; let rest 5 minutes. Divide dough in half. Roll each half to an oval about 1-inch thick. Brush with 2 tablespoons butter. Combine 2 tablespoons sugar and cinnamon; sprinkle over dough. Fold ovals in half lengthwise, pressing edges to seal. Place on greased baking sheets, curving ends slightly toward folded edge. Cover; let rise in a warm place, free from drafts, 1 hour or until doubled in bulk. Bake at 350° for 30 minutes or until golden. Drizzle frosting over stollen. Garnish, if desired. Yield: 2 loaves.

Frosting

1 cup sifted powdered sugar
3 tablespoons butter, melted

1 tablespoon half-and-half or
milk

Combine all ingredients; stir until smooth. Yield: ⅓ cup.

The Golden Apple Collection
White Plains Auxiliary of the White Plains Hospital Center
White Plains, New York

Norand 20th Anniversary Cookbook *was created by Norand Cares, a group whose members are employees of the Norand Corporation in Cedar Rapids, Iowa. On a volunteer basis, employees work to help families in need by providing them with food baskets at Thanksgiving and Christmas. Also, toys are collected and distributed to needy children at Christmas.*

Black Forest Cake

2 (1-ounce) squares
  unsweetened chocolate
1¾ cups sifted cake flour
1 cup sugar
1 teaspoon salt
¾ teaspoon baking soda
1 cup milk, divided
⅓ cup vegetable oil
2 eggs, separated

½ cup sugar
Butter frosting (recipe
  follows)
Cherry filling (recipe follows)
Chocolate Mousse
Whipped Cream Frosting
Powdered sugar
Maraschino cherries
Chocolate curls

Place unsweetened chocolate in top of a double boiler; bring water to a boil. Reduce heat to low; cook until chocolate melts, stirring occasionally. Set aside, and let cool.

Combine flour, 1 cup sugar, salt, and soda in a large mixing bowl. Add ½ cup milk and oil; beat 1 minute at medium speed of an electric mixer. Add remaining ½ cup milk, egg yolks, and melted chocolate; beat until thoroughly combined.

Beat egg whites (at room temperature) at high speed until soft peaks form. Gradually add ½ cup sugar, 1 tablespoon at a time, beating until stiff peaks form and sugar dissolves (2 to 4 minutes). Gently fold egg whites into chocolate mixture.

Pour batter into 2 greased and floured 9-inch round cakepans. Bake at 350° for 30 to 35 minutes or until a wooden pick inserted in center comes out clean. Let cool in pans 10 minutes; remove from pans, and let cool completely on wire racks.

Split cake layers in half horizontally to make 4 layers. Place 1 layer, cut side up, on a cake platter; spread with ½ cup butter frosting. Pipe remaining butter frosting in a ring ½-inch wide and ¾-inch high around outside edge of cake layer; pipe an additional ring 2 inches from outside edge. Chill 30 minutes. Fill space between rings with cherry filling.

Place second cake layer, cut side down, gently on top of frosting and filling; spread with Chocolate Mousse.

Place third cake layer, cut side up, gently on top of Chocolate Mousse. Spread with 1½ cups Whipped Cream Frosting. Top with fourth cake layer, cut side down. Frost sides with remaining Whipped Cream Frosting, reserving ¼ cup frosting for garnish.

Sift powdered sugar over cake. Pipe rosettes of Whipped Cream Frosting around top of cake. Top rosettes with maraschino cherries and chocolate curls; chill. Yield: one 4-layer cake.

Butter Frosting

¼ cup plus 2 tablespoons butter, softened

4 cups sifted powdered sugar

2 to 4 tablespoons whipping cream

1½ teaspoons vanilla extract

Cream butter; gradually add sugar, beating until light and fluffy. Add whipping cream, 1 tablespoon at a time, beating until spreading consistency. Stir in vanilla. Yield: 2⅓ cups.

Cherry Filling

1 (16-ounce) can pitted tart cherries, drained

½ cup port wine

1 tablespoon kirsch or other cherry-flavored brandy

⅛ teaspoon almond extract

Place all ingredients in a small bowl; stir gently to combine. Cover and chill at least 3 hours. Drain well. Yield: 2 cups.

Chocolate Mousse

3 (1-ounce) squares semisweet chocolate

3 tablespoons kirsch or other cherry-flavored brandy

1 egg, beaten

1 cup whipping cream

2 tablespoons sugar

Combine chocolate and brandy in top of a double boiler; bring water to a boil. Reduce heat to low; cook until chocolate melts and mixture is smooth, stirring occasionally. Remove from heat, and let cool. Gradually stir chocolate mixture into beaten egg.

Beat whipping cream until foamy; gradually add sugar, beating until stiff peaks form. Gently fold whipped cream into chocolate mixture. Cover and chill thoroughly. Yield: 2½ cups.

Whipped Cream Frosting

2 cups whipping cream

1 teaspoon vanilla extract

2 tablespoons sugar

Beat whipping cream and vanilla at medium speed of an electric mixer until foamy; gradually add sugar, beating at high speed until stiff peaks form. Yield: 4 cups.

Terry Home Presents Food & Fun from Celebrities & Us
Terry Home, Inc.
Sumner, Washington

Greek Cuisine

Greeks came to America to seek a better life for themselves and for political reasons. Many Greek dishes like Greek salads, stuffed grape leaves, shish kabob, moussaka, gyros, rice pilaf, and baklava have become part of America's cuisine. Ingredients commonly used in Greek cooking, such as artichokes, eggplants, tomatoes, lemons, onions, yogurt, feta cheese, olive oil, garlic, cinnamon, parsley, dillweed, mint, and oregano, are now deeply ingrained in the American way of cooking.

Avgolemono Soup

4½ cups canned diluted
   chicken broth
3½ tablespoons long-grain
   rice, uncooked
1 egg, beaten

¼ cup plus 2 tablespoons
   lemon juice
¼ teaspoon salt
¼ teaspoon pepper
Garnish: lemon slices

Place chicken broth in a medium saucepan; bring to a boil. Add rice; cover, reduce heat, and cook 15 minutes.

Combine egg and lemon juice, stirring with a wire whisk. Gradually stir about one-fourth of hot mixture into egg mixture; add to remaining hot mixture, stirring constantly. Stir in salt and pepper. Serve warm or cold. Garnish, if desired. Yield: 3½ cups.

Merrymeeting Merry Eating
The Regional Memorial Hospital Auxiliary
Brunswick, Maine

Stuffed Grape Leaves

2 (7-ounce) jars grape leaves
4 medium onions, chopped
3 tablespoons vegetable oil
⅓ cup minced fresh parsley
2 cups long-grain rice,
   uncooked

¼ cup pine nuts
3 cups canned diluted
   chicken or beef broth
Juice of 2 medium lemons

Separate grape leaves; rinse with cold water, and drain well. Set leaves aside.

Sauté chopped onion in oil in a large nonstick skillet until tender. Add minced parsley, and cook 1 minute. Add rice, and sauté 8 minutes or until rice is lightly browned. Stir in pine nuts. Remove from heat, and let cool.

Place grape leaves, stem side up, on a flat surface. Place about one tablespoon rice mixture in center of each leaf. Fold right and left sides of each leaf over filling; then fold bottom and top of leaf over filling, forming a square. Place stuffed leaves, seam side down, in a large saucepan.

Combine broth and lemon juice; pour over stuffed leaves. Bring to a boil; cover, reduce heat, and simmer 20 minutes or until liquid is absorbed. Yield: 5½ dozen.   Jacqueline Greene

Ex Libris, A Treasury of Recipes
The Friends of the Wellesley Free Libraries
Wellesley, Massachusetts

Souvlakia

1½ cups olive oil
1 cup Burgundy or other dry
  red wine
⅔ cup lemon juice
2 cloves garlic, minced
2 bay leaves

1 tablespoon dried whole
  oregano
½ teaspoon salt
¼ teaspoon pepper
1 (6-pound) leg of lamb, cut
  into 1-inch cubes

Combine first 8 ingredients in a large bowl; stir with a wire whisk. Add lamb, stirring gently to combine. Cover and marinate in refrigerator 8 hours.

Remove lamb from marinade, reserving marinade. Set meat aside. Place marinade in a saucepan; bring to a boil, reduce heat, and simmer 5 minutes. Remove from heat; set aside.

Place lamb on metal skewers; grill over medium coals or broil 4 to 6 inches from heat 8 to 10 minutes on each side or to desired degree of doneness, basting frequently with marinade. Yield: 8 to 10 servings.

World Heritage of Cooking
Friends of the World Heritage Museum
Urbana, Illinois

Moussaka

2 large eggplants (about 3
  pounds)
1 cup butter, melted
1 cup Italian-seasoned
  breadcrumbs
2 large onions, chopped
1 large clove garlic, crushed
¼ cup olive oil
2 pounds ground lamb or
  chuck
1 (28-ounce) can Italian-style
  tomatoes, undrained and
  chopped

1 (15-ounce) can tomato sauce
2 teaspoons salt
1 teaspoon dried whole
  oregano
½ teaspoon dried whole basil
½ teaspoon dried whole
  thyme
¼ teaspoon freshly ground
  pepper
Salt and pepper
Béchamel Sauce
½ cup grated Parmesan
  cheese

Peel eggplants, and cut into ¼-inch-thick slices. Brush eggplant
slices with butter; dredge in breadcrumbs. Place on a rack in a
broiler pan; broil 4 inches from heat 2 minutes on each side or until
golden brown. Set aside.

Sauté onion and garlic in oil in a large skillet until tender. Add
meat, and cook until browned, stirring to crumble meat. Drain well;
return meat mixture to skillet. Add tomatoes and next 6 ingredients.
Bring to a boil; cover, reduce heat, and simmer 2 hours, stirring
occasionally.

Place one-third of reserved eggplant slices in a buttered 15- x 11-
x 2½-inch oval baking dish or two 11- x 7- x 1½-inch baking dishes.
Sprinkle with salt and pepper. Cover eggplant slices with half of
meat sauce. Repeat layers, ending with eggplant slices. Top with
Béchamel Sauce. Sprinkle with Parmesan cheese. Bake at 350° for
35 to 45 minutes or until golden brown. Serve immediately. Yield:
12 to 14 servings.

Béchamel Sauce

½ cup butter, melted
½ cup all-purpose flour
4 cups half-and-half
¼ teaspoon salt

¼ teaspoon ground white
  pepper
4 egg yolks

Combine butter and flour in a Dutch oven. Cook over medium
heat, stirring constantly, until roux is caramel colored (20 to 30
minutes). Gradually stir in half-and-half; cook, stirring constantly,

until mixture thickens. Add salt and pepper. Add egg yolks, one at a time, stirring with a wire whisk. Cook 1 minute, stirring constantly. Yield: 4½ cups.   Toula Patsalis

Joy of Greek Cooking (With an American Accent)
The Annunciation Cathedral Philoptochos Society
Detroit, Michigan

Baklava

1 (17¼-ounce) package frozen phyllo pastry, thawed	1 teaspoon ground cinnamon
2 cups butter, melted	¼ teaspoon ground cloves
1 pound walnuts, finely chopped and toasted	¼ teaspoon freshly grated nutmeg
½ pound finely chopped blanched almonds	2 cups sugar
½ cup sugar	1 cup water
	1 tablespoon lemon juice
	¼ cup honey

Cut phyllo in half crosswise; trim phyllo to fit a 13- x 9- x 2-inch baking pan. Cover phyllo with a slightly damp towel. Lightly butter bottom of 13- x 9- x 2-inch baking pan. Layer 20 sheets of phyllo in pan (keep remaining phyllo covered), brushing each sheet with melted butter.

Combine walnuts and next 5 ingredients; stir well. Sprinkle nut mixture over phyllo in pan. Top with remaining 20 sheets of phyllo, brushing each sheet with melted butter. Cut into diamond shapes, using a sharp knife. Bake at 350° for 30 minutes. Reduce temperature to 300°, and bake 30 minutes or until golden brown. Let cool completely.

Combine 2 cups sugar and water in a medium saucepan; bring to a boil. Add lemon juice, and cook over low heat 10 to 15 minutes, stirring occasionally. Remove from heat, and stir in honey. Drizzle syrup over phyllo. Cover and let stand at room temperature 4 hours. Yield: 3 dozen.

Very Innovative Parties
The Loma Linda University School of Dentistry Auxiliary
Loma Linda, California

Italian Cuisine

Almost 4 million Italian farmers immigrated to America between 1880 and 1914 to escape prejudice, trade wars, epidemics, overpopulation, and starvation. Many turned to mining, working in steel mills, and building railroads for their livelihood. The Italian immigrants expanded American tastes with inexpensive and flavorful fare such as minestrone, osso buco, chicken cacciatore, veal parmesan, spaghetti with tomato sauce and meatballs, lasagna, ravioli, pizza, macaroni and cheese, spumoni, and cappuccino. In addition, Italian cheeses such as mozzarella, Parmesan, Romano, and ricotta became part and parcel of the American cuisine.

Pasta Primavera

2 medium carrots, scraped and cut into thin strips
1 cup broccoli flowerets
½ cup frozen English peas
1 small sweet red pepper, cut into thin strips
1 small green pepper, cut into thin strips
3 tablespoons olive oil
½ pound fresh asparagus spear tips
2 medium zucchini, sliced diagonally into ¼-inch slices
4 ripe Italian-style tomatoes, chopped
1 (12-ounce) package pasta
½ cup grated Parmesan cheese
¼ cup chopped fresh parsley
¼ cup olive oil
2 to 3 tablespoons lemon juice
1 teaspoon salt
¼ teaspoon ground white pepper

Cook carrot in a small amount of boiling water 1 minute. Add broccoli and peas; cook 2 minutes. Drain and set aside.

Sauté peppers in 3 tablespoons oil 1 minute. Add asparagus tips and zucchini, and sauté 2 minutes or until vegetables are crisp-tender. Remove from heat; add reserved carrot mixture and tomato. Set aside.

Cook pasta according to package directions; drain. Place in a serving dish. Add vegetable mixture, Parmesan cheese, and remaining ingredients; toss gently. Yield: 8 to 10 servings.

Wild about Texas
The Cypress-Woodlands Junior Forum
Houston, Texas

Eggplant Parmigiana

1 pound ground round
1 pound mild Italian sausage
1 (28-ounce) can Italian-style tomatoes, undrained
1 (28-ounce) can tomato puree
1 (6-ounce) can tomato paste
3½ cups water
¼ cup sugar
2 cloves garlic, crushed
3 bay leaves
1 tablespoon plus 1 teaspoon chopped fresh basil
1 tablespoon plus 1 teaspoon chopped fresh oregano
Salt and pepper to taste
1 large eggplant
½ cup olive oil
2 cups (8 ounces) shredded mozzarella cheese
1½ cups grated Parmesan or Romano cheese
1 (6-ounce) package mozzarella cheese slices, cut into thin strips

Cook ground round in a skillet until browned, stirring to crumble meat. Drain, reserving 3 tablespoons drippings. Set meat and drippings aside. Cook sausage in skillet until browned, stirring to crumble meat. Drain; set aside.

Combine ground round, reserved drippings, tomatoes, and next 9 ingredients in a Dutch oven. Cook, uncovered, over medium-low heat 2 hours. Remove and discard bay leaves.

Cut eggplant into ¼-inch slices. Sauté eggplant in olive oil in a large skillet over medium-high heat until almost tender; drain.

Spread 1½ cups tomato mixture in a 13- x 9- x 2-inch baking dish. Layer half each of eggplant slices, shredded mozzarella cheese, grated Parmesan cheese, reserved sausage, and tomato mixture; repeat layers. Top with mozzarella cheese strips. Bake at 350° for 45 minutes or until lightly browned and thoroughly heated. Yield: 8 servings.

Ruth Giammusso

East Cooper Cuisine
Christ Our King Ladies Club
Mt. Pleasant, South Carolina

Almond-Anise Biscotti

½ cup unsalted butter, softened
¾ cup sugar
3 eggs
2 tablespoons brandy
1 tablespoon grated lemon rind

3 cups all-purpose flour
2 teaspoons baking powder
½ teaspoon salt
1 cup coarsely ground blanched almonds, toasted
1 tablespoon anise seeds

Cream butter; gradually add sugar, beating well at medium speed of an electric mixer. Add eggs, one at a time, beating well after each addition. Stir in brandy and lemon rind.

Combine flour, baking powder, and salt; gradually add to creamed mixture, stirring well. Stir in almonds and anise seeds. Cover and chill dough at least 1 hour.

Divide dough in half. Shape each half into a 16- x 2½- x ¾-inch loaf on a lightly greased cookie sheet. Bake at 350° for 15 to 20 minutes or until lightly browned. Remove from oven; let cool slightly on cookie sheets. Cut loaves into ½-inch diagonal slices. Place slices on cookie sheets, cut side down. Bake an additional 15 minutes or until lightly browned. Let cool on wire racks. Yield: about 5½ dozen.

Catherine Tripalin Murray

A Taste of Memories from the Old "Bush"
The Italian-American Women's Mutual Aid Society
Madison, Wisconsin

La Cucina Sammarinese *is a collection of recipes shared by members of the San Marino Ladies Auxiliary of Troy, Michigan. The auxiliary members hold dear to their hearts the traditions, values, and Sammarinese cuisine of the Republic of San Marino in northern Italy, the smallest and oldest republic in the world.*

"Lift Me Up" Torte — Tiramisu

1 (16-ounce) container
  mascarpone cheese
½ cup sifted powdered sugar
⅓ cup plus 3 tablespoons
  Kahlúa or other
  coffee-flavored liqueur
2 (1-ounce) squares semisweet
  chocolate, coarsely grated
1½ teaspoons vanilla extract,
  divided
½ teaspoon salt

1½ cups whipping cream,
  divided
2 tablespoons water
2 teaspoons instant espresso
  coffee granules
2 (3- to 4½-ounce) packages
  ladyfingers
1 (1-ounce) square semisweet
  chocolate, coarsely grated
2 tablespoons powdered sugar

Combine mascarpone cheese, ½ cup powdered sugar, 3 table-spoons Kahlúa, 2 ounces grated chocolate, 1 teaspoon vanilla, and salt; stir well with a wire whisk.

Beat 1 cup whipping cream until soft peaks form. Gently fold whipped cream into cheese mixture. Set aside.

Combine remaining ⅓ cup Kahlúa, water, espresso granules, and remaining ½ teaspoon vanilla; stir well.

Separate ladyfingers in half lengthwise. Line the bottom of a 10-cup glass bowl with one-fourth of ladyfingers; brush with 2 tablespoons espresso mixture. Spoon one-third of cheese mixture over ladyfingers. Repeat layering procedure twice. Top with re-maining ladyfingers. Gently press ladyfingers into cheese mixture. Brush with remaining espresso mixture. Sprinkle top with 1 ounce grated chocolate, reserving 1 tablespoon for garnish.

Beat remaining ½ cup whipping cream until foamy; gradually add 2 tablespoons powdered sugar, beating until soft peaks form. Using a No. 132 metal tip, pipe sweetened whipped cream in rosettes over top of dessert. Sprinkle reserved 1 tablespoon grated chocolate over rosettes. Cover and chill at least 6 hours. Yield: 8 to 10 servings.

Vinci Crescentini

La Cucina Sammarinese
The San Marino Ladies Auxiliary
Troy, Michigan

Jewish Cuisine

Between 1880 and 1927, millions of Jews from Eastern Europe and Russia made the journey to America. Most came in family groups, and sometimes entire communities crossed the Atlantic together. They had a high rate of literacy but lacked experience as farmers. Many earned a living in tailoring, dressmaking, and shoemaking, or as merchants or moneylenders.

Jewish tastes and dietary rules gave America new additions to their tables. Soda water, pickles, chopped chicken livers, smoked fish, the Reuben sandwich, pastrami, cream cheese, lox, and New York cheesecake appeared in delicatessens. Bagels topped with garlic, onion, salt, poppy seeds, or sesame seeds are now an American classic. Challah (the traditional braided egg bread), potato latkes (crispy little potato pancakes served with sour cream or applesauce), tsimmes, chicken soup with matzo balls, fruit kugel, and cheese blintzes were also introduced to the American palate by the Jewish immigrants.

Chopped Chicken Livers

2 medium onions, chopped
¼ cup rendered chicken fat, divided
1 pound chicken livers
3 hard-cooked egg yolks
1 teaspoon salt
¼ teaspoon pepper

Sauté onion in 2 tablespoons chicken fat in a large skillet until tender. Remove from skillet, and set aside.

Cook chicken livers in remaining 2 tablespoons chicken fat 10 to 15 minutes or until done. Remove from heat, and let cool slightly.

Position knife blade in food processor bowl. Add reserved onion, chicken livers, hard-cooked egg yolks, salt, and pepper; process until mixture is smooth. Cover and chill thoroughly. Serve with crackers. Yield: 2⅓ cups.   Barbara Amundsen

Down East Jewish Cooking
The Rockland Chapter of Hadassah
Rockland, Maine

Fannie's Chicken Soup

1 (4-pound) broiler-fryer, cut up
3 quarts water
3 carrots, scraped and cut
  into 1-inch pieces
2 stalks celery, cut into
  1-inch pieces
2 green onions, cut into
  1-inch pieces
1 onion, peeled and quartered

1 parsnip, scraped and cut
  into 1-inch pieces
8 fresh dillweed sprigs
2 fresh parsley sprigs
1 small bay leaf
1 tablespoon salt
¼ teaspoon pepper
Garnish: chopped fresh
  parsley

Combine chicken and water in a large Dutch oven; bring to a boil. Skim foam off top of soup and discard. Add carrot and remaining ingredients except chopped parsley; cover, reduce heat, and simmer 3 hours. Remove chicken, reserving broth. Remove and discard skin from chicken. Bone chicken, and cut meat into pieces.

Strain chicken broth reserving carrot, celery, onion, and parsnip; return chicken and vegetables to broth. Garnish, if desired. Yield: 16 cups.   Lynn Budnick

What's Cooking?
The Sisterhood of Temple Shalom
Succasunna, New Jersey

Potato Latkes

5 medium baking potatoes,
  peeled and shredded
1 medium onion, grated
2 eggs, beaten
¾ cup all-purpose flour

¼ teaspoon baking powder
1 teaspoon salt
Dash of pepper
Vegetable oil
Commercial applesauce

Press potato between paper towels to remove excess moisture. Combine potato and next 6 ingredients. Drop ¼ cup potato mixture at a time into ⅛ inch hot oil; press into 3-inch rounds with the back of a fork. Fry until golden, turning once. Drain. Serve with applesauce. Yield: 6 to 8 servings.   Pat Spetter

What's Cooking?
The Sisterhood of Temple Shalom
Succasunna, New Jersey

Brisket

¼ cup all-purpose flour
½ teaspoon salt, divided
¼ teaspoon pepper
1 (4- to 5-pound) beef
  brisket
3 tablespoons vegetable oil
3 onions, chopped
1 clove garlic, minced

1½ cups sliced fresh
  mushrooms
2 tablespoons all-purpose
  flour
1 cup chili sauce
1 cup Burgundy or other dry
  red wine

Combine ¼ cup flour, ¼ teaspoon salt, and pepper. Dredge brisket in flour mixture.

Brown brisket in 3 tablespoons hot oil in a large Dutch oven; remove brisket, reserving drippings. Set brisket aside.

Sauté onion, garlic, and mushrooms in drippings in Dutch oven until tender. Add 2 tablespoons flour and remaining ¼ teaspoon salt, stirring constantly. Stir in chili sauce and wine. Return brisket to Dutch oven. Cover and bake at 325° for 3½ to 4 hours or until meat is tender. Yield: 8 to 10 servings.   Adele Fox

What's Cooking?
The Sisterhood of Temple Shalom
Succasunna, New Jersey

Sweet Potato Tzimmes

1 cup water
¼ teaspoon salt
1½ pounds sweet potatoes,
  peeled and cut into
  ¼-inch-thick slices
4 large carrots, scraped and
  cut into ¼-inch-thick slices

¼ cup honey
2 tablespoons vegetable oil
½ teaspoon ground cinnamon
¼ teaspoon ground ginger
1 cup pitted prunes, halved

Place water and salt in a large saucepan; bring to a boil. Add potato and carrot slices; cover, reduce heat, and simmer 12 to 14 minutes or until tender. Drain and set aside.

Combine honey and next 3 ingredients in a large skillet. Cook over medium heat, stirring constantly, until mixture is thickened and bubbly. Add potato and carrot slices, stirring until glazed.

Gently stir in prunes, and cook 1 minute or until thoroughly heated. Yield: 6 servings.   Jill Goldman

East Cooper Cuisine
Christ Our King Ladies Club
Mt. Pleasant, South Carolina

Deluxe Braided Challah

3 packages dry yeast
1 tablespoon sugar
1⅓ cups warm water (105° to 115°)
3 eggs, beaten
3 tablespoons margarine, melted and cooled
1 tablespoon salt
6 to 6½ cups all-purpose flour
1 egg yolk
1 teaspoon water
Poppy seeds or sesame seeds

Dissolve yeast and sugar in 1⅓ cups warm water in a large bowl; let stand 5 minutes. Add eggs, margarine, and salt to yeast mixture; stir well. Add 3 cups flour, 1 cup at a time, beating well at medium speed of an electric mixer until mixture is smooth. Gradually stir in enough remaining 3½ cups flour to make a soft dough.

Turn dough out onto a lightly floured surface; knead until smooth and elastic (about 10 minutes). Place in a well-greased bowl, turning to grease top. Cover and let rise in a warm place (85°), free from drafts, 1 hour or until doubled in bulk.

Punch dough down; divide into 6 equal portions for two 3-braid challahs or 8 equal portions for two 4-braid challahs. Shape each portion into a 15-inch rope. Place ropes on greased baking sheets (do not stretch); pinch ends together at one end to seal. Braid ropes; pinch loose ends together to seal. Tuck ends under. Cover and let rise in a warm place, free from drafts, 1 hour or until loaves are doubled in bulk.

Combine egg yolk and 1 teaspoon water; stir well. Brush top and sides of loaves with egg mixture; sprinkle with poppy seeds. Bake at 350° for 30 to 35 minutes or until loaves sound hollow when tapped. Let cool on wire racks. Yield: 2 loaves.   Denise Sutton

Deal Delights II
Sephardic Women's Organization
Deal, New Jersey

Scandinavian Cuisine

The shortage of land, a population explosion, and crop failures were the principal reasons many Norwegians, Swedes, Finns, and Danes left their homelands. The Scandinavians often found work in America as farmers, lumbermen, fishermen, shipbuilders, miners, and railroad workers, settling in the Midwest and Pacific Northwest.

Scandinavian women quickly gained a reputation for being excellent cooks, and their cooking methods and recipes became part of American kitchens. The Swedes especially enjoyed the celebration of Christmas, when friends and relatives would drop by for a cup of strong coffee, a slice of Julekage (Scandinavian Christmas bread), and a glass of warm glogg. The Scandinavian immigrant brought us the smorgasbord, open-faced sandwiches, potato sausage, fruit soup, limpa rye bread, lefse, Swedish pancakes, Danish pastries, rosettes, and pepparkakor (gingersnaps).

Pooh's Glogg

20 whole cloves
2 (3-inch) sticks cinnamon
1 cup water
2 quarts Burgundy or other
   dry red wine
1 (750-milliliter) bottle port
   wine

1 cup brandy
1 cup light rum
1 cup raisins
⅔ cup slivered almonds
Garnish: orange slices

Combine cloves, cinnamon, and water in a saucepan. Bring to a boil; cover, reduce heat, and simmer 30 minutes. Remove and discard spices. Combine spiced water, Burgundy, and remaining ingredients except orange slices in a Dutch oven; cook over low heat until thoroughly heated (do not boil). Garnish, if desired. Serve warm. Yield: 14 cups.   Lori Metcalf

eating
First Lutheran Church
Mission Hills, Kansas

Kaernemaelkssuppe (Buttermilk Soup)

8 cups buttermilk, divided
¼ cup all-purpose flour
1½ cups sugar
½ cup golden raisins
1 (3-inch) stick cinnamon
6 (4- x ¼-inch) slices lemon
    rind

¼ cup sliced blanched
    almonds
¾ cup whipping cream,
    whipped
Garnish: grated lemon rind

Combine 1 cup buttermilk and flour in a Dutch oven; stir until smooth. Gradually add remaining 7 cups buttermilk, stirring well. Add sugar and next 3 ingredients; cook over medium heat 20 minutes. Remove from heat. Remove and discard cinnamon and lemon rind. Add almonds and whipped cream; stir gently to combine. Garnish, if desired. Yield: 10 cups.   Inge Salmonsen

Calvary Collections
Calvary Lutheran Church
Kalispell, Montana

Fillets of Sole Poached in White Wine

¼ cup butter or margarine,
    melted
4 (4-ounce) sole fillets
⅔ cup Chablis or other dry
    white wine
1 tablespoon lemon juice
1 tablespoon chopped fresh
    dillweed

1 tablespoon chopped fresh
    parsley
¼ teaspoon dried whole
    thyme
1 tablespoon chopped green
    onion tops
1 tablespoon butter
Salt to taste

Place ¼ cup butter in a 13- x 9- x 2-inch dish. Add fillets; turn to coat. Combine wine and lemon juice; pour over fish. Sprinkle herbs and onions over fish. Bake at 350° for 10 minutes or until fish flakes easily when tested with a fork, basting once with liquid. Set fish aside, and keep warm. Place liquid in a saucepan. Bring to a boil; cover, reduce heat, and simmer 5 minutes. Add 1 tablespoon butter; stir until butter melts. Remove from heat; add salt. Spoon sauce over fish. Yield: 4 servings.   Esther Wagner Ellingson

Rosemalers' Recipes
The Vesterheim-Norwegian American Museum
Decorah, Iowa

St. Lucia Ring

1 package dry yeast
1 teaspoon sugar
¼ cup warm water (105° to 115°)
1 tablespoon boiling water
1 teaspoon saffron threads
¾ cup milk
¼ cup unsalted butter
¼ cup sugar
1 egg, lightly beaten
¼ teaspoon ground cardamom
4 to 4½ cups all-purpose flour
1 egg, lightly beaten
1 teaspoon sugar
1 tablespoon raisins
1 tablespoon slivered almonds

Dissolve yeast and 1 teaspoon sugar in warm water in a large bowl; let stand 5 minutes.

Pour boiling water over saffron threads; let stand 4 minutes or until saffron dissolves.

Combine milk and butter in a saucepan; heat until butter melts, stirring occasionally. Let cool to 120° to 130°. Add saffron mixture, milk mixture, ¼ cup sugar, 1 egg, and cardamom to yeast mixture; beat at medium speed of an electric mixer until well blended. Gradually stir in enough flour to make a soft dough.

Turn dough out onto a well-floured surface, and knead until smooth and elastic (about 5 minutes). Place in a well-greased bowl, turning to grease top. Cover and let rise in a warm place (85°), free from drafts, 1 hour or until doubled in bulk.

Punch dough down. Divide dough into 12 equal portions. Roll each portion into a 5-inch rope. Tightly coil one end of rope toward center. Bring other end of rope around curl forming a coil. Pinch ends to seal. Arrange coiled rolls in a circle with sides slightly touching on a greased baking sheet. Brush dough with 1 beaten egg; sprinkle with 1 teaspoon sugar. Place several raisins and almonds in the center of each coil. Cover and let rise in a warm place, free from drafts, 30 minutes or until dough is doubled in bulk. Bake at 375° for 20 minutes or until golden brown. Let cool on a wire rack. Yield: 1 dozen rolls (1 ring).   Jerome Grunes

Hemi-demi-semi Flavors
The Chamber Music Society of the North Shore
Glencoe, Illinois

Pepparkakor

1 cup butter, softened	1 teaspoon baking soda
½ cup sugar	1 teaspoon ground cinnamon
½ cup molasses	1 teaspoon ground cloves
1 tablespoon whipping cream	1 teaspoon ground ginger
3¼ cups all-purpose flour	

Cream butter; gradually add sugar, beating at medium speed of an electric mixer until light and fluffy. Add molasses and whipping cream, beating well. Combine flour and remaining ingredients in a medium bowl; stir well. Add to creamed mixture, beating well. Cover and chill at least 2 hours.

Divide dough into 4 equal portions. Work with one portion of dough at a time, and store remainder in refrigerator. Roll dough to ¼-inch thickness on a lightly floured surface. Cut with a 2-inch cookie cutter; place on lightly greased cookie sheets. Repeat procedure with remaining dough.

Bake at 375° for 6 to 8 minutes or until cookies are lightly browned. Let cool on wire racks. Yield: 6 dozen.

Ancestral Stirrings
The New England Historic Genealogical Society
Boston, Massachusetts

Ancestral Stirrings *features family recipes, stories, letters, and early cookbooks donated by members and friends of the New England Historic Genealogical Society of Boston, Massachusetts. The society was founded to collect, study, and preserve the history of families and communities. Monies earned from the cookbook sales will go toward collecting and publishing valuable records, thereby helping thousands discover their New England heritage.*

Norwegian Nut Cake

4 eggs, separated
1 cup sifted powdered sugar
¼ cup all-purpose flour
1 teaspoon baking powder
1 cup finely chopped
  blanched almonds,
  hazelnuts, or walnuts
1 teaspoon vanilla extract

½ cup sugar
¼ cup chopped blanched
  almonds, hazelnuts, or
  walnuts
1 (16-ounce) jar apricot or
  raspberry jam
1 cup whipping cream,
  whipped

Grease bottoms only of two 8-inch round cakepans. Line bottoms with wax paper. Grease and flour wax paper; set aside.

Beat egg yolks at high speed of an electric mixer until thick and lemon colored. Combine 1 cup sugar, flour, and baking powder in a large mixing bowl; gradually add beaten egg yolks, beating well at medium speed until blended. Stir in 1 cup finely chopped nuts and vanilla.

Pour batter into prepared cakepans. Bake at 325° for 20 to 22 minutes or until cake springs back when lightly touched. When cake is done, immediately loosen from sides of pan, and turn out onto a sugared towel. Carefully peel off wax paper. Let cake layers cool completely on wire racks.

Combine ½ cup sugar and ¼ cup nuts in a heavy saucepan; cook over medium heat, stirring constantly, until sugar melts and mixture turns golden brown. Pour into a large shallow pan; let cool. Break into small pieces. Set aside.

Split cake layers in half horizontally to make 4 layers. Spread jam between layers. Frost sides and top edge of cake with whipped cream. Sprinkle unfrosted center of top layer with nut topping. Chill 12 to 24 hours. Yield: one 8-inch cake.   Pat Virch

Rosemalers' Recipes
The Vesterheim-Norwegian American Museum
Decorah, Iowa

Appetizers & Beverages

*Just outside of Des Moines, Iowa, is a living history village
called Walnut Hill. The village includes a cabinetmaking
shop, smithy, veterinary clinic, and general store stocked with
a variety of goods and a big red coffee grinder. Costumed
interpreters demonstrate crafts and explain the displays which
trace the evolution of agriculture in the region.*

Brie and Easy

1 (2-pound) round fully
  ripened Brie, chilled
½ cup chopped green onions

½ cup walnuts, chopped
¼ cup raisins

Remove rind from top of cheese. Place cheese on a baking sheet; top with onions, walnuts, and raisins. Bake at 350° for 12 minutes or until cheese softens. Serve warm with crackers or sliced Granny Smith apples. Yield: 12 appetizer servings.

Hearts and Flours
The Junior League of Waco, Texas

Layered Brie and Pesto

1 cup packed fresh basil sprigs
¾ cup grated Parmesan
  cheese
½ cup chopped fresh parsley
¼ cup pine nuts or chopped
  walnuts
2 cloves garlic, halved
⅓ cup olive oil

1 (8-ounce) package cream
  cheese, softened
4½ ounces fully ripened Brie
  with rind removed, softened
½ cup whipping cream,
  whipped
Garnishes: fresh basil and
  parsley sprigs

Remove and discard stems from 1 cup basil sprigs. Wash leaves, and drain well. Position knife blade in food processor bowl; add basil leaves, and process until finely chopped. Add Parmesan cheese and next 3 ingredients; process until smooth. With processor running, pour olive oil through food chute in a slow, steady stream, processing until combined. Set pesto aside.

Combine cream cheese and Brie; beat at medium speed of an electric mixer until smooth. Fold in whipped cream.

Line a 3½-cup mold or bowl with plastic wrap, leaving a 1-inch overhang of plastic wrap around edges. Spread one-fourth of cheese mixture in prepared mold. Spread one-third of pesto over cheese mixture. Repeat layers twice. Top with remaining cheese mixture. Cover and chill at least 8 hours.

Unmold onto a serving platter; carefully peel off plastic wrap. Garnish, if desired. Serve with unsalted crackers. Yield: 3½ cups.

A Matter of Taste
The Junior League of Morristown, New Jersey

Four Cheese Ball

2 cups (8 ounces) shredded
  Colby cheese
1 cup (4 ounces) shredded
  provolone cheese
1 cup small-curd cottage
  cheese

1 (8-ounce) package cream
  cheese, softened
1 teaspoon prepared mustard
1 teaspoon Worcestershire
  sauce
Paprika

Position knife blade in food processor bowl; add all ingredients except paprika, and process until combined. Wrap cheese mixture in plastic wrap, and chill 2 to 3 hours. Shape mixture into a 6-inch ball, and sprinkle with paprika. Let stand at room temperature about 20 minutes before serving. Serve with crackers. Yield: one 6-inch cheese ball.   Terry and Cindy Schwab

Centennial Cookbook: 100 Years of Freemasonry in North Dakota
The Masonic Grand Lodge
Fargo, North Dakota

Bacon and Almond Cheese Ball

4 cups (16 ounces) shredded
  process American cheese
1 (8-ounce) package cream
  cheese, softened
1 cup finely chopped
  blanched almonds, toasted
1 cup finely chopped green
  onions

6 slices bacon, cooked and
  crumbled
Dash of salt
½ cup mayonnaise
Additional finely chopped
  blanched almonds, toasted

Combine first 6 ingredients in a medium bowl; mix well. Add mayonnaise; mix well. Shape mixture into two 4-inch balls. Roll cheese balls in finely chopped almonds. Wrap cheese balls in plastic wrap, and chill 2 to 3 hours. Serve with crackers. Yield: two 4-inch cheese balls.   Buna Patterson

Aggies, Moms, and Apple Pie
The Federation of Texas A&M University Mothers' Clubs
College Station, Texas

Summer Garden Appetizer

2 large tomatoes, peeled, seeded, and chopped
1 cup minced celery
1 cup peeled, seeded, and chopped cucumber
1 cup chopped green pepper
¾ cup minced onion
½ cup scraped, shredded carrot
1 (4-ounce) can chopped green chiles, drained
2 tablespoons minced fresh parsley
1 envelope unflavored gelatin
¼ cup cold water
¼ cup boiling water
1 cup mayonnaise
1 tablespoon Worcestershire sauce
1 teaspoon salt
1 teaspoon dried whole dillweed
1 teaspoon paprika
½ teaspoon hot sauce
½ teaspoon ground red pepper (optional)
Garnish: fresh dillweed or parsley sprigs

Drain first 6 ingredients on paper towels 30 minutes; pat dry with paper towels, and place in a large bowl. Add green chiles and minced parsley; stir well, and set aside. Combine gelatin and cold water. Add boiling water; stir until gelatin dissolves. Let cool.

Combine mayonnaise and next 5 ingredients; stir in red pepper, if desired. Stir in gelatin mixture.

Fold mayonnaise mixture into vegetable mixture. Spoon into an oiled 6-cup mold. Cover and chill 8 hours. Garnish, if desired. Serve with crackers. Yield: 5½ cups.   Eleanor D. Hughes

Gracious Goodness: The Taste of Memphis
The Symphony League of Memphis, Tennessee

Aggies, Moms, and Apple Pie *was compiled by the Federation of Texas A&M University Mothers' Clubs. The Federation focuses on the needs of college students and their families. Proceeds will go toward the funding of student scholarships and loans.*

Radish Spread

1 (3-ounce) package cream
cheese, softened
2 tablespoons butter or
margarine, softened
1 teaspoon prepared
mustard
1 clove garlic, crushed

¼ teaspoon salt
⅛ teaspoon pepper
½ cup finely shredded
radishes
2 tablespoons chopped fresh
parsley

Combine cream cheese and butter in a small mixing bowl; beat well at medium speed of an electric mixer. Add mustard and next 3 ingredients, beating well. Stir in radishes and parsley. Cover and chill at least 1 hour. Serve with crackers or an assortment of fresh vegetables. Yield: ¾ cup.   Blanche Larson

eating
First Lutheran Church
Mission Hills, Kansas

Avocado and Pine Nut Dip

2 medium-size ripe avocados,
peeled and mashed
1 medium tomato, coarsely
chopped
½ cup chopped pine nuts
3 green onions, chopped
1 small clove garlic, crushed
2 tablespoons mayonnaise

2 tablespoons lemon juice
2 teaspoons lime juice
¾ teaspoon salt
¼ teaspoon ground
coriander
¼ teaspoon pepper
Dash of hot sauce

Combine all ingredients in a medium bowl, stirring until well blended. Cover and chill thoroughly. Serve dip with tortilla chips. Yield: 1½ cups.   Arlene Harris

The Best Specialties of the House . . . and More
North Suburban Guild of Children's Memorial Medical Center
Chicago, Illinois

Smoked Oyster Dip

1 (8-ounce) package cream
  cheese, softened
1½ cups mayonnaise
1 tablespoon lemon juice
⅛ teaspoon hot sauce

1 (4¼-ounce) can chopped
  ripe olives, drained
1 (3.6-ounce) can smoked
  oysters, drained and
  chopped

Beat cream cheese at medium speed of an electric mixer. Add mayonnaise, lemon juice, and hot sauce; beat until smooth. Add olives and oysters, stirring gently to combine. Serve with crackers. Yield: 3 cups.   Brenda Tunstill

In the Pink of Things
The Muskogee Regional Medical Center Auxiliary
Muskogee, Oklahoma

Sombrero Dip

1 pound lean ground beef
½ cup chopped onion
½ cup hot catsup
1 tablespoon chili powder
1 teaspoon salt
1 (15-ounce) can kidney
  beans, undrained

1 cup (4 ounces) shredded
  Cheddar cheese
½ cup chopped onion
½ cup chopped ripe olives
  (optional)

Cook ground beef and ½ cup chopped onion in a large skillet until beef is browned, stirring to crumble meat. Drain well, and return to skillet. Stir in catsup, chili powder, and salt.

Place beans in container of an electric blender, and process until smooth; add to meat mixture. Bring to a boil; reduce heat, and simmer 30 minutes or until mixture thickens, stirring occasionally.

Spoon meat mixture into a chafing dish, if desired. Sprinkle with cheese, ½ cup chopped onion, and, if desired, olives. Serve with corn chips. Yield: 3 cups.

Terry Home Presents Food & Fun from Celebrities & Us
Terry Home, Inc.
Sumner, Washington

Cheese Icebox Wafers

½ cup butter, softened
2 cups (8 ounces) shredded
 sharp Cheddar cheese
1½ cups all-purpose flour
½ teaspoon salt

Pinch of ground red pepper
Pecan halves
Paprika
Additional salt to taste

Cream butter; add next 4 ingredients, and mix until blended. Shape dough into two 6-inch rolls; wrap in wax paper, and chill 2 hours. Unwrap rolls, and cut into ¼-inch slices; place cut side down on ungreased baking sheets.

Bake at 350° for 12 minutes or until lightly browned. Top each wafer with a pecan half; sprinkle with paprika and salt. Let cool on wire racks. Yield: 4 dozen.   Mrs. Edward S. T. Hale

Critics' Choice
The Corinth Theatre Arts Guild
Corinth, Mississippi

Green Chile Wontons

4 cups (16 ounces) shredded
 Monterey Jack cheese
⅔ cup diced green chiles
⅓ cup diced jalapeño
 peppers

1 (1-pound) package frozen
 wonton skins, thawed
Peanut oil
Salt

Combine cheese, chiles, and pepper; stir well. Working with one wonton skin at a time, spoon about 1½ teaspoons cheese mixture in center of each wonton. Moisten edges of wonton lightly with water. Fold wonton in half to form a triangle, pressing edges together to seal. Repeat procedure with remaining wonton skins and cheese mixture. Chill 20 minutes.

Fry wontons in a small amount of hot oil (375°) until golden brown, turning once. Drain on paper towels. Sprinkle with salt. Serve with avocado dip. Yield: 6½ dozen.   Mary Jane Groesch

Secret Recipes II
4450th Tactical Group, Nellis Air Force Base
Las Vegas, Nevada

Hot Cheddar-Stuffed Mushrooms

18 large fresh mushrooms
2 tablespoons butter or
  margarine, melted
1 cup chopped onion
¼ cup butter or margarine,
  melted
1 cup soft breadcrumbs

1 cup (4 ounces) shredded
  Cheddar cheese
½ cup chopped walnuts
¼ cup chopped fresh parsley
½ teaspoon salt
¼ teaspoon pepper

Clean mushrooms with damp paper towels. Remove and chop stems; set aside. Brush mushroom caps with 2 tablespoons melted butter; place in a lightly buttered shallow baking pan. Set aside.

Sauté onion and chopped mushroom stems in ¼ cup melted butter in a large skillet over medium heat until vegetables are tender. Remove from heat. Add breadcrumbs and remaining ingredients; stir well.

Spoon cheese mixture evenly into mushroom caps. Bake, uncovered, at 350° for 20 minutes or until cheese melts and mushrooms are thoroughly heated. Yield: 1½ dozen.   Judy Mahoney

641.5 "Show Me" Recipes
The Missouri Association of School Librarians
Glen Carbon, Illinois

The cookbook 641.5 "Show Me" Recipes was created for the Missouri Association of School Librarians. The professional organization is devoted to the continued education and training of Missouri school librarians, recognizing contributions to the profession, and improving school library media programs. The Mark Twain Award is presented annually by the association to a favored author that has been chosen by the children of Missouri.

Black-Eyed Peawheels

1 (15-ounce) can black-eyed
  peas, drained
¼ cup butter or margarine,
  melted
¼ teaspoon ground red
  pepper
¼ teaspoon seasoned salt

Dash of garlic powder
2 (3-ounce) packages cream
  cheese, softened
1 (1-pound) package sliced
  cooked ham (16 slices)
16 green onions

Combine peas and butter in a saucepan. Cook over medium-high heat until mixture boils. Add red pepper, seasoned salt, and garlic powder; reduce heat, and simmer 10 minutes. Let cool.

Position knife blade in food processor bowl. Add pea mixture and cream cheese, and process until mixture is smooth. Spread cream cheese mixture evenly over ham slices. Place a green onion on long edge of each ham slice, and roll up jellyroll fashion; cover with plastic wrap. Chill at least 1 hour. Cut ham rolls into ½-inch slices. Yield: 6½ dozen.

Betty Barrett

The Cookbook
East Lake United Methodist Church
Birmingham, Alabama

Spiced Meatballs

1 pound ground chuck
½ pound ground pork
¾ cup fine, dry breadcrumbs
2 tablespoons finely chopped
  onion
1 tablespoon catsup
4 drops of hot sauce
½ teaspoon prepared
  horseradish
2 eggs, beaten
½ teaspoon salt
¼ teaspoon pepper
1 tablespoon grated Parmesan
  cheese
1 to 2 tablespoons butter or
  margarine, melted

½ cup catsup
½ cup chili sauce
¼ cup cider vinegar
½ cup firmly packed brown
  sugar
2 tablespoons finely chopped
  onion
1 tablespoon Worcestershire
  sauce
4 drops of hot sauce
½ teaspoon dry mustard
3 drops of aromatic bitters
1 teaspoon salt
¼ teaspoon pepper
Garnish: chopped green
  onions

Combine first 11 ingredients in a large bowl; stir well. Shape meat mixture into 1-inch balls. Cook meatballs in melted butter in a large skillet over medium-high heat until browned on all sides. Drain well; set aside.

Combine catsup, chili sauce, vinegar, brown sugar, 2 tablespoons chopped onion, Worcestershire sauce, 4 drops hot sauce, dry mustard, bitters, 1 teaspoon salt, and ¼ teaspoon pepper in a large saucepan; stir well. Bring to a boil; reduce heat, and simmer 10 minutes or until sauce is thoroughly heated. To serve, combine meatballs and sauce in a chafing dish. Serve warm. Garnish, if desired. Yield: about 6 dozen.   Laura Powell Whitlock

Georgia on My Menu
The Junior League of Cobb-Marietta, Georgia

Silver Spoon Angel Wings

18 chicken wings (about 3 pounds)
½ cup sugar
½ cup water
½ cup soy sauce
¼ cup pineapple juice
2 tablespoons vegetable oil
1 teaspoon grated ginger
½ teaspoon garlic powder

Remove and discard chicken wing tips. Place wings in a 13- x 9- x 2-inch baking dish; set aside.

Combine sugar and remaining ingredients in a small bowl, stirring until sugar dissolves.

Pour marinade over chicken. Cover and marinate in refrigerator 8 hours, turning occasionally.

Drain chicken wings, reserving marinade. Place marinade in a small saucepan. Bring to a boil; reduce heat, and simmer 5 minutes. Place wings in a 15- x 10- x 1-inch jellyroll pan. Bake at 350° for 40 minutes or until done, basting frequently with reserved marinade. Yield: 6 appetizer servings.   Angeline Grooms Proctor

A Samford Celebration Cookbook
Samford University Auxiliary
Birmingham, Alabama

Authentic Buffalo Wings

24 chicken wings (about 4
  pounds)
Salt and freshly ground
  pepper
Peanut oil

¼ cup butter, melted
2 to 5 tablespoons hot sauce
1 tablespoon vinegar
Celery sticks
Blue Cheese Dressing

Remove and discard chicken wing tips. Cut wings in half at joint.
Sprinkle with salt and pepper. Fry 8 wings at a time in deep hot oil
(375°) 10 minutes or until golden brown, turning occasionally. Drain
on paper towels. Combine butter, hot sauce, and vinegar; stir well.
Pour over wings, tossing to coat. Serve warm with celery sticks and
Blue Cheese Dressing. Yield: 6 appetizer servings.

Blue Cheese Dressing

1 cup mayonnaise
½ cup sour cream
¼ cup crumbled blue cheese
¼ cup chopped fresh parsley
2 tablespoons finely chopped
  onion

1 tablespoon lemon juice
1 tablespoon vinegar
1 teaspoon minced garlic
¼ teaspoon salt
¼ teaspoon black pepper
Dash of ground red pepper

Combine all ingredients in a small bowl; stir well. Cover and chill
at least 1 hour. Yield: 2¼ cups.

Cardinal Cuisine
The Mount Vernon Hospital Auxiliary
Alexandria, Virginia

Chicken Liver Strudel Slices

1 onion, finely chopped
¼ cup butter, melted and
  divided
1 pound chicken livers
1½ cups sliced fresh
  mushrooms
¼ cup soft breadcrumbs
1 egg, lightly beaten
2 tablespoons chopped fresh
  parsley

2 tablespoons cognac
½ teaspoon salt
⅛ teaspoon ground allspice
⅛ teaspoon pepper
10 sheets commercial frozen
  phyllo pastry, thawed
Additional melted butter

Sauté onion in 2 tablespoons melted butter in a medium skillet until tender. Add remaining 2 tablespoons melted butter and chicken livers; cook over medium-high heat until livers are browned on all sides. Add mushrooms, and cook 3 minutes. Remove from heat, and let cool slightly.

Finely chop liver mixture; place in a large bowl. Add breadcrumbs and next 6 ingredients; stir well. Set aside, and let cool completely.

Place 2 sheets of phyllo pastry on a damp towel, keeping remaining phyllo covered. Lightly brush phyllo with melted butter. Top with 2 sheets phyllo; brush with melted butter. Repeat layers, with remaining phyllo and butter.

Place liver mixture on phyllo layers. Shape mixture into a log down long side of phyllo layers; roll up jellyroll fashion, starting at long side. Carefully place roll, seam side down, on a large ungreased baking sheet. Bake at 375° for 30 to 40 minutes or until pastry is crisp and golden brown. Cut into slices, and serve immediately. Yield: 18 appetizer servings.   Jandi Dille

Port's Galley
The Port Council of Port of Portland, Oregon

Apple Knockers

3 (3-inch) sticks cinnamon, broken into pieces
2 teaspoons whole cloves
1 cup sugar
½ teaspoon ground nutmeg
2 quarts apple cider
2 cups orange juice
½ cup lemon juice

Place cinnamon sticks and cloves in a large tea ball, or tie in a cheesecloth bag. Set aside.

Combine sugar and nutmeg in a large Dutch oven, stirring well. Gradually add apple cider, orange juice, and lemon juice, stirring well. Add tea ball. Bring mixture to a boil; reduce heat, and simmer 15 minutes. Remove tea ball; discard spices. Serve beverage warm. Yield: 2½ quarts.   Kathleen Spires

Central Texas Style
The Junior Service League of Killeen, Texas

Cranberry Spiced Tea

2 cups boiling water
5 regular-size tea bags
¼ teaspoon ground cinnamon
¼ teaspoon ground nutmeg
⅓ cup sugar

1 (48-ounce) bottle cranberry
  juice cocktail
⅔ cup orange juice
½ cup water
¼ cup lemon juice

Pour boiling water over tea bags; add cinnamon and nutmeg. Let steep 5 minutes. Remove tea bags, squeezing gently. Add sugar and remaining ingredients; stir until sugar dissolves. Serve warm. Yield: 2 quarts.

Hearts & Flour
The Women's Club of Pittsford, New York

Mint Sparkle

1 (10-ounce) jar mint jelly
1 cup water
2 (12-ounce) cans
  unsweetened pineapple
  juice

1 cup water
½ cup lemon juice
1 (12-ounce) bottle ginger ale,
  chilled

Combine jelly and 1 cup water in a medium saucepan. Cook over low heat, stirring constantly, until jelly melts. Let cool. Stir in pineapple juice, 1 cup water, and lemon juice; chill thoroughly. Gently stir in ginger ale just before serving. Yield: about 2 quarts.

Visions of Sugarplums
The Parents' Association, Charlotte Country Day School
Charlotte, North Carolina

Lavender and Old Lace Punch

2 cups water
1 (6-inch) stick cinnamon
7 whole cloves
2 (12-ounce) cans frozen
  grape juice, thawed and
  undiluted

½ cup lime juice
Ice cubes
2 (32-ounce) bottles ginger
  ale, chilled

Combine water, cinnamon, and cloves in a large saucepan. Bring to a boil; remove from heat, and let cool. Remove and discard cinnamon stick and cloves. Add grape juice and lime juice; stir well.

To serve, pour grape juice mixture over ice cubes in a large punch bowl. Gently stir in chilled ginger ale just before serving. Yield: about 3½ quarts. Wava Apelgreen

Aspic and Old Lace
The Northern Indiana Historical Society
South Bend, Indiana

Pink Debutante Punch

2 (64-ounce) bottles cranberry or cranapple juice cocktail, chilled
2 (12-ounce) cans frozen pink lemonade concentrate, undiluted
2 (6-ounce) cans frozen orange juice concentrate, undiluted

1 gallon water
2 (32-ounce) bottles lemon-lime carbonated beverage or carbonated sparkling water, chilled
Ice ring (recipe follows)

Combine cranberry juice cocktail, lemonade concentrate, and orange juice concentrate in a large punch bowl; stir until concentrates are dissolved. Add water, stirring well. Gently stir in chilled lemon-lime beverage just before serving. Carefully float ice ring in punch. Yield: 3 gallons.

Ice Ring

1 (6-ounce) can frozen pink lemonade concentrate, thawed and diluted

⅓ cup green seedless grapes
⅓ cup purple seedless grapes
⅓ cup red seedless grapes

Pour 3 cups lemonade into a 6-cup ring mold; arrange grapes in mold and freeze. Fill mold to top with remaining lemonade; freeze. Let ice ring stand at room temperature 5 minutes before unmolding. Yield: one 6-cup ice ring.

Twickenham Tables
Twickenham Historic Preservation District Association, Inc.
Huntsville, Alabama

Sparkling Pink Party Punch

3 tablespoons red cinnamon
  candies
¼ cup sugar
½ cup warm water
1 (46-ounce) can pineapple
  juice, chilled

1 (32-ounce) bottle ginger ale
  or lemon-lime carbonated
  beverage, chilled

Combine first 3 ingredients in a small saucepan. Bring to a boil; reduce heat, and simmer until candy dissolves, stirring occasionally. Let cool completely.

Combine syrup mixture and pineapple juice in a large punch bowl; stir well. Gently stir in chilled ginger ale just before serving. Yield: 2½ quarts.   Ian and Craig Hasund

Symphony of Tastes
The Youth Symphony of Anchorage, Alaska

Sparkling Strawberry Punch

2 (10-ounce) packages frozen
  strawberries, slightly
  thawed
1 (6-ounce) can frozen
  lemonade concentrate,
  slightly thawed and
  undiluted
1 (25.4-ounce) bottle rosé or
  other dry pink wine, chilled

4 cups ice cubes
¼ cup sugar
2 (28-ounce) bottles ginger
  ale, chilled
1 (28-ounce) bottle club soda,
  chilled
Garnish: orange slices

Combine strawberries and lemonade concentrate in container of an electric blender; process until smooth.

Combine strawberry mixture, wine, ice cubes, and sugar; stir until sugar dissolves. Pour into punch bowl. Gently stir in chilled ginger ale and club soda just before serving. Garnish, if desired. Yield: about 1¼ gallons.   Carolyn Bracken

Black-Eyed Susan Country
The Saint Agnes Hospital Auxiliary
Baltimore, Maryland

Perfect Lemonade

5 cups water, divided
1 cup lemon juice

3 lemons
1 cup sugar

Combine 4 cups water and lemon juice. Chill 30 minutes. Peel lemons, leaving inner white pith on fruit. Reserve lemons for other uses. Cut lemon rind into strips. Combine rind, sugar, and remaining 1 cup water in a saucepan. Cook over medium-low heat, stirring constantly, until sugar dissolves. Bring to a boil; boil 7 minutes. Let cool. Add to lemon juice mixture; stir. Chill 2 hours before serving. Yield: 1½ quarts.   Fran Zurilgen

Crème de la Congregation
Our Saviors Lutheran Church
Lafayette, California

Frozen Peach Daiquiris

3 large fresh peaches, peeled
  and halved
3 tablespoons sugar

½ cup light rum or vodka
2 tablespoons fresh lime juice
3 cups crushed ice

Place first 4 ingredients in container of an electric blender; process at high speed until smooth. Add ice, and process until slushy. Yield: 1½ quarts.   Carol Harnois Potter

With Great Gusto
The Junior League of Youngstown, Ohio

Beer Margaritas

¾ cup beer
¾ cup tequila
1 (6-ounce) can frozen
  limeade concentrate, thawed
  and undiluted

4 cups crushed ice
Garnish: lime wedges

Combine beer, tequila, and limeade concentrate in container of an electric blender. Add crushed ice, and process until smooth. Garnish, if desired. Yield: 1½ quarts.

Gourmet LA
The Junior League of Los Angeles, California

Brandy Freeze

½ gallon vanilla ice cream,
  softened
6 to 7½ ounces brandy or
  amaretto

3 to 4 ounces crème de cacao
Ground nutmeg

Combine first 3 ingredients; stir well to combine. Position knife blade in food processor bowl; add one-third of ice cream mixture, and process until smooth. Transfer ice cream mixture to a freezer container. Repeat procedure twice. Freeze until firm.

Serve in brandy snifters or wine glasses. Top each serving with a dash of ground nutmeg. Yield: 1½ quarts.

Celebrations on the Bayou
The Junior League of Monroe, Louisiana

Cafe Granite

1 cup sugar
2 cups boiling water
2 teaspoons instant espresso
  coffee granules

1 cup hot water
¼ cup crème de cacao
Whipped cream or vanilla ice
  cream

Dissolve sugar in 2 cups boiling water. Dissolve espresso granules in 1 cup hot water. Combine sugar and coffee mixtures; freeze 8 hours or until slushy. Stir in crème de cacao. Spoon into cups, and top each serving with whipped cream or a scoop of ice cream. Yield: 3¾ cups.   Sandra Uelner and Jane Trishman Heaton

World Heritage of Cooking
Friends of the World Heritage Museum
Urbana, Illinois

Breads

FRENCH MARKET

The French Market in colorful New Orleans, Louisiana, is the oldest "trading post" in the city. Vendors once advertised their wide variety of goods in song. The French Market contains all the flavorful ingredients needed to create the Creole cuisine for which New Orleans is famous.

Buttermilk Prune Bread

1 cup all-purpose flour
1 cup yellow cornmeal
1 teaspoon baking soda
1¼ teaspoons salt
1½ cups buttermilk

⅓ cup molasses
1 cup pitted prunes, chopped
1½ teaspoons grated orange
  rind

Combine first 4 ingredients in a medium bowl; stir well. Add buttermilk and molasses, stirring until blended. Stir in prunes and orange rind. Pour batter into a well-greased 6-cup mold or coffee can; cover tightly with mold lid or aluminum foil.

Place mold on a shallow rack in a large Dutch oven; add enough boiling water to come halfway up sides of mold. Return water to a boil; cover and steam in continuously boiling water, replacing water as necessary, 1 hour and 45 minutes to 2 hours or until a wooden pick inserted in center of bread comes out clean. Remove mold from water, and let stand 10 minutes. Unmold bread; serve with butter or cream cheese. Yield: 1 loaf.   Cheri Adams

Our Town Cookbook
The Historical Society of Peterborough, New Hampshire

Pueblo Pumpkin Raisin Bread

1¾ cups cooked, mashed
  pumpkin
1½ cups firmly packed brown
  sugar
½ cup butter, melted
3 eggs, lightly beaten

3 cups all-purpose flour
2 teaspoons baking powder
1 teaspoon ground cinnamon
½ teaspoon ground nutmeg
1 cup raisins
½ cup chopped pecans

Combine first 4 ingredients; stir well. Combine flour, baking powder, cinnamon, and nutmeg; stir well. Add raisins and pecans, stirring gently to combine. Add flour mixture to pumpkin mixture, stirring until well blended.

Pour batter into 2 greased and floured 8½- x 4½- x 3-inch loafpans. Bake at 350° for 55 minutes or until a wooden pick inserted in center comes out clean. Let cool in pans 10 minutes. Serve warm. Yield: 2 loaves.   Sharon Howell

In the Pink of Things
The Muskogee Regional Medical Center Auxiliary
Muskogee, Oklahoma

Rhubarb Bread

2 cups diced fresh rhubarb
1½ cups sugar
1 cup vegetable oil
½ cup milk
3 eggs
3 cups plus 2 tablespoons
    all-purpose flour
2 teaspoons baking soda
½ teaspoon baking powder
½ teaspoon salt
1 tablespoon ground
    cinnamon
½ cup chopped pecans or
    walnuts (optional)

Place first 5 ingredients in container of an electric blender, and process until smooth.

Combine flour, soda, baking powder, salt, and cinnamon in a large bowl; stir well. Add rhubarb mixture to flour mixture, stirring just until dry ingredients are moistened. Stir in pecans, if desired.

Pour batter into 2 greased 8½- x 4½- x 3-inch loafpans. Bake at 325° for 1 hour or until a wooden pick inserted in center comes out clean. Let cool in pans 10 minutes; remove from pans, and let cool on wire racks. Yield: 2 loaves.   The Family of Erin Whitney

Symphony of Tastes
The Youth Symphony of Anchorage, Alaska

Peanut Butter Bread with Bacon

1 cup creamy peanut butter
1 tablespoon butter, melted
2 cups all-purpose flour
1 tablespoon baking powder
1 teaspoon salt
1 cup sugar
1 cup milk
1 egg, lightly beaten
1 cup chopped unsalted
    roasted peanuts
16 slices bacon, cooked and
    crumbled (about 1 cup)

Cream peanut butter and butter in a large mixing bowl. Combine flour and next 3 ingredients; stir. Add flour mixture to creamed mixture, stirring well.

Combine milk and egg; add to creamed mixture, stirring to combine. Stir in peanuts and bacon. Pour batter into a greased 9- x 5- x 3-inch loafpan. Bake at 350° for 1 hour and 15 minutes or until a wooden pick inserted in center comes out clean. Let cool in pan 10 minutes; remove from pan, and let cool on a wire rack. Yield: 1 loaf.

From Scratch Cookbook
The Assistance League® of Glendale, California

Gourmet Cornbread

2½ cups yellow cornmeal
1 cup all-purpose flour
1 tablespoon plus 1 teaspoon
 baking powder
1 teaspoon salt
2 tablespoons sugar
1½ cups milk
½ cup vegetable oil

3 eggs
2 cups (8 ounces) shredded
 sharp Cheddar cheese
1 large onion, grated
1 (17-ounce) can cream-style
 corn
6 to 8 chopped green chiles

Combine cornmeal, flour, baking powder, salt, and sugar in a large bowl; stir well.

Combine milk, oil, and eggs in a medium mixing bowl; beat well at medium speed of an electric mixer. Add milk mixture, cheese, and remaining ingredients to cornmeal mixture, stirring just until dry ingredients are moistened. Pour batter into a greased 13- x 9- x 2-inch baking pan. Bake at 425° for 25 to 30 minutes or until golden brown. Yield: 15 servings.   Marcelle Phillips

Pioneers of Alaska Cookbook
The Pioneers of Alaska Auxiliary #4
Anchorage, Alaska

From Scratch Cookbook *was compiled by the* **Assistance League®** *of Glendale, California. The league is engaged in providing volunteer service to the community through such offerings as SAT seminars for young adults entering college and Operation School Bell, which provides clothing, toothbrushes, and other supplies to school-age children. Their motto All for Service and Service for All exemplifies the commitment of the organization to the Glendale Community.*

Coffee Lovers' Coffee Cake

2 cups all-purpose flour
2 teaspoons instant coffee granules
2 cups firmly packed brown sugar
1 teaspoon ground cinnamon
½ teaspoon salt
¼ teaspoon ground nutmeg
½ cup butter
1 (8-ounce) carton sour cream
1 teaspoon baking soda
1 egg, beaten
½ cup chopped pecans or walnuts

Combine flour and coffee granules in a large bowl. Add brown sugar and next 3 ingredients; stir well. Cut in butter with a pastry blender until mixture resembles coarse meal. Press half of crumb mixture into a greased 9-inch square baking pan; set aside.

Combine sour cream and baking soda, stirring well. Add to remaining crumb mixture, stirring just until dry ingredients are moistened. Add egg, stirring gently to combine. Pour sour cream mixture over crumb mixture in pan; sprinkle with pecans. Bake at 350° for 45 minutes. Yield: one 9-inch coffee cake.

Honest to Goodness
The Junior League of Springfield, Illinois

Fresh Peach Coffee Cake

½ cup butter or margarine, softened
1 cup sugar
1 egg
2 cups all-purpose flour
2 teaspoons baking powder
½ teaspoon salt
⅔ cup milk
1 large fresh ripe peach, peeled and thinly sliced
Ground cinnamon
1 cup sifted powdered sugar
1 tablespoon plus 1 teaspoon milk
½ teaspoon vanilla extract

Cream butter; gradually add 1 cup sugar, beating well at medium speed of an electric mixer. Add egg, beating well.

Combine flour, baking powder, and salt; stir well. Add to creamed mixture alternately with ⅔ cup milk, beginning and ending with flour mixture. Pour batter into a greased and floured 13- x 9- x 2-inch baking pan. Arrange peach slices over batter; sprinkle with cinnamon. Bake at 350° for 30 to 35 minutes or until a wooden pick inserted in center comes out clean.

Combine powdered sugar, 1 tablespoon plus 1 teaspoon milk, and vanilla in a small bowl; stir until smooth. Drizzle glaze over warm coffee cake. Yield: 15 servings.

From a Lighthouse Window
The Chesapeake Bay Maritime Museum
St. Michaels, Maryland

Orange Bran Muffins

5 cups all-purpose flour	4 cups buttermilk
1 tablespoon plus 2 teaspoons baking soda	1 large orange, peeled and coarsely chopped
1 teaspoon salt	1½ cups sugar
7 cups unprocessed wheat bran, uncooked	1 cup butter, melted
2 cups boiling water	1 cup vegetable oil
4 eggs	2 cups raisins or chopped dried fruit

Combine flour, soda, and salt in a large bowl; make a well in center of mixture. Set aside.

Combine wheat bran and boiling water in a large bowl; stir well, and set aside.

Place eggs, buttermilk, and chopped orange in container of an electric blender or food processor; process until smooth. Add buttermilk mixture to bran mixture; stir well. Add sugar, butter, and oil; stir well. Add buttermilk mixture to flour mixture, stirring just until dry ingredients are moistened. Add raisins; stir well. Cover batter, and store in refrigerator up to 1 month.

When ready to bake, spoon batter into greased muffin pans, filling two-thirds full. Bake at 400° for 20 minutes or until a wooden pick inserted in center of muffin comes out clean. Remove from pans immediately, and let muffins cool completely on wire racks. Yield: about 6 dozen.   Kate Munger

Home on the Range
West Marin Health Project and Dance Palace Community Center
Point Reyes, California

Coffee Cake Muffins

½ cup firmly packed brown sugar
½ cup chopped pecans or walnuts
2 tablespoons all-purpose flour
2 tablespoons butter or margarine, melted

2 teaspoons ground cinnamon
1½ cups all-purpose flour
2 teaspoons baking powder
½ teaspoon salt
½ cup sugar
¼ cup shortening
½ cup milk
1 egg, beaten

Combine first 5 ingredients in a small bowl; stir well, and set side.

Combine 1½ cups flour, baking powder, salt, and ½ cup sugar in a large bowl; stir well. Cut in shortening with a pastry blender until mixture resembles coarse meal. Combine milk and egg; add to flour mixture, stirring just until dry ingredients are moistened.

Spoon 1 tablespoon batter into paper-lined muffin pans; sprinkle with 1 tablespoon reserved brown sugar mixture. Top with remaining batter; sprinkle with remaining brown sugar mixture. Bake at 375° for 20 to 25 minutes or until a wooden pick inserted in center comes out clean. Yield: 1 dozen.   Mary Pankiewicz

Favorite Recipes from Fishers Island
The Island Bowling Center
Fishers Island, New York

The idea for **The Farmer's Daughters** *originated when two sisters, raised on a small farm in Point DeLuce, Arkansas, tried to think of a way to help the Multiple Sclerosis Society in it's fight against the disease with which their older sister had been diagnosed. Proceeds will benefit efforts of the local chapter of the National Multiple Sclerosis Society.*

Country Biscuits

2½ cups all-purpose flour
1 tablespoon baking powder
½ teaspoon baking soda
½ teaspoon salt

2 tablespoons shortening
1 cup buttermilk
¼ cup butter, melted

Combine first 4 ingredients in a large bowl, stir well. Cut in shortening with a pastry blender until mixture resembles coarse meal. Add buttermilk and melted butter, stirring until dry ingredients are moistened.

Turn dough out onto a floured surface, and knead lightly 4 or 5 times. Roll dough to ½-inch thickness; cut with a 2-inch biscuit cutter. Place on a lightly greased baking sheet. Bake at 400° for 15 to 18 minutes or until lightly browned. Yield: 2 dozen.

The Farmer's Daughters
The National Multiple Sclerosis Society
St. Charles, Arkansas

Cheddar Cheese Crackers

1 cup butter, softened
2 cups (8 ounces) shredded
  sharp Cheddar cheese
1 tablespoon chopped fresh
  chives
1 teaspoon caraway seeds

½ teaspoon dry mustard
⅛ teaspoon ground red
  pepper
1 teaspoon commercial steak
  sauce
2⅔ cups all-purpose flour

Cream butter; gradually add cheese and next 5 ingredients, beating well at medium speed of an electric mixer. Gradually stir in flour. Shape dough into four 7-inch rolls; wrap in wax paper, and chill at least 3 hours.

Unwrap rolls, and cut into ¼-inch slices. Place slices, cut side down, on greased baking sheets. Bake at 375° for 18 to 20 minutes or until lightly browned. Let cool completely on baking sheets. Store crackers in an airtight container. Yield: 9 dozen.

Central Texas Style
The Junior Service League of Killeen, Texas

Gingerbread Pancakes

2¼ cups all-purpose flour
1½ teaspoons baking powder
1½ teaspoons baking soda
½ teaspoon salt
1 tablespoon instant coffee
  granules
1 teaspoon ground cinnamon
1 teaspoon ground ginger
1 teaspoon ground nutmeg

½ teaspoon ground cloves
1 egg, beaten
¾ cup buttermilk
¾ cup water
¼ cup butter, melted
¼ cup firmly packed brown
  sugar
Lemon Hard Sauce

Sift together first 9 ingredients in a large bowl. Add egg, buttermilk, water, melted butter, and brown sugar, stirring until blended.

For each pancake, pour about ¼ cup batter onto a hot, lightly greased griddle. Turn pancakes when tops are covered with bubbles and edges look cooked. Serve with Lemon Hard Sauce. Yield: 12 (4-inch) pancakes.

Lemon Hard Sauce

½ cup butter, softened
2½ cups sifted powdered
  sugar

Grated rind of 1 lemon
3 tablespoons fresh lemon
  juice

Cream butter; gradually add sugar, beating until light and fluffy. Add lemon rind and lemon juice; beat until smooth. Yield: 1¼ cups.

Hearts and Flours
The Junior League of Waco, Texas

Peach Waffles

⅓ cup shortening
½ cup sugar
2 eggs
2 cups all-purpose flour
1 tablespoon baking powder
½ teaspoon salt

1 cup milk
1½ cups peeled, diced
  peaches
½ teaspoon lemon juice
½ teaspoon vanilla extract
Powdered sugar

Cream shortening; gradually add ½ cup sugar, beating well at low speed of an electric mixer. Add eggs, one at a time, beating well after each addition.

Combine flour, baking powder, and salt; add to creamed mixture alternately with milk, beginning and ending with flour mixture. Mix after each addition. Stir in peaches, lemon juice, and vanilla.

Bake in preheated oiled waffle iron. Sprinkle with powdered sugar. Serve waffles with sliced fresh fruit or whipped cream. Yield: 16 (4-inch) waffles.   Mrs. Helene Sailer

Aspic and Old Lace
The Northern Indiana Historical Society
South Bend, Indiana

Oatmeal Waffles with Orange-Maple Sauce

1½ cups all-purpose flour	½ teaspoon ground cinnamon
1 tablespoon baking powder	2 eggs, lightly beaten
½ teaspoon salt	1½ cups milk
1 tablespoon sugar	¼ cup butter, melted
½ cup quick-cooking oats, uncooked	¼ cup raisins, chopped
	Orange-Maple Sauce

Combine first 6 ingredients in a medium bowl; stir well.

Combine eggs, milk, and butter; stir well. Add milk mixture to dry ingredients, stirring until blended. Stir in raisins. Bake in preheated, oiled waffle iron. Serve waffles with warm Orange-Maple Sauce. Yield: 12 (4-inch) waffles.

Orange-Maple Sauce

1½ cups maple-flavored syrup	1 tablespoon grated orange rind

Combine syrup and orange rind in a small saucepan. Bring to a boil over medium heat; reduce heat, and simmer 5 minutes. Yield: 1½ cups.   Ray Hume

Port's Galley
The Port Council of Port of Portland, Oregon

Dilly Casserole Bread

1 package dry yeast
1 tablespoon sugar
¼ cup warm water (105° to 115°)
1 cup cottage cheese
1 egg, beaten
1½ tablespoons butter
1 tablespoon sugar

2 teaspoons instant minced onion
2 teaspoons dillseeds
1 teaspoon salt
¼ teaspoon baking soda
2½ cups all-purpose flour
Melted butter
Additional salt

Dissolve yeast and 1 tablespoon sugar in warm water; let stand 5 minutes. Combine cottage cheese and next 7 ingredients in a saucepan. Cook over medium heat until butter melts, stirring occasionally. Let cool to 105° to 115°.

Combine cottage cheese mixture, yeast mixture, and flour; stir well (dough will be sticky). Cover and let rise in a warm place (85°), free from drafts, 1 hour or until doubled in bulk. Stir well; spoon into a well-greased 2-quart soufflé dish. Cover and let rise in a warm place, free from drafts, 40 minutes or until doubled in bulk.

Bake at 350° for 30 minutes or until golden brown. Brush with melted butter, and sprinkle with salt. Remove from dish; let cool on a wire rack. Yield: 1 loaf.   Ella Haag Smith

200th Anniversary Year Cookbook
Christ Evangelical Lutheran Church
Jeffersontown, Kentucky

Oregano Bread

2 packages dry yeast
2 cups warm water (105° to 115°)
4½ cups all-purpose flour, divided
2 tablespoons sugar
2 teaspoons salt
1 tablespoon grated onion

2 tablespoons butter, softened
½ cup grated Parmesan cheese
1½ tablespoons dried whole oregano
1 tablespoon grated Parmesan cheese

Dissolve yeast in warm water; let stand 5 minutes. Combine yeast mixture, 3 cups flour, and next 6 ingredients in a mixing bowl. Beat at low speed of an electric mixer 2 minutes. Gradually stir in remaining 1½ cups flour. Shape dough into a ball; place in a well-greased bowl, turning to grease top. Cover and let rise in a warm place (85°), free from drafts, 45 to 50 minutes or until doubled in bulk.

Stir dough 25 strokes. Place in a greased 2-quart casserole. Sprinkle with 1 tablespoon Parmesan cheese. Bake at 350° for 35 minutes. Cover loosely with aluminum foil; bake an additional 20 minutes or until lightly browned. Yield: 1 loaf.   Patty Johnson

Texas Hill Country Wine & Food Festival: A Cookbook
The Texas Hill Country Wine and Food Festival
Austin, Texas

Prosciutto Bread

1 package dry yeast
⅛ teaspoon sugar
¾ cup warm water (105° to 115°)
2 eggs, beaten
2 teaspoons fennel seeds
1 teaspoon salt
3 to 3½ cups all-purpose flour

1 cup minced onion
2 tablespoons olive oil
½ pound prosciutto, cut into julienne strips
8 ounces provolone cheese, cut into julienne strips
1 egg yolk
1 teaspoon water

Dissolve yeast and sugar in ¾ cup warm water in a large bowl; let stand 5 minutes. Add eggs, fennel seeds, and salt; stir well. Gradually stir in enough flour to make a soft dough.

Turn dough out onto a well-floured surface, and knead until smooth and elastic (8 to 10 minutes). Place in a well-greased bowl, turning to grease top. Cover and let rise in a warm place (85°), free from drafts, 1 hour or until doubled in bulk.

Sauté minced onion in olive oil until tender. Let cool slightly. Add onion, prosciutto, and cheese to dough; knead gently to combine. Shape into a 7-inch round loaf; place on a greased baking sheet. Let rise in a warm place, free from drafts, 30 minutes or until doubled in bulk.

Combine egg yolk and 1 teaspoon water; brush on loaf. Bake at 350° for 30 to 40 minutes or until golden. Let cool 10 minutes on a wire rack. Yield: 1 loaf.   Lynn Moss

Greetings from Atlantic City
The Ruth Newman Shapiro Cancer and Heart Fund
Atlantic City, New Jersey

Christopsomo (Christmas Bread)

1⅓ cups milk	2 packages dry yeast
½ cup butter	4 eggs
6 to 7 cups all-purpose flour	5 unshelled walnuts
¼ cup plus 2 tablespoons	1 egg, beaten
sugar	1 teaspoon sesame seeds
1 teaspoon salt	

Combine milk and butter in a saucepan; heat until butter melts, stirring occasionally. Let cool to 120° to 130°.

Combine 3 cups flour, sugar, salt, and yeast in a large mixing bowl; stir well.

Gradually add milk mixture to flour mixture, beating well at medium speed of an electric mixer. Add eggs, one at a time, beating well after each addition. Beat at medium speed an additional 2 minutes. Gradually add ¾ cup flour, beating 2 minutes. Stir in enough remaining 3¼ cups flour to make a soft dough.

Turn dough out onto a floured surface, and knead until smooth and elastic (about 10 minutes). Place in a well-greased bowl, turning to grease top. Cover and let rise in a warm place (85°), free from drafts, 1¼ hours or until doubled in bulk.

Punch dough down. Let rest 10 minutes. Divide one-third of dough into 8 equal portions. Shape each portion into a 15-inch rope. Twist 2 ropes together; repeat with remaining ropes, making 4 twisted ropes. Place two of the twisted ropes around the inside edge of a greased 12-inch round cakepan. Set remaining twists aside. Shape remaining two-thirds of dough into a ball; place in cakepan, and flatten to an 11-inch round loaf. With remaining twists, form a cross on top of loaf. Press one walnut into the center and into each end of cross.

Cover and let rise in a warm place, free from drafts, 45 minutes or until doubled in bulk. Brush top of loaf with beaten egg. Sprinkle with sesame seeds.

Bake at 350° for 35 to 45 minutes or until loaf is golden brown. Cover bread loosely with aluminum foil during last 15 minutes of baking to prevent excessive browning, if necessary. Let cool on a wire rack. Yield: 1 loaf.   Ritsa Economakis

Favorite Recipes from St. Demetrios Church
St. Demetrios Greek Orthodox Church
Baltimore, Maryland

Baked Spicy Twists

2 packages dry yeast
½ cup warm water (105° to
  115°)
¾ cup milk
½ cup butter or margarine
½ cup sugar
1 egg

2 teaspoons salt
4¼ to 5¼ cups all-purpose
  flour
¼ cup butter or margarine,
  melted and divided
½ cup sugar
½ teaspoon ground cinnamon

Dissolve yeast in warm water in a large bowl; let stand 5 minutes.

Combine milk and ½ cup butter in a saucepan; heat until butter melts, stirring occasionally. Let cool to 105° to 115°.

Add milk mixture, ½ cup sugar, egg, and salt to yeast mixture; beat at medium speed of an electric mixer until blended. Stir in 2 cups flour, beating 2 minutes at medium speed. Gradually stir in enough remaining 3¼ cups flour to make a soft dough. Cover and chill 2 hours. (Dough may be stored in refrigerator up to 3 days.)

Punch dough down; turn out onto a lightly floured surface, and knead lightly 4 or 5 times. Divide dough in half. Roll one portion of dough to a 16- x 8-inch rectangle. Brush with 2 tablespoons melted butter. Combine ½ cup sugar and cinnamon; sprinkle half of cinnamon mixture over dough. Fold dough in thirds crosswise. Cut crosswise into 24 strips. Twist each strip, and place on greased baking sheets. Bake at 375° for 10 to 12 minutes or until lightly browned. Repeat procedure with remaining dough, butter, and cinnamon mixture. Yield: 4 dozen.

Seasoned with Sun
The Junior League of El Paso, Texas

Proceeds from the sale of **Favorite Recipes from St. Demetrios Church,** *compiled by the members of the St. Demetrios Greek Orthodox Church of Baltimore, will benefit the church's building fund.*

Caramel Pecan Rolls

1 package dry yeast
¼ cup warm water (105° to 115°)
1 cup milk
⅓ cup butter or margarine
⅓ cup sugar
2 eggs
1 teaspoon salt
4 to 5 cups all-purpose flour
1 cup chopped pecans, divided
¾ cup dark corn syrup
⅓ cup firmly packed brown sugar
3 tablespoons butter or margarine
2 tablespoons butter or margarine, melted
1 cup raisins
½ cup firmly packed brown sugar
1 tablespoon ground cinnamon

Dissolve yeast in warm water in a large mixing bowl; let stand 5 minutes.

Combine milk and ⅓ cup butter in a small saucepan; heat until butter melts, stirring occasionally. Let mixture cool to 105° to 115°. Add milk mixture, ⅓ cup sugar, eggs, salt, and 1 cup flour to yeast mixture, beating at medium speed of an electric mixer until mixture is smooth. Gradually stir in enough remaining 4 cups flour to make a soft dough.

Turn dough out onto a floured surface, and knead until smooth and elastic (about 5 minutes). Place in a well-greased bowl, turning to grease top. Cover and let rise in a warm place (85°), free from drafts, 1 hour or until doubled in bulk.

Sprinkle ½ cup pecans over the bottom of a 13- x 9- x 2-inch baking pan. Combine syrup, ⅓ cup brown sugar, and 3 tablespoons butter in a saucepan. Cook over medium heat until sugar and butter melt, stirring frequently. Pour syrup mixture evenly over pecans in baking pan; set aside.

Punch dough down; turn out onto a lightly floured surface. Roll dough to a 15- x 12-inch rectangle; brush with 2 tablespoons melted butter. Combine raisins, ½ cup brown sugar, remaining ½ cup pecans, and cinnamon in a small bowl; sprinkle raisin mixture evenly over rectangle. Roll up dough, jellyroll fashion, starting at long side. Pinch seam to seal (do not seal ends). Cut into 1-inch slices. Place slices, cut side down, in prepared pan. Cover and chill at least 12 hours.

When ready to bake, uncover and let stand at room temperature 15 minutes. Bake at 350° for 35 to 40 minutes or until rolls are golden brown. Immediately invert pan onto a serving plate. Let stand 1 minute to allow caramel mixture to drizzle over rolls. Remove pan. Yield: 15 rolls.   Joan Cannon

Heavenly Delights
United Methodist Women, First United Methodist Church
Noblesville, Indiana

Orange Rolls

2 packages dry yeast
⅔ cup warm water (105° to 115°)
⅓ cup orange juice
¼ cup sugar
¼ cup shortening, melted and cooled
2 eggs

1½ teaspoons salt
4 to 4½ cups all-purpose flour
¼ cup butter or margarine, melted and divided
¼ cup sugar
Grated rind of 1 large orange

Dissolve yeast in warm water in a large bowl; let stand 5 minutes. Add orange juice and next 4 ingredients; beat at medium speed of an electric mixer until well blended. Gradually add ¾ cup flour, beating 2 minutes at medium speed. Gradually stir in enough remaining 3¾ cups flour to make a soft dough.

Turn dough out onto a well-floured surface, and knead until smooth and elastic (about 5 minutes). Place in a well-greased bowl, turning to grease top. Cover and let rise in a warm place (85°), free from drafts, 45 minutes or until doubled in bulk.

Punch dough down, and divide in half. Roll one portion of dough to a 12- x 8-inch rectangle; brush with 2 tablespoons melted butter. Combine ¼ cup sugar and orange rind; sprinkle half of mixture over dough. Roll up jellyroll fashion, starting at long side. Pinch seam to seal (do not seal ends). Cut roll into 1-inch-thick slices. Place slices, cut side down, in greased muffin pans. Repeat procedure with remaining dough, melted butter, and sugar mixture.

Cover and let rise in a warm place, free from drafts, 30 minutes or until doubled in bulk. Bake at 375° for 15 minutes or until rolls are golden brown. Yield: 2 dozen.   Joe Grove

Bethany Christian Community, A Recipe Collection
Bethany Christian Community
Anchorage, Alaska

Moravian Love Feast Buns

2 packages dry yeast
1 cup warm water (105° to 115°)
½ cup plus ½ teaspoon sugar, divided
5 to 5½ cups all-purpose flour, divided
3 tablespoons instant nonfat dry milk powder
3 tablespoons instant potato flakes
1 teaspoon salt
½ teaspoon ground mace
½ teaspoon ground nutmeg
2 eggs
½ cup butter or margarine, melted and cooled
2 teaspoons grated orange rind
⅓ cup freshly squeezed orange juice
Additional melted butter (optional)

Dissolve yeast in warm water in a large mixing bowl; stir in ½ teaspoon sugar, and let stand 5 minutes. Add 2½ cups flour, remaining ½ cup sugar, dry milk powder, and next 4 ingredients. Beat at medium speed of an electric mixer until smooth. Add eggs, ½ cup melted butter, orange rind, and orange juice; beat at high speed 5 minutes. Stir in 2 cups flour. Gradually stir in enough remaining 1 cup flour to make a soft dough.

Turn dough out onto a lightly floured surface. Cover and let rest 10 minutes. Knead until smooth and elastic (about 5 minutes).

Place dough in a well-greased bowl, turning to grease top. Cover and let rise in a warm place (85°), free from drafts, 1 hour or until doubled in bulk.

Punch dough down; cover and let rest 10 minutes. Divide dough into 18 equal portions. Shape each portion of dough into a ball. Place dough balls 3 inches apart on greased baking sheets. Cover and let rise 1 hour or until doubled in bulk. Slash an "M" in top of each bun with a sharp knife or razor blade, if desired. Bake at 375° for 12 minutes or until lightly browned. Brush with melted butter, if desired. Yield: 1½ dozen.   Donnie Erwin-Brown

The Cookbook
East Lake United Methodist Church
Birmingham, Alabama

Cakes

The restored Victorian bandstand was part of a revitalization program of the business district in Medina, Ohio. One can almost hear the rhythmic, lively notes of the John Philip Sousa march, **The Stars and Stripes Forever.**

Southern Gingerbread with Lemon Sauce

½ cup butter, melted
¼ cup shortening, melted
¾ cup firmly packed brown
 sugar
¾ cup molasses
2 eggs, beaten
2½ cups all-purpose flour
2 teaspoons baking soda

½ teaspoon baking powder
2 teaspoons ground ginger
1½ teaspoons ground
 cinnamon
½ teaspoon ground cloves
½ teaspoon ground nutmeg
1 cup boiling water
Lemon Sauce

Combine butter, shortening, brown sugar, molasses, and eggs; beat well at medium speed of an electric mixer. Combine flour and next 6 ingredients; stir well. Add flour mixture to molasses mixture, stirring well. Stir in boiling water.

Pour batter into a greased 13- x 9- x 2-inch baking pan. Bake at 350° for 30 to 40 minutes or until a wooden pick inserted in center comes out clean. Let cool in pan on a wire rack. Serve with Lemon Sauce. Yield: 15 servings.

Lemon Sauce

1 cup sugar
1 egg, lightly beaten
½ cup butter

½ cup boiling water
Juice of 1 lemon

Combine sugar and beaten egg in top of a double boiler, and stir well. Add butter, boiling water, and lemon juice, and stir well. Bring water in bottom of double boiler to a boil; reduce heat to low, and cook, stirring constantly, until mixture is smooth and slightly thickened. Yield: 1¾ cups.   Mary Alice Coulter

Twickenham Tables
Twickenham Historic Preservation District Association, Inc.
Huntsville, Alabama

White Cake with Lemon Filling

½ cup shortening
1½ cups sugar
2½ cups sifted cake flour
2 teaspoons baking powder
⅛ teaspoon salt
1 cup milk

1 teaspoon vanilla extract
½ teaspoon lemon extract
4 egg whites
Lemon Filling
Seven-Minute Frosting

Cream shortening; gradually add sugar, beating well at medium speed of an electric mixer.

Combine flour, baking powder, and salt; stir well. Add to creamed mixture alternately with milk, beginning and ending with flour mixture. Mix after each addition. Stir in flavorings.

Beat egg whites (at room temperature) at high speed until stiff peaks form. Gently fold into flour mixture.

Pour batter into a greased and floured 13- x 9- x 2-inch baking pan. Bake at 325° for 25 to 30 minutes or until a wooden pick inserted in center comes out clean. Let cool in pan 10 minutes; remove from pan, and let cool completely on a wire rack.

Split cake in half horizontally; spread filling between layers. Spread frosting on top and sides of cake. Yield: 15 servings.

Lemon Filling

1½ cups hot water
½ cup sugar
⅓ cup lemon juice

4 egg yolks
3 tablespoons cornstarch

Combine all ingredients in top of a double boiler; bring water in bottom of double boiler to a boil. Reduce heat to low; cook, stirring constantly, until mixture is thickened. Let cool. Yield: 2 cups.

Seven-Minute Frosting

1½ cups sugar
⅓ cup water

2 egg whites
1 teaspoon light corn syrup

Combine all ingredients in top of a double boiler; place over boiling water. Beat at high speed of an electric mixer 7 minutes or until stiff peaks form. Yield: 3 cups.   Mary Dukeminier

In the Pink of Things
The Muskogee Regional Medical Center Auxiliary
Muskogee, Oklahoma

Scandinavian Apple Cake

4 large tart cooking apples, peeled, cored, and finely chopped
1 cup sugar
⅔ cup butter or margarine, melted
2 eggs, beaten
2 teaspoons vanilla extract
2 cups all-purpose flour
2 teaspoons baking soda
½ teaspoon salt
2 teaspoons ground allspice
2 teaspoons ground cinnamon
1 cup chopped pecans
1 (8-ounce) package cream cheese, softened
¼ cup butter or margarine, softened
2 tablespoons lemon juice
2 cups sifted powdered sugar

Combine chopped apple, 1 cup sugar, and melted butter in a large bowl; stir well. Add eggs and vanilla, stirring well. Combine flour and next 4 ingredients; add to apple mixture, stirring well. Stir in pecans. Spoon batter into a greased 13- x 9- x 2-inch baking pan. Bake at 350° for 45 minutes or until a wooden pick inserted in center comes out clean. Let cool in pan on a wire rack.

Combine cream cheese and ¼ cup butter, beating well at medium speed of an electric mixer. Add lemon juice and powdered sugar; beat until light and fluffy. Spread frosting on top of cake. Yield: 15 servings.

Southern California Style
The Assistance League® of Anaheim, California

The rich cooking heritage of early Spanish settlers is spotlighted in a special chapter in Southern California Style. *The Assistance League® of Anaheim is dedicated to acting as a friend at any and all times to men, women, and children in need of care and guidance as well as spiritual, material, and physical assistance.*

Orange-Zucchini Cake

1½ cups vegetable oil
1½ cups sugar
3 eggs
¼ cup Grand Marnier or
other orange-flavored
liqueur
1 teaspoon grated orange rind
1 teaspoon vanilla extract
3 cups all-purpose flour
2 teaspoons baking soda

1 teaspoon baking powder
1 teaspoon salt
2 teaspoons ground cinnamon
2 cups coarsely grated
zucchini
1 cup raisins
1 cup chopped pecans or
walnuts
Frosting (recipe follows)

Combine oil and sugar in a large mixing bowl, and beat at medium speed of an electric mixer until blended. Add eggs, one at a time, beating well after each addition. Stir in liqueur, orange rind, and vanilla.

Combine flour and next 4 ingredients; stir well. Add to creamed mixture, beating until well blended. Add zucchini, raisins, and pecans; stir well.

Pour batter into a greased and floured 13- x 9- x 2-inch baking pan. Bake at 350° for 40 to 45 minutes or until a wooden pick inserted in center comes out clean. Let cool completely in pan on a wire rack. Spread frosting on top of cake. Yield: 15 servings.

Frosting

1 (8-ounce) package cream
cheese, softened
½ cup butter or margarine,
softened
2 cups sifted powdered
sugar

2 tablespoons Grand Marnier
or other orange-flavored
liqueur
1 tablespoon grated orange
rind
1 teaspoon vanilla extract

Combine softened cream cheese and butter in a large mixing bowl; beat at medium speed of an electric mixer until smooth. Add powdered sugar and remaining ingredients; beat until mixture is smooth. Yield: 2⅓ cups.   Martha Merza and Nellie Jacobs

Feed My People
Carter-Westminster United Presbyterian Church
Skokie, Illinois

Mother's Orange Bonbon Cake

¾ cup shortening
1½ cups sugar
2 tablespoons grated orange
   rind
3 eggs
3 cups all-purpose flour

1 tablespoon baking powder
¾ teaspoon salt
⅓ cup fresh orange juice
2 tablespoons lemon juice
½ cup orange marmalade
Bonbon Frosting

Cream shortening; gradually add sugar, beating well at medium speed of an electric mixer. Add orange rind, mixing well. Add eggs, one at a time, beating well after each addition.

Combine flour, baking powder, and salt; stir well. Combine orange juice and lemon juice; add enough water to make 1 cup. Add flour mixture to creamed mixture alternately with juice, beginning and ending with flour mixture. Mix after each addition.

Pour batter into 2 greased and floured 9-inch round cakepans. Bake at 375° for 25 minutes or until a wooden pick inserted in center comes out clean. Let cool in pans 10 minutes. Remove from pans; let cool on wire racks. Spread marmalade between layers. Spread frosting on top and sides of cake. Yield: one 2-layer cake.

Bonbon Frosting

2 teaspoons grated orange
   rind
¼ cup plus 2 tablespoons
   fresh orange juice
2 tablespoons shortening
1 tablespoon butter or
   margarine, softened

3 cups sifted powdered sugar,
   divided
¼ teaspoon salt
2 (1-ounce) squares semisweet
   chocolate, melted
2 tablespoons whipping
   cream

Combine orange rind and orange juice in a small bowl; let stand 10 minutes.

Cream shortening and butter; add ½ cup powdered sugar and salt, beating at medium speed of an electric mixer until smooth. Add chocolate, and mix well.

Strain juice mixture, discarding rind. Add juice, remaining 2½ cups powdered sugar, and cream, beating until smooth. Yield: about 1½ cups.   Lorraine and Gene Holderman

Centennial Cookbook
The Orange County Pioneer Council
Newport Beach, California

Mama's Japanese Fruitcake

1 cup butter, softened
2 cups sugar
4 eggs, separated
3 cups all-purpose flour
2 teaspoons baking powder
½ teaspoon salt
1 cup milk
1½ teaspoons vanilla extract

1 cup raisins
1 cup chopped pecans
1 teaspoon ground allspice
1 teaspoon ground cinnamon
1 teaspoon ground nutmeg
½ to 1 teaspoon ground
   cloves
Filling (recipe follows)

Cream butter; gradually add sugar, beating at medium speed of an electric mixer until light and fluffy. Add egg yolks, beating well. Combine flour, baking powder, and salt; stir well. Add to creamed mixture alternately with milk, beginning and ending with flour mixture. Stir in vanilla.

Beat egg whites (at room temperature) at high speed until stiff peaks form. Gently fold into batter.

Pour half of batter into 2 greased and floured 9-inch round cakepans. Add raisins and next 5 ingredients to remaining half of batter; stir well. Pour batter into 2 additional greased and floured 9-inch round cakepans. Bake at 350° for 25 to 30 minutes or until a wooden pick inserted in center comes out clean. Let cool in pans 10 minutes; remove from pans, and let cool completely on wire racks.

Spread 1 cup filling on top of 1 plain cake layer. Top with 1 spiced cake layer, and spread with 1 cup filling. Repeat procedure with remaining cake layers and filling. Yield: one 4-layer cake.

Filling

2 (20-ounce) cans
   unsweetened crushed
   pineapple, undrained
1 (12-ounce) package frozen
   flaked coconut, thawed
2 cups sugar

2 teaspoons grated lemon
   rind
¼ cup plus 2 tablespoons
   fresh lemon juice
2 tablespoons all-purpose
   flour

Combine all ingredients in a saucepan; stir well. Cook over medium heat, stirring occasionally, 45 minutes or until thick enough to spread. Yield: 4 cups.   Mrs. James H. Daughdrill, Jr.

Gracious Goodness: The Taste of Memphis
The Symphony League of Memphis, Tennessee

Blitzkuchen (Lightning Cake)

½ cup butter, softened
½ cup sugar
4 eggs, separated
1½ teaspoons grated lemon
   rind
1 tablespoon lemon juice
1 cup all-purpose flour
1¼ teaspoons baking powder
¼ cup plus 2 tablespoons
   milk

1 cup sugar
½ cup chopped pecans or
   walnuts
1 egg
1 cup milk
2 tablespoons all-purpose
   flour
½ cup sugar
⅛ teaspoon salt
½ teaspoon vanilla extract

Cream butter; add ½ cup sugar, 4 egg yolks, grated lemon rind, and lemon juice, beating at medium speed of an electric mixer until blended.

Combine 1 cup flour and baking powder; add to creamed mixture alternately with ¼ cup plus 2 tablespoons milk, beginning and ending with flour mixture. Mix well after each addition. Pour batter into 2 greased and floured 8-inch round cakepans.

Beat remaining 4 egg whites (at room temperature) at high speed just until foamy. Gradually add 1 cup sugar, 1 tablespoon at a time, beating until stiff peaks form and sugar dissolves (2 to 4 minutes). Gently fold in pecans.

Carefully spread meringue over batter in cakepans. Bake at 350° for 30 minutes or until meringue is lightly browned. Let cake layers cool in pans 10 minutes; remove from pans, and let cool completely on wire racks.

Combine 1 egg, 1 cup milk, 2 tablespoons flour, ½ cup sugar, and salt in a saucepan; cook over medium heat, stirring constantly, until mixture is thickened. Remove from heat; stir in vanilla. Set filling aside, and let cool.

Invert 1 cake layer onto a serving platter, meringue side down. Spread filling evenly over top. Place second cake layer on top of filling, meringue side up. Chill cake thoroughly before serving. Yield: one 2-layer cake.   Charlene Fischer

Aggies, Moms, and Apple Pie
The Federation of Texas A&M University Mothers' Clubs
College Station, Texas

Cocoa Apple Cake

1 cup butter or margarine, softened
2 cups sugar
3 eggs
2½ cups all-purpose flour
1 teaspoon baking soda
2 tablespoons cocoa
1 teaspoon ground allspice
1 teaspoon ground cinnamon
1 tablespoon vanilla extract
2 cups peeled, cored, and shredded Red Delicious or Golden Delicious apples
1 cup chopped pecans or walnuts
1 cup semisweet chocolate morsels
Powdered sugar
Vanilla ice cream (optional)

Cream butter; gradually add 2 cups sugar, beating at medium speed of an electric mixer until light and fluffy. Add eggs, one at a time, beating after each addition.

Combine flour, soda, cocoa, allspice, and cinnamon; add to creamed mixture, beating well. Stir in vanilla. Stir in shredded apple, pecans, and chocolate morsels.

Spoon batter into a greased and floured 12-cup Bundt pan. Bake at 325° for 60 to 70 minutes or until a wooden pick inserted in center comes out clean. Let cool in pan 10 minutes; remove from pan, and let cool completely on a wire rack. Sprinkle with powdered sugar. Serve with vanilla ice cream, if desired. Yield: one 10-inch cake.

Only in California
The Children's Home Society of California
Los Angeles, California

Funds raised from the sale of **Only in California** *will benefit the Children's Home Society of California, which offers families and children programs that include adoption, child care, foster care, group home care, family support, and shelter care services.*

Cranberry Swirl Cake

½ cup unsalted butter,
  softened
1 cup sugar
2 eggs
2 cups all-purpose flour
1 teaspoon baking
  powder
1 teaspoon baking soda

1 (8-ounce) carton sour cream
1 teaspoon almond extract
½ (8-ounce) can whole-berry
  cranberry sauce
½ cup chopped pecans or
  walnuts
Glaze (recipe follows)

Cream butter; gradually add sugar, beating well at medium speed of an electric mixer. Add eggs, one at a time, beating well after each addition.

Combine flour, baking powder, and soda in a medium bowl; stir well. Add flour mixture to creamed mixture alternately with sour cream, beginning and ending with flour mixture. Mix after each addition. Stir in almond extract.

Pour half of batter into a greased and floured 12-cup Bundt or 10-inch tube pan. Spoon half of cranberry sauce over batter. Repeat layers, using remaining batter and cranberry sauce. Sprinkle with chopped pecans.

Bake at 350° for 50 to 60 minutes or until a wooden pick inserted in center comes out clean. Let cool in pan 10 minutes; remove from pan, and let cool completely on a wire rack. Drizzle with glaze. Yield: one 10-inch cake.

Glaze

¾ cup sifted powdered
  sugar

1 tablespoon water
½ teaspoon almond extract

Combine all ingredients in a small bowl, stirring until smooth. Yield: ¼ cup.

Jean Collins

Favorite Recipes from St. Paul's
St. Paul's Episcopal Church
Millis, Massachusetts

Pear Cake with Caramel Drizzle

1 cup vegetable oil
1¾ cups sugar
3 eggs, beaten
1 tablespoon vanilla extract
1½ cups all-purpose flour
1 cup whole wheat flour
2 teaspoons baking powder

1 teaspoon baking soda
1 teaspoon ground allspice
3 cups peeled, cored, and
   chopped ripe pears (about
   4 medium)
1 cup chopped pecans
Caramel Drizzle

Combine vegetable oil, sugar, and beaten eggs in a large mixing bowl; beat at medium speed of an electric mixer until well blended. Stir in vanilla.

Combine flours, baking powder, baking soda, and allspice in a medium bowl; stir well. Add flour mixture to sugar mixture alternately with chopped pear, beating at medium speed until blended. Stir in chopped pecans.

Pour batter into a greased and floured 12-cup Bundt pan. Bake at 375° for 55 minutes or until a wooden pick inserted in center comes out clean. Let cool in pan 10 minutes; remove from pan, and let cool completely on a wire rack. Spoon Caramel Drizzle over cake. Yield: one 10-inch cake.

Caramel Drizzle

¼ cup butter
¼ cup firmly packed dark
   brown sugar
2 tablespoons milk

1 cup sifted powdered sugar
½ teaspoon vanilla extract
Pinch of salt

Melt butter in a small saucepan; add brown sugar, and cook over medium heat, stirring constantly, until sugar melts. Remove from heat; add milk, stirring constantly. Add powdered sugar, vanilla, and salt; beat at medium speed of an electric mixer until smooth. Yield: ⅔ cup.

Gloria Pedersen

Rebel Recipes
Department of Home Economics, University of Mississippi
Oxford, Mississippi

Chocolate Chip Pound Cake

1 cup butter, softened
1 tablespoon shortening
1½ cups sugar
6 eggs, separated
3 cups all-purpose flour
¼ teaspoon baking soda
½ teaspoon salt
1 (8-ounce) carton sour cream
1 teaspoon vanilla extract

1 (12-ounce) package
   semisweet chocolate
   morsels, divided
1 (4-ounce) package sweet
   baking chocolate, grated
½ cup sugar
1 cup sifted powdered sugar
1 tablespoon milk

Cream butter and shortening; gradually add 1½ cups sugar, beating well at medium speed of an electric mixer. Add egg yolks, and beat at medium-high speed 5 minutes.

Combine flour, baking soda, and salt in a medium bowl; stir well. Add flour mixture to creamed mixture alternately with sour cream, beginning and ending with flour mixture, mixing just until blended after each addition. Stir in vanilla, 1⅓ cups chocolate morsels, and grated chocolate.

Beat egg whites (at room temperature) at high speed until soft peaks form. Gradually add ½ cup sugar, 2 tablespoons at a time, beating until stiff peaks form and sugar dissolves (2 to 4 minutes). Stir one-third of beaten egg whites into batter. Fold in remaining egg whites.

Pour batter into a greased and floured 10-inch tube pan. Bake at 325° for 1 hour and 25 minutes or until a wooden pick inserted in center comes out clean. Let cool in pan 10 minutes; remove from pan, and let cool on a wire rack.

Combine powdered sugar and milk in a small bowl; stir until mixture is smooth. Spoon glaze over warm cake. Sprinkle with remaining ⅔ cup chocolate morsels, and let cool completely. Yield: one 10-inch cake.

Donnie Huckaby

Central Texas Style
The Junior Service League of Killeen, Texas

Apricot Brandy Pound Cake

1 cup butter or margarine,
   softened
3 cups sugar
6 eggs
1 (8-ounce) carton sour cream
½ cup apricot brandy
1 teaspoon orange extract

1 teaspoon vanilla extract
½ teaspoon lemon extract
½ teaspoon rum flavoring
¼ teaspoon almond extract
3 cups all-purpose flour
¼ teaspoon baking soda
½ teaspoon salt

Cream butter; gradually add sugar, beating well at medium speed of an electric mixer. Add eggs, one at a time, beating after each addition.

Combine sour cream and next 6 ingredients in a small bowl; stir with a wire whisk. Combine flour, baking soda, and salt; stir well. Add to creamed mixture alternately with sour cream mixture, beginning and ending with flour mixture.

Pour batter into a greased and floured 10-inch tube pan. Bake at 325° for 1 hour and 45 minutes or until a wooden pick inserted in center of cake comes out clean. Let cake cool in pan 10 minutes; remove from pan, and let cool completely on a wire rack. Yield: one 10-inch cake.

Estelle Zagorin

A Taste of Hope
The Camarillo Chapter of City of Hope
Camarillo, California

Peach Pound Cake

1 cup butter or margarine,
   softened
3 cups sugar
6 eggs
3 cups all-purpose flour
¼ teaspoon baking soda

¼ teaspoon salt
2 cups peeled, chopped fresh
   ripe peaches
½ cup sour cream
1 teaspoon vanilla extract
1 teaspoon almond extract

Cream butter; gradually add sugar, beating well at medium speed of an electric mixer. Add eggs, one at a time, beating after each addition.

Combine flour, soda, and salt; stir well. Combine peaches and sour cream. Add flour mixture to creamed mixture alternately with peach mixture, beginning and ending with flour mixture. Mix just until blended after each addition. Stir in flavorings.

Pour batter into a greased and floured 10-inch tube pan. Bake at 350° for 1 hour and 10 minutes or until a wooden pick inserted in center of cake comes out clean. Let cake cool in pan 10 minutes; remove from pan, and let cool completely on a wire rack. Yield: one 10-inch cake.   Celestine Sibley

Georgia on My Menu
The Junior League of Cobb-Marietta, Georgia

Peach Praline Shortcake

1½ cups all-purpose flour
1 tablespoon baking powder
¼ teaspoon baking soda
½ teaspoon salt
½ cup firmly packed brown
  sugar
⅓ cup shortening
½ cup coarsely chopped
  pecans

¾ cup milk
1 egg, beaten
4 cups peeled, sliced fresh
  ripe peaches
1 (8-ounce) carton sour cream
½ cup firmly packed brown
  sugar

Combine first 5 ingredients in a medium bowl; stir well. Cut in shortening with a pastry blender until mixture resembles coarse meal. Stir in pecans.

Combine milk and egg; stir with a wire whisk until blended. Add to flour mixture, stirring just until blended. Pour batter into a greased 9-inch round cakepan.

Bake at 375° for 20 to 25 minutes or until a wooden pick inserted in center comes out clean. Let cool in pan 10 minutes; remove from pan, and let cool slightly on a wire rack.

Split warm cake in half horizontally to make 2 layers. Place one layer, cut side up, on a cake plate; spoon half of peaches over layer. Place remaining layer, cut side down, on top of peaches. Spoon remaining peaches on top of cake.

Combine sour cream and ½ cup brown sugar in a small bowl; stir until smooth. Serve sour cream mixture with cake. Yield: one 2-layer cake.   Deborah Camea

An Apple a Day Cookbook
Children's Hospital at Santa Rosa
San Antonio, Texas

Coffee Cheesecake

¾ cup all-purpose flour
3 tablespoons brown sugar
¼ cup plus 2 tablespoons
  butter or margarine
1 egg yolk, lightly beaten
¼ teaspoon vanilla extract
¼ cup milk
1 tablespoon instant coffee
  granules
3 (8-ounce) packages cream
  cheese, softened

½ cup sugar
½ cup firmly packed brown
  sugar
2 tablespoons all-purpose
  flour
2 teaspoons vanilla extract
3 eggs
Coffee-Walnut Sauce
Whipped cream
Praline Fans

Combine ¾ cup flour and 3 tablespoons brown sugar; stir well. Cut in butter with a pastry blender until mixture resembles coarse meal. Stir in egg yolk and ¼ teaspoon vanilla.

Remove sides of a 9-inch springform pan. Press one-third of flour mixture on bottom of pan. Bake crust at 400° for 5 minutes. Let cool. Grease sides of pan with butter, and attach to bottom of pan. Press remaining flour mixture 1½ inches up sides of pan; set aside.

Combine milk and coffee granules; let stand, stirring occasionally.

Beat cream cheese at high speed of an electric mixer until light and fluffy; gradually add ½ cup sugar and ½ cup brown sugar, mixing well. Add 2 tablespoons flour and 2 teaspoons vanilla; beat well. Add 3 eggs, beating just until blended. Stir in milk mixture.

Pour batter into prepared pan. Bake at 350° for 45 to 55 minutes or until cheesecake is almost set. Turn oven off. Partially open oven door, and let cheesecake cool in oven 1 hour. Let cool to room temperature on a wire rack; chill at least 8 hours.

Drizzle Coffee-Walnut Sauce over cheesecake; top with whipped cream. Arrange Praline Fans in whipped cream. Yield: 12 servings.

Coffee-Walnut Sauce

⅔ cup sugar
1 cup hot water
2 teaspoons instant coffee
  granules
2 tablespoons cold water

1 tablespoon cornstarch
2 tablespoons butter
⅓ cup coarsely chopped
  walnuts

Sprinkle sugar in a cast-iron skillet; cook over medium-low heat, stirring constantly with a wooden spoon, until sugar melts and turns golden brown. Remove from heat; stir in 1 cup hot water and coffee granules. Return to heat; cook over medium-low heat, stirring constantly, until coffee granules dissolve.

Combine 2 tablespoons water and cornstarch, stirring until smooth. Stir cornstarch mixture into sugar mixture; cook, stirring constantly, until mixture is bubbly. Cook an additional 2 minutes, stirring constantly. Remove from heat; add butter and walnuts, stirring until butter melts. Yield: 1½ cups.

Praline Fans

½ cup sugar

2 teaspoons finely chopped walnuts

Sprinkle sugar in a small cast-iron skillet. Cook over medium-low heat, stirring constantly with a wooden spoon, until sugar melts and turns golden brown. Remove from heat; let cool 1 minute. Drizzle sugar by teaspoonfuls in a fan-shaped design onto an aluminum foil-lined baking sheet; sprinkle with walnuts. Let cool completely; carefully peel off foil. Yield: 3 fans.   Edward Robbins

Something Entertaining to Cook
The Southeastern Theatre Conference, Inc.
Greensboro, North Carolina

The Southeastern Theatre Conference, Inc., was organized in Chapel Hill, North Carolina, in 1949 in recognition of the importance of the theatre arts to the community. Their purpose is to provide services and educational programs for those individuals and organizations engaged in theatre in the southeast. Proceeds from the sale of **Something Entertaining to Cook** *go to the Southeastern Theatre Conference Endowment Fund for scholarships and awards.*

Grapefruit Chiffon Loaf Cake

1 cup all-purpose flour
1½ teaspoons baking powder
¼ teaspoon salt
¾ cup sugar
1½ teaspoons grated
   grapefruit rind

⅓ cup grapefruit juice
¼ cup vegetable oil
3 eggs, separated
¼ teaspoon cream of tartar

Sift together flour, baking powder, salt, and sugar in a mixing bowl. Make a well in center; add grapefruit rind, grapefruit juice, oil, and egg yolks. Beat at high speed of an electric mixer 5 minutes or until satiny smooth.

Beat egg whites (at room temperature) and cream of tartar in a large mixing bowl at high speed until stiff peaks form.

Pour egg yolk mixture in a thin, steady stream over entire surface of egg whites; gently fold egg whites into yolk mixture.

Pour batter into an ungreased 9- x 5- x 3-inch loafpan. Bake at 350° for 35 minutes or until golden brown. Let cool in pan 40 minutes. Loosen cake from sides of pan, using a narrow metal spatula; remove from pan. Yield: 8 servings.

Connecticut Cooks III
The American Cancer Society, Connecticut Division, Inc.
Wallingford, Connecticut

Slices of Sin

8 (1-ounce) squares semisweet
   chocolate
½ cup strong brewed coffee
1 cup butter
1 cup sugar

4 eggs
1 cup whipping cream
2 to 3 teaspoons
   brandy

Line an 8½- x 4½- x 3-inch glass loafpan with aluminum foil; grease foil with butter. Set aside.

Combine chocolate and coffee in top of a double boiler. Bring water to a boil; reduce heat to low, and cook until chocolate melts, stirring occasionally. Add butter and sugar to melted chocolate mixture, stirring until butter melts. Let cool. Add eggs, one at a time, beating well after each addition.

Pour batter into prepared loafpan. Bake at 350° for 35 to 45 minutes or until a crust forms on top. Let cool completely on a wire rack. Cover tightly; chill at least 2 days.

Beat whipping cream until soft peaks form. Gently fold in brandy. Unmold loaf onto a serving platter. Serve with whipped cream. Yield: 10 to 12 servings.

Capital Classics
The Junior League of Washington, DC

Gooey Butter Cake

3 cups sifted cake flour	2 eggs
2½ teaspoons baking powder	1½ teaspoons vanilla extract
1 teaspoon salt	1 (8-ounce) package cream cheese, softened
1¾ cups sugar	2 eggs
⅓ cup instant nonfat dry milk powder	1 teaspoon vanilla extract
1 cup plus 2 tablespoons butter, melted	1 (16-ounce) package powdered sugar, sifted

Combine flour, baking powder, salt, 1¾ cups sugar, and milk powder in a large mixing bowl; stir well. Add melted butter, 2 eggs, and 1½ teaspoons vanilla; beat at medium speed of an electric mixer until mixture is well blended. Pour batter into a greased 15- x 10- x 1-inch jellyroll pan.

Beat cream cheese at medium speed of electric mixer until smooth. Add 2 eggs and 1 teaspoon vanilla; beat well. Add powdered sugar, and beat until mixture is smooth. Spread cream cheese mixture evenly over batter. Bake at 350° for 25 to 30 minutes or until top is golden brown. Let cake cool in pan on a wire rack; cut into squares. Yield: 40 servings.

Honest to Goodness
The Junior League of Springfield, Illinois

Date-Nut Cake Roll

1 cup chopped dates
1 cup water
¼ cup sugar
⅛ teaspoon salt
3 eggs
½ cup sugar
1 cup all-purpose flour
1 teaspoon baking powder
½ teaspoon salt
½ teaspoon ground allspice
¾ cup finely chopped
  walnuts
1 to 2 tablespoons powdered
  sugar
Cream Cheese Filling

Grease bottom and sides of a 15- x 10- x 1-inch jellyroll pan with vegetable oil; line with wax paper, and grease wax paper with oil. Set pan aside.

Combine first 4 ingredients in a saucepan. Cook over medium heat 3 minutes or until thickened, stirring constantly. Let cool.

Beat eggs in a large bowl at high speed of an electric mixer until thick and lemon colored; gradually add ½ cup sugar, beating well.

Combine flour, baking powder, ½ teaspoon salt, and allspice; stir well. Gradually fold into egg mixture. Fold in date mixture.

Spread batter evenly in prepared pan. Sprinkle with walnuts. Bake at 375° for 12 to 15 minutes.

Sift powdered sugar in a 15- x 10-inch rectangle on a towel. When cake is done, immediately loosen from sides of pan, and turn out onto sugared towel. Carefully peel off wax paper. Starting at narrow end, roll up cake and towel together; let cool completely on a wire rack, seam side down. Unroll cake. Spread with Cream Cheese Filling, and carefully reroll cake without towel. Chill. Yield: 8 to 10 servings.

Cream Cheese Filling

2 (3-ounce) packages cream
  cheese, softened
¼ cup butter or margarine,
  softened
1 cup sifted powdered
  sugar
½ teaspoon vanilla extract

Combine cream cheese and butter, and beat at medium speed of an electric mixer until smooth. Add sugar and vanilla; beat until light and fluffy. Yield: about 1 cup.   Helen Bardwell

This Side of the River Cookbook
The Hatfield Book Club
Hatfield, Massachusetts

Walnut Sponge Cake Roll

7 eggs, separated
¼ cup plus 3 tablespoons
  sugar
¼ cup plus 3 tablespoons
  all-purpose flour
1 teaspoon vanilla extract
  (optional)
1 to 2 tablespoons powdered
  sugar

1 cup sugar
¾ cup half-and-half
3 cups ground walnuts
1 teaspoon rum or lemon
  extract (optional)
Additional powdered sugar

Grease bottom and sides of an 18- x 12- x 1-inch jellyroll pan with vegetable oil; line with wax paper, and grease wax paper with oil. Set pan aside.

Beat egg yolks in a large mixing bowl at high speed of an electric mixer until thick and lemon colored. Gradually add ¼ cup plus 3 tablespoons sugar and flour, beating well. Stir in vanilla, if desired. Set aside.

Beat egg whites (at room temperature) at high speed until stiff peaks form. Gently fold egg whites into yolks. Spread batter evenly in prepared pan. Bake at 350° for 15 minutes.

Sift 1 to 2 tablespoons powdered sugar in an 18- x 12-inch rectangle on a towel. When cake is done, immediately loosen from sides of pan, and turn out onto sugared towel. Carefully peel off wax paper. Starting at narrow end, roll up cake and towel together; let cake cool completely on a wire rack, seam side down.

Combine 1 cup sugar and half-and-half in a medium saucepan; cook over medium-high heat, stirring constantly, until sugar dissolves. Stir in walnuts and, if desired, rum extract.

Unroll cake. Spread walnut filling over cake, and carefully reroll cake without towel. Place cake on a serving plate, seam side down. Sprinkle cake with additional powdered sugar. Yield: 10 to 12 servings.   Marija Longnecker

Dobar Tek
The Yugoslav Women's Club
Seattle, Washington

Victorian Sponge Cake with Lemon Curd

1 cup all-purpose flour
1 teaspoon baking powder
¼ teaspoon salt
3 eggs
¾ cup sugar
¼ cup butter or margarine, softened

2 tablespoons sour cream
1 tablespoon plus 1 teaspoon lemon juice
Lemon Curd

Sift together flour, baking powder, and salt; set aside.

Beat eggs at high speed of an electric mixer until thickened; add sugar, and beat until thick and lemon colored. Add butter and sour cream; beat at medium speed until blended. Stir in lemon juice.

Sprinkle one-fourth of flour mixture at a time over egg mixture; gently fold in with a rubber spatula after each addition.

Pour batter into a wax paper-lined 15- x 10- x 1-inch jellyroll pan. Bake at 350° for 15 to 18 minutes or until cake springs back when lightly touched. Let cool completely in pan on a wire rack. Remove from pan; carefully peel off wax paper.

Cut cake crosswise into 4 rectangles. Gently spread ⅓ cup Lemon Curd on top of 3 rectangles; stack the rectangles, Lemon Curd side up. Top with fourth rectangle. Chill thoroughly. Cut cake into thin slices, and serve with remaining Lemon Curd. Yield: 16 servings.

Lemon Curd

⅓ cup butter
1 cup superfine sugar
¼ cup grated lemon rind

3 eggs
1 cup lemon juice

Cream butter; gradually add sugar, beating well at medium speed of an electric mixer. Add lemon rind and eggs; beat until thick and lemon colored. Gradually add lemon juice, beating well.

Transfer lemon mixture to top of a double boiler. Bring water to a boil; reduce heat, and cook, stirring constantly, until mixture thickens and coats the back of a metal spoon (about 15 minutes). Remove from heat; let cool slightly. Cover and chill. Yield: 2 cups.

Recipes & Recollections from Terrace Hill
The Terrace Hill Society
Des Moines, Iowa

Butterscotch-Nut Torte

6 eggs, separated
1½ cups sugar
1 teaspoon baking powder
2 teaspoons vanilla extract
1 teaspoon almond extract
2 cups graham cracker
  crumbs

1 cup finely chopped pecans
  or walnuts
3 cups whipping cream
¼ cup plus ½ tablespoon
  sifted powdered sugar
Butterscotch Sauce

Grease two 9-inch round cakepans; line with wax paper, and grease and flour wax paper. Set aside.

Beat egg yolks at medium speed of an electric mixer until thick and lemon colored; gradually add 1½ cups sugar, beating well. Add baking powder and flavorings, beating well. Set aside.

Beat egg whites (at room temperature) at high speed until stiff peaks form; fold into egg yolk mixture. Fold in graham cracker crumbs and pecans.

Pour batter into prepared pans. Bake at 325° for 30 to 35 minutes or until a wooden pick inserted in center comes out clean. Let cake layers cool in pans 10 minutes; remove from pans, and let cool completely on wire racks.

Beat whipping cream until foamy; gradually add powdered sugar, beating until soft peaks form.

Spread half of sweetened whipped cream between layers; spread remaining whipped cream over top. Drizzle Butterscotch Sauce over torte. Yield: one 9-inch torte.

Butterscotch Sauce

1 cup firmly packed brown
  sugar
¼ cup butter, melted
¼ cup water

1 tablespoon all-purpose flour
1 egg, beaten
¼ cup orange juice
½ teaspoon vanilla extract

Combine first 4 ingredients in a medium saucepan, stirring well. Add egg, orange juice, and vanilla; bring mixture to a boil over medium-low heat, stirring constantly. Cook 3 to 5 minutes or until mixture thickens, stirring constantly. Remove from heat, and let cool completely. Yield: about ¾ cup.

"One Lump or Two?"
All Children's Hospital Guild
St. Petersburg, Florida

Ricotta Torte

1 (14-ounce) loaf commercial
  pound cake
¼ cup plus 2 tablespoons
  Grand Marnier or other
  orange-flavored liqueur
1 (15-ounce) carton ricotta
  cheese
½ cup sugar
1½ teaspoons vanilla extract
4 (1-ounce) squares semisweet
  chocolate, chopped
  (optional)

2 tablespoons cocoa
½ cup sifted powdered sugar
1 tablespoon butter or
  margarine, melted
1 tablespoon plus 1 teaspoon
  boiling water
2 tablespoons chopped pecans
  or walnuts

Slice cake horizontally into 3 layers. Drizzle 2 tablespoons liqueur
on one side of each layer; set aside.

Combine ricotta cheese, ½ cup sugar, vanilla, and, if desired,
chocolate in a small bowl, stirring well.

Place bottom cake layer on a serving plate, liqueur side up. Spread
1 cup cheese mixture over layer. Repeat procedure with second
layer and remaining cheese mixture. Top with remaining layer, cut
side down; set aside.

Combine cocoa, powdered sugar, and butter; beat at medium
speed of an electric mixer until smooth. Add boiling water, stirring
until smooth. (If necessary, add more boiling water to reach glaze
consistency.) Drizzle glaze over torte. Sprinkle with pecans. Chill 30
minutes. Yield: 6 servings.

Thymes Remembered
The Junior League of Tallahassee, Florida

Cookies &
Candies

The Betsy Ross House is a modest brick townhouse built around 1740 in Philadelphia, Pennsylvania. The first floor contains the upholstery shop where the seamstress-patriot Betsy Ross reputedly stitched the first American flag in 1776. Congress formally adopted this flag as the national symbol on June 14, 1777.

Devil's Food Frosted Cookies

2 (1-ounce) squares
  unsweetened chocolate
½ cup butter or margarine,
  softened
1 cup firmly packed brown
  sugar
1 egg
1 teaspoon vanilla extract

2 cups all-purpose flour
½ teaspoon baking soda
¼ teaspoon salt
1 (8-ounce) carton sour cream
½ cup chopped pecans or
  walnuts (optional)
Frosting (recipe follows)

Place chocolate in top of a double boiler; bring water to a boil. Reduce heat to low; cook until chocolate melts, stirring occasionally. Remove from heat; set aside, and let cool.

Cream butter; gradually add brown sugar, beating well at medium speed of an electric mixer. Add egg and vanilla, beating well.

Combine flour, soda, and salt in a medium bowl; stir well. Add to creamed mixture alternately with sour cream, beginning and ending with flour mixture. Mix well after each addition. Stir in chopped pecans, if desired.

Drop dough by rounded teaspoonfuls 2 inches apart onto greased cookie sheets. Bake at 350° for 10 minutes. Let cool on wire racks; spread frosting over tops of cookies. Yield: 4½ dozen.

Frosting

¼ cup butter or margarine,
  softened
2 tablespoons cocoa
2 teaspoons instant coffee
  granules

Dash of salt
3 cups sifted powdered sugar
3 tablespoons milk
1½ teaspoons vanilla extract

Cream butter; add cocoa, coffee granules, and salt, beating well at medium speed of an electric mixer. Gradually add powdered sugar, 1 cup at a time, beating well after each addition. Add milk and vanilla, beating until smooth. Yield: 2 cups.   Linda Pope

Out of This World
Wood Acres Elementary School
Bethesda, Maryland

Miss Freedom's Chocolate Crab Cake Cookies

½ cup butter, softened
½ cup sugar
1 (15-ounce) can cream of
  coconut
1 teaspoon vanilla extract
2 eggs
1½ cups all-purpose flour
½ cup cocoa

2 teaspoons baking powder
½ teaspoon baking soda
¼ teaspoon salt
1 (14-ounce) package
  shredded coconut
1 (12-ounce) package
  semisweet chocolate
  morsels

Cream butter in a large mixing bowl; gradually add sugar, beating well at medium speed of an electric mixer. Add cream of coconut and vanilla, beating well. Add eggs, one at a time, beating well after each addition.

Combine flour, cocoa, baking powder, soda, and salt; stir well. Add to creamed mixture, mixing well. Stir in shredded coconut and chocolate morsels.

Drop dough by rounded tablespoonfuls 2 inches apart onto aluminum foil-lined cookie sheets. Bake at 375° for 15 minutes or until cookies spring back when lightly touched. Let cool completely on wire racks. Yield: 5 dozen.

From a Lighthouse Window
The Chesapeake Bay Maritime Museum
St. Michaels, Maryland

Chocolate Double Delights

1½ cups firmly packed brown
  sugar
¾ cup butter or margarine
2 tablespoons water
1 (12-ounce) package
  semisweet chocolate
  morsels

2 eggs, beaten
3 cups all-purpose flour
1¼ teaspoons baking soda
1 teaspoon salt
Peppermint Cream Filling

Combine brown sugar and butter in a heavy saucepan; cook over medium heat until butter melts, stirring occasionally. Remove from heat, and stir in water. Add chocolate morsels, stirring until chocolate melts. Add eggs, stirring well.

Combine flour, baking soda, and salt; stir well. Add to chocolate mixture, stirring well.

Drop dough by heaping teaspoonfuls onto greased cookie sheets. Bake at 350° for 8 to 10 minutes. Let cool on wire racks. Spread half of cookies with Peppermint Cream Filling; top with remaining cookies. Yield: about 3½ dozen.

Peppermint Cream Filling

3 cups sifted powdered sugar, divided
⅓ cup butter, softened

⅛ teaspoon peppermint extract
2 to 3 tablespoons milk

Combine 1½ cups powdered sugar, butter, and peppermint extract; beat at medium speed of an electric mixer until smooth. Add remaining 1½ cups powdered sugar and milk; beat until smooth. Yield: 1½ cups.

Terry Home Presents Food & Fun from Celebrities & Us
Terry Home, Inc.
Sumner, Washington

Yankee Molasses Chip Cookies

¾ cup butter or margarine, softened
1 cup sugar
1 egg
¼ cup molasses
2 cups all-purpose flour
2 teaspoons baking soda

¼ teaspoon salt
1 teaspoon ground cinnamon
¾ teaspoon ground ginger
½ teaspoon ground cloves
1¼ cups semisweet chocolate morsels

Cream butter; gradually add sugar, beating well at medium speed of an electric mixer. Add egg and molasses, beating well. Combine flour and next 5 ingredients; add to creamed mixture, mixing well. Stir in chocolate morsels.

Drop dough by heaping teaspoonfuls onto lightly greased cookie sheets. Bake at 350° for 8 to 10 minutes. Let cool slightly on cookie sheets; transfer cookies to wire racks, and let cool completely. Yield: about 4½ dozen.

More Than a Tea Party
The Junior League of Boston, Massachusetts

Cranberry Drops

½ cup butter or margarine,
  softened
1 cup sugar
¾ cup firmly packed brown
  sugar
¼ cup milk
1 egg
2 tablespoons orange juice

3 cups all-purpose flour
½ teaspoon baking powder
¼ teaspoon baking soda
½ teaspoon salt
2¼ cups coarsely chopped
  cranberries
1 cup chopped pecans or
  walnuts

Cream butter; gradually add sugars, beating at medium speed of an electric mixer until light and fluffy. Add milk, egg, and orange juice; beat well.

Combine flour and next 3 ingredients; add to creamed mixture, beating well. Stir in cranberries and pecans.

Drop dough by rounded teaspoonfuls onto greased cookie sheets. Bake at 375° for 12 to 14 minutes or until lightly browned. Let cool slightly on cookie sheets; transfer to wire racks, and let cool completely. Yield: 7½ dozen.   John and Enid Morris

Capital Connoisseur
The Lawrence Center Independence House
Schenectady, New York

Gumdrop Cookies

¾ cup shortening
1 cup sugar
1 egg
2 cups all-purpose flour
1 teaspoon baking powder
½ teaspoon salt

1 cup assorted colored, spicy
  gumdrops, chopped
¼ cup milk
1½ teaspoons vanilla extract
36 assorted colored, spicy
  gumdrops

Cream shortening; gradually add sugar, beating well at medium speed of an electric mixer. Add egg; beat well.

Combine flour, baking powder, and salt in a medium bowl; stir well. Combine ½ cup flour mixture and chopped gumdrops; toss gently to coat well. Set aside.

Add remaining flour mixture to creamed mixture alternately with milk, beginning and ending with flour mixture. Mix after each addition. Stir in vanilla.

Drop dough by tablespoonfuls 2 inches apart onto greased cookie sheets. Press 1 gumdrop in center of each cookie. Bake at 400° for 15 to 17 minutes or until lightly browned. Let cool on wire racks. Yield: 3 dozen.   Fran Robinson

RSVP: Recipes Shared Very Proudly
First Church of Christ
Simsbury, Connecticut

Oatmeal Jim Jams

1 cup butter or margarine, softened

1 cup firmly packed brown sugar

2 cups quick-cooking oats, uncooked

2 cups all-purpose flour

1 teaspoon baking soda

1 teaspoon salt

½ cup buttermilk

1¾ cups chopped dates or raisins

¾ cup sugar

½ cup boiling water

½ teaspoon vanilla extract

Cream butter in a large mixing bowl; gradually add 1 cup brown sugar, beating at medium speed of an electric mixer until mixture is light and fluffy.

Combine oats, flour, soda, and salt; stir well. Add to creamed mixture alternately with buttermilk, beginning and ending with flour mixture.

Drop dough by tablespoonfuls onto ungreased cookie sheets. Bake at 350° for 12 to 15 minutes. Let cool slightly on cookie sheets; transfer to wire racks, and let cool completely.

Combine chopped dates, ¾ cup sugar, boiling water, and vanilla in a small saucepan. Cook over low heat, stirring constantly, until mixture is thickened. Remove from heat, and let cool. Spread half of cookies with date mixture. Top with remaining cookies. Yield: about 2 dozen.   Hulda Thompson

Mothers of Twins Cookbook
Twice as Nice, Mothers of Twins Club
Gillette, Wyoming

World's Best Sugar Cookies

1 cup sugar	1 cup vegetable oil
1 cup sifted powdered sugar	4 cups all-purpose flour
2 eggs	1 teaspoon baking soda
2 tablespoons butter or	¼ teaspoon salt
margarine, melted	1 teaspoon cream of tartar
2 teaspoons vanilla extract	½ cup sugar
1 teaspoon lemon extract	½ teaspoon ground cinnamon

Combine first 6 ingredients; beat well at medium speed of an electric mixer. Add oil, beating well. Combine flour, soda, salt, and cream of tartar, stirring well. Gradually add to creamed mixture; mix well.

Combine ½ cup sugar and cinnamon. Shape dough into 1-inch balls; roll in sugar mixture. Place balls 3 inches apart on ungreased cookie sheets. Dip a flat-bottomed glass in sugar mixture; flatten balls to ¼-inch thickness. Bake at 350° for 12 minutes. Let cool on wire racks. Yield: 6 dozen.   Virginia Lee Graves Pettengill

Centennial Cookbook
The Orange County Pioneer Council
Newport Beach, California

Chocolate-Covered Cherry Cookies

½ cup butter or margarine,	¼ teaspoon baking soda
softened	2 (10-ounce) jars maraschino
1 cup sugar	cherries, undrained
1 egg	1 (6-ounce) package
2 teaspoons vanilla extract	semisweet chocolate
1½ cups all-purpose flour	morsels
½ cup cocoa	½ cup sweetened condensed
¼ teaspoon baking powder	milk

Cream butter; gradually add sugar, beating well at medium speed of an electric mixer. Add egg and vanilla; beat well. Combine flour and next 3 ingredients; stir well. Gradually add to creamed mixture, beating well.

Shape dough into 1-inch balls; place on ungreased cookie sheets. Press thumb into each ball of dough, leaving an indentation. Drain cherries, reserving 1 tablespoon plus 1 teaspoon juice. Press 1 cherry into indentation of each cookie.

Combine reserved cherry juice, chocolate morsels, and milk in a small saucepan. Cook over medium heat, stirring constantly, until chocolate melts. Spread about 1 teaspoon frosting over each cherry. Bake at 350° for 10 to 12 minutes. Let cool completely on cookie sheets. Yield: 4 dozen.

Hearts and Flours
The Junior League of Waco, Texas

Almond Dunking Cookies

1 cup butter, softened
1 cup sugar
2 eggs
3 tablespoons sour cream
½ teaspoon almond extract
3 cups all-purpose flour
1 teaspoon baking powder
¼ teaspoon baking soda
⅔ cup slivered almonds

Cream butter; gradually add sugar, beating well at medium speed of an electric mixer. Add eggs, one a time, beating well after each addition. Stir in sour cream and almond extract.

Combine flour, baking powder, and soda; stir well. Add to creamed mixture, stirring well. Stir in almonds.

Divide dough into thirds. With floured hands, shape each portion into a 10-inch log on a large greased cookie sheet. Flatten logs to ½-inch thickness. Bake at 350° for 20 to 25 minutes or until golden brown. Cut logs diagonally into ½-inch slices. Place slices, cut side down, on ungreased cookie sheets; bake 10 minutes. Let cool on wire racks. Yield: 5 dozen.   Kristine Kolstad

Crème de la Congregation
Our Saviors Lutheran Church
Lafayette, California

Speculaas

1 cup butter, softened	2 teaspoons ground cinnamon
¾ cup firmly packed brown sugar	¾ teaspoon ground cloves
1 egg, beaten	¼ teaspoon ground nutmeg
¼ teaspoon anise extract	⅛ teaspoon cocoa
⅛ teaspoon almond extract	⅛ teaspoon pepper
3 cups all-purpose flour	½ teaspoon grated lemon rind
1 tablespoon baking powder	¼ cup finely chopped blanched almonds
Pinch of salt	

Cream butter; gradually add brown sugar, beating well at medium speed of an electric mixer. Add egg and flavorings, beating well. Combine flour and next 8 ingredients; stir well. Add to creamed mixture, mixing well. Stir in almonds.

Shape dough into a ball; knead 3 or 4 times. Roll dough to ¼-inch thickness on a large cookie sheet. Press into floured cookie boards or cut with cookie cutters. Chill 1 hour. Place cookies on buttered cookie sheets. Bake at 350° for 25 minutes. Let cool on wire racks. Yield: 2 dozen.   Claudie J. Brock

The Delaware Heritage Cookbook
The Delaware Heritage Commission
Wilmington, Delaware

Peek-A-Boos

½ cup butter, softened	2½ cups all-purpose flour
¾ cup sugar	1½ teaspoons baking powder
2 eggs	¼ teaspoon salt
1 teaspoon lemon extract	½ cup fruit preserves

Cream butter; gradually add sugar, beating well at medium speed of an electric mixer. Add eggs, one at a time, beating well after each addition. Stir in extract. Combine flour, baking powder, and salt; stir well. Add to creamed mixture; mix well. Cover and chill.

Divide dough in half, storing remaining half of dough in refrigerator. Roll half of dough to ⅛-inch thickness on a lightly floured surface. Cut with a 2-inch cookie cutter, and place on ungreased cookie sheets. Place 1 teaspoon preserves in center of each cookie.

Repeat rolling and cutting procedure with remaining half of dough. Cut out a star design in center of each plain cookie. Top each preserve-topped cookie with a cut-out cookie. Seal edges with a fork. Bake at 375° for 12 to 15 minutes or until lightly browned. Let cool on wire racks. Yield: 2 dozen.   Jo Faimon

Heritage of Red Cloud
Heritage of Red Cloud
Red Cloud, Nebraska

Cookie Turnovers

½ cup shortening
1½ cups firmly packed brown
  sugar
1 egg
⅓ cup buttermilk
3½ cups all-purpose flour

1 teaspoon baking powder
½ teaspoon baking soda
½ teaspoon salt
½ teaspoon ground cinnamon
Filling (recipe follows)

Cream shortening; gradually add brown sugar, beating well at medium speed of an electric mixer. Add egg, and beat well. Add buttermilk, mixing well. Combine flour and next 4 ingredients; stir well. Add to creamed mixture, beating well. Cover and chill 2 hours.

Divide dough into fourths. Work with one portion of dough at a time, storing remaining dough in refrigerator. Roll dough to ⅛-inch thickness on a lightly floured surface. Cut with a 2-inch cookie cutter, and place on greased cookie sheets. Place about 1 teaspoon filling in center of half of cookies; top with remaining cookies. Bake at 375° for 15 minutes. Let cool on wire racks. Yield: 3 dozen.

Filling

1 cup chopped dates
1 cup chopped prunes
1 cup chopped raisins

1 cup brewed coffee
1 cup firmly packed brown
  sugar

Combine first 4 ingredients in a medium saucepan. Cook over medium heat, stirring constantly, 3 to 5 minutes or until liquid is absorbed and mixture is thickened. Remove from heat; stir in brown sugar. Let cool. Yield: about 2 cups.   Ellen West

The Florida Cooking Adventure
The Florida Federation of Women's Clubs
Lakeland, Florida

Fruitcake Gems

½ cup chopped red candied
  cherries
½ cup chopped green
  candied cherries
1 cup slivered candied
  pineapple
¼ cup finely chopped
  candied orange peel
¼ cup raisins (optional)
2 cups chopped walnuts
2 cups chopped pecans
½ cup butter, softened

3 tablespoons brown sugar
3 eggs
¼ cup brandy, ginger-
  flavored brandy, or fruit
  juice
3 tablespoons honey
½ cup all-purpose flour
½ teaspoon baking powder
½ teaspoon salt
¼ teaspoon ground allspice
¼ teaspoon ground nutmeg

Combine candied cherries, pineapple, orange peel, and, if desired, raisins in a large bowl. Add nuts, tossing gently to combine.

Cream butter; gradually add brown sugar, beating well at medium speed of an electric mixer. Add eggs, one at a time, beating well after each addition. Stir in brandy and honey.

Combine flour and remaining ingredients; stir well. Add to creamed mixture; mix well. Add fruit mixture, stirring to combine. Spoon batter into greased miniature (1¾-inch) muffin pans, filling to top (batter will not rise).

Cover pans with greased parchment or brown paper, placing paper greased side down. Bake at 300° for 40 to 45 minutes. Remove from oven. Remove and discard paper; let cookies cool in pans 10 minutes. Remove from pans, and let cool completely on wire racks. Yield: about 4½ dozen.   Betty Totten

Mountain Memories
The American Cancer Society, West Virginia Division, Inc.
Charleston, West Virginia

Chocolate Pecan Bars

1¼ cups all-purpose flour
1 cup sifted powdered
  sugar
½ cup cocoa
1 cup butter or margarine

1 (14-ounce) can sweetened
  condensed milk
1 egg, lightly beaten
2 teaspoons vanilla extract
1½ cups chopped pecans

Combine flour, sugar, and cocoa in a medium bowl; stir well. Cut in butter with a pastry blender until mixture resembles coarse meal. Press mixture into a 13- x 9- x 2-inch baking pan. Bake at 350° for 15 minutes; let cool on a wire rack 10 minutes.

Combine condensed milk, egg, and vanilla; stir until blended. Stir in pecans. Pour over prepared crust. Bake at 350° for 25 minutes. Let cool completely in pan on wire rack; cut into bars. Cover and store in refrigerator. Yield: 2½ dozen.   Rayna Larson

Alaska's Cooking, Volume II
The Woman's Club of Anchorage, Alaska

Rebel Peanut Butter Brownies

½ cup butter, softened
½ cup creamy peanut butter
1½ cups firmly packed brown
  sugar
2 eggs
1 teaspoon vanilla extract
1½ cups all-purpose flour
2 teaspoons baking powder
2 teaspoons salt

½ cup chopped salted roasted
  peanuts
½ cup firmly packed brown
  sugar
3 tablespoons butter
1 tablespoon honey
1 tablespoon milk
¼ cup finely chopped salted
  roasted peanuts

Cream ½ cup butter and peanut butter; gradually add 1½ cups brown sugar, ½ cup at a time, beating well at medium speed of an electric mixer. Add eggs and vanilla; beat well.

Combine flour, baking powder, and salt; stir well. Add to creamed mixture, mixing well. Stir in ½ cup chopped peanuts.

Spread batter in a greased 13- x 9- x 2-inch pan. Bake at 350° for 30 minutes or until a wooden pick inserted in center comes out clean. Remove from oven; let cool slightly in pan on a wire rack.

Combine ½ cup brown sugar, 3 tablespoons butter, honey, and milk in a small saucepan. Bring to a boil; reduce heat, and simmer 5 minutes, stirring constantly. Remove from heat; stir in ¼ cup finely chopped peanuts.

Spread topping over warm brownies. Let cool completely in pan on a wire rack; cut into squares. Yield: 2 dozen.   Lisa Quinn

Island Born and Bred
The Harkers Island United Methodist Women
Harkers Island, North Carolina

Tonia's Badge of Honour Brownies

4 eggs
2 cups sugar
⅔ cup vegetable oil
4 (1-ounce) squares
  unsweetened chocolate,
  melted and cooled
2 teaspoons vanilla extract

1⅓ cups all-purpose flour
1 teaspoon baking powder
1 cup chopped pecans or
  walnuts, divided
1 cup semisweet chocolate
  morsels, divided

Beat eggs in a large bowl at medium speed of an electric mixer until thick and lemon colored; gradually add sugar, beating well. Add oil, melted chocolate, and vanilla, stirring well to combine.

Combine flour and baking powder; stir well. Add to chocolate mixture, beating well at medium speed. Stir in ⅔ cup pecans and ½ cup chocolate morsels. Spread batter in a buttered and floured 13- x 9- x 2-inch baking dish. Sprinkle remaining ⅓ cup pecans and ½ cup chocolate morsels on top of batter, pressing lightly into batter. Bake at 350° for 30 to 35 minutes. Let cool in pan on a wire rack; cut into squares. Yield: 1½ dozen.   Tonia Sedlock

The Galloping Chef
The Combined Training Equestrian Team Alliance
Woodside, California

Triple Treats

1 (11½-ounce) package milk
  chocolate morsels
2 tablespoons shortening
30 caramels
3 tablespoons butter

2 tablespoons water
1 cup coarsely chopped
  unsalted dry roasted
  peanuts

Combine milk chocolate morsels and shortening in top of a double boiler; bring water to a boil. Reduce heat to low; cook until chocolate and shortening melt, stirring occasionally. Spread half of chocolate mixture evenly in an aluminum foil-lined 8-inch square pan. Chill 15 minutes or until firm. (Keep remaining chocolate mixture warm.)

Combine caramels, butter, and water in top of a double boiler; bring water in bottom of double boiler to a boil. Reduce heat to low; cook, stirring occasionally, until smooth. Stir in peanuts; let cool slightly. Spread caramel mixture over chilled chocolate mixture.

Chill 15 minutes; spread remaining warm chocolate mixture evenly over caramel mixture. Chill 1 hour or until firm. Cut into squares. Yield: about 1¾ pounds.   Kathy Radulovich

Aggies, Moms, and Apple Pie
The Federation of Texas A&M University Mothers' Clubs
College Station, Texas

Golden Butterscotch Fudge

2¼ cups firmly packed brown sugar
1 cup sugar
1 cup evaporated milk
½ cup butter, melted
1 (12-ounce) package butterscotch morsels

1 (10-ounce) jar marshmallow cream
1 cup chopped walnuts
½ cup golden raisins
1 teaspoon rum extract
½ teaspoon vanilla extract

Combine first 4 ingredients in a saucepan; stir well. Cook over medium heat to soft ball stage (238°), stirring occasionally. Remove from heat; add butterscotch morsels and marshmallow cream, stirring until melted. Add walnuts, raisins, and flavorings; stir well. Spread in two greased 8-inch square pans. Let cool in pans on a wire rack; cut into squares. Yield: 3 pounds.   Clara Browne

Favorite Recipes from Our Best Cooks, Volume II
Frederick Chopin Choir, St. Valentine's Polish National
Catholic Church
Northampton, Massachusetts

Proceeds generated from the sale of **The Galloping Chef** *will go to the Western America Equestrian Performing Arts Education Center, the United States Equestrian Team, and the CTETA Horse Park.*

Sugarplums

2 cups pitted prunes, finely chopped
2 cups raisins
1⅓ cups finely chopped walnuts
2 cups sugar
½ cup light corn syrup
½ cup water
½ teaspoon vanilla extract
¼ teaspoon salt
2 (3½-ounce) cans flaked coconut

Combine prunes, raisins, and chopped walnuts; stir well.

Combine sugar, corn syrup, and water in a saucepan; cook over low heat, stirring gently, until sugar dissolves. Cover and cook over medium heat 2 to 3 minutes to wash down sugar crystals from sides of pan. Uncover and cook until mixture reaches soft ball stage (238°). Remove from heat; let cool 10 minutes. Pour sugar mixture into a bowl; add vanilla and salt. Beat at high speed of an electric mixer 5 minutes or until light and fluffy. Stir in prune mixture. Press into a lightly greased 9-inch square pan. Chill 1 hour.

Position knife blade in food processor bowl; add coconut, and process until finely chopped. Cut candy into 64 squares. Shape each square into a ball; roll in coconut. Store candy in an airtight container. Yield: 1¼ pounds.   Jerry and Sheri Wiener

Aspic and Old Lace
The Northern Indiana Historical Society
South Bend, Indiana

Sour Cream-Glazed Pecans

3 cups sugar
1 (8-ounce) carton sour cream
2 teaspoons vanilla extract
5 cups pecan halves

Combine sugar and sour cream in a heavy 2½-quart saucepan. Cook over low heat, stirring constantly, until mixture reaches soft ball stage (240°). Remove from heat, and stir in vanilla. Continue stirring until mixture begins to cool. Add pecans, stirring well. Spread in a single layer on wax paper; let cool completely. Yield: about 6 cups.   Janice A. McKinney

Calling All Cooks Two
The Telephone Pioneers of America
Birmingham, Alabama

Desserts

Belle Meade, located in Nashville, Tennessee, was the nation's "oldest and greatest" Thoroughbred horse farm in the 1880s. The Victorian carriage house and stable is home to a notable collection of horse-drawn vehicles. Also on display are Belle Meade's maroon racing silks, the first racing silks to be registered in America.

Cantaloupe Balls

2 cantaloupes
1 (6-ounce) can frozen orange
  juice concentrate, thawed
  and undiluted

1 (6-ounce) can frozen
  lemonade concentrate,
  thawed and undiluted
1 cup water

Cut cantaloupes in half, and remove seeds. Carefully scoop out cantaloupe balls. Place cantaloupe balls in a large bowl; set aside.

Combine juices and water; stir well. Pour orange juice mixture over cantaloupe, stirring gently to combine. Cover and chill at least 2 hours. Yield: 8 to 10 servings.

Wild about Texas
The Cypress-Woodlands Junior Forum
Houston, Texas

Cranberry-Apricot Fool

1 (8¾-ounce) can apricot
  halves, drained
1 (8-ounce) can jellied
  cranberry sauce

¾ cup whipping cream
1 teaspoon vanilla extract
Crisp cookies or ladyfingers
  (optional)

Divide apricot halves evenly among 4 dessert dishes, and chill thoroughly.

Place cranberry sauce in a small bowl; stir well, and set aside.

Combine whipping cream and vanilla; beat at high speed of an electric mixer until soft peaks form. Fold cranberry sauce into whipped cream, creating a marbled effect.

Spoon whipped cream mixture evenly over apricots. Serve immediately. If desired, serve with crisp cookies or ladyfingers. Yield: 4 servings.   The Family of Gerhard Hahn

Symphony of Tastes
The Youth Symphony of Anchorage, Alaska

Chilled Zabaglione

6 egg yolks
⅔ cup Marsala wine
½ cup sugar
½ teaspoon vanilla extract
Dash of ground cinnamon

½ cup whipping cream, whipped
8 to 10 canned peach halves, chilled

Combine egg yolks and wine in top of a double boiler; beat at medium speed of an electric mixer until blended. Add sugar, beating well. Bring water to a boil; reduce heat to low, and beat 8 minutes at high speed or until mixture thickens and stiff peaks form. Remove from heat; gently fold in vanilla and cinnamon.

Set top of double boiler in a large bowl of ice; beat egg yolk mixture at medium speed until thoroughly chilled. Fold in whipped cream; chill. To serve, place peach halves in dessert dishes; top with chilled mixture. Yield: 8 to 10 servings.   Betty O'Neill

Our Favorite Recipes
St. Edmond's Church
Philadelphia, Pennsylvania

Pears in Chocolate

12 medium-size, firm, ripe pears with stems
8 cups water
2 cups sugar
½ cup lemon juice

4 (3-inch) sticks cinnamon
8 (1-ounce) squares semisweet chocolate
½ cup unsalted butter
Garnish: fresh mint sprigs

Peel pears; remove core from bottom end and cut to, but not through, the stem end. Slice ¼ inch from bottom of each pear to make a flat base. Set pears aside.

Combine water and next 3 ingredients in a large Dutch oven; bring to a boil, stirring until sugar dissolves. Add pears; cover, reduce heat, and simmer 20 minutes or until pears are tender but still hold their shape. Let pears cool in liquid. Transfer pears and liquid to a large bowl. Cover and chill 12 hours.

Drain pears; discard syrup. Gently press pears between paper towels to remove excess moisture.

Combine chocolate and butter in top of a double boiler; bring water to a boil. Reduce heat to low; cook until chocolate and butter melt, stirring occasionally. Dip pears in chocolate mixture. If necessary, spoon chocolate mixture over pears to coat well. Place coated pears on wax paper; let stand until chocolate is set.

Transfer pears to individual dessert dishes. Garnish, if desired. Yield: 12 servings.   Martha Buller

Favorite Recipes from Fishers Island
The Island Bowling Center
Fishers Island, New York

Baked Pears with Lemon Sauce

½ cup honey
2 tablespoons lemon juice
6 large, firm, ripe pears, peeled and cored
1½ cups graham cracker crumbs
2 tablespoons sugar
1 teaspoon grated lemon rind
¼ cup butter, melted
½ cup water
½ cup sugar
1 tablespoon all-purpose flour
2 egg yolks, lightly beaten
3 tablespoons lemon juice
2 tablespoons butter
1 teaspoon grated lemon rind

Combine honey and 2 tablespoons lemon juice in a small bowl; stir well. Dip pears in honey mixture; coat with cracker crumbs. Place pears, upright, in an 11- x 7- x 1½-inch baking dish.

Combine 2 tablespoons sugar and 1 teaspoon lemon rind, stirring well. Place 1 teaspoon sugar mixture in cavity of each pear. Pour ¼ cup melted butter in bottom of baking dish. Bake, uncovered, at 325° for 25 to 30 minutes or until pears are tender.

Combine water, ½ cup sugar, and flour in a small saucepan; stir well. Cook over medium heat, stirring constantly, until sugar dissolves and mixture comes to a boil; boil 1 minute. Gradually stir about one-fourth of hot mixture into egg yolks; add to remaining hot mixture, stirring constantly. Cook over medium heat, stirring constantly, until mixture is thickened and bubbly. Boil 2 minutes, stirring constantly. Remove from heat. Add 3 tablespoons lemon juice, 2 tablespoons butter, and 1 teaspoon lemon rind, stirring until butter melts. Serve pears with sauce. Yield: 6 servings.

Recipes & Recollections from Terrace Hill
The Terrace Hill Society
Des Moines, Iowa

Penny's Strawberry Brûlée

1 (8-ounce) package cream
  cheese, softened
1½ cups sour cream
¼ cup plus 2 tablespoons
  sugar

1 quart fresh strawberries,
  hulled and sliced
1 cup firmly packed brown
  sugar

Combine cream cheese and sour cream in a small bowl; beat at medium speed of an electric mixer until light and fluffy. Gradually add ¼ cup plus 2 tablespoons sugar, beating well.

Place strawberries in a 13- x 9- x 2-inch baking dish; spread cream cheese mixture evenly over strawberries. Sprinkle with brown sugar. Broil 3 to 4 inches from heat 2 minutes or until sugar melts and mixture is bubbly. Yield: 10 servings.   Pam Jenkins

Gingerbread . . . and all the trimmings
The Junior Service League of Waxahachie, Texas

Baked Apple Tapioca

3 large cooking apples,
  peeled, cored, and sliced
3 tablespoons lemon juice
3 cups water
1 cup firmly packed brown
  sugar
½ cup quick-cooking tapioca,
  uncooked

½ teaspoon salt
¼ teaspoon ground mace
2 tablespoons butter or
  margarine, melted
Whipping cream

Place apple slices in a 13- x 9- x 2-inch baking dish. Combine lemon juice and water; stir well. Pour lemon juice mixture over apple slices. Cover and bake at 375° for 45 minutes.

Combine brown sugar and next 3 ingredients; stir well. Sprinkle sugar mixture over apple mixture; stir gently. Add butter, and stir gently. Cover and bake 10 minutes. Remove cover and stir. Cover and bake an additional 5 minutes. Serve warm with whipping cream. Yield: 6 servings.

Ancestral Stirrings
The New England Historic Genealogical Society
Boston, Massachusetts

Apricot Rice Pudding

1½ cups cooked long-grain
    rice
½ cup shredded coconut
1½ cups apricot nectar
⅔ cup sugar, divided
2 tablespoons water

½ teaspoon salt
3 eggs, separated
1 teaspoon grated lemon rind
1 teaspoon vanilla extract
½ cup apricot preserves

Combine rice and coconut; spoon mixture into an 11- x 7- x 1½-inch baking dish. Set aside.

Combine apricot nectar, ⅓ cup sugar, and 2 tablespoons water in a medium saucepan; bring to a boil. Stir in salt, and remove from heat. Set aside.

Beat egg yolks at high speed of an electric mixer until thick and lemon colored. Stir in lemon rind and vanilla. Gradually stir about one-fourth of hot mixture into egg yolks; add to remaining hot mixture, stirring constantly. Pour egg yolk mixture over rice mixture in baking dish.

Place baking dish in a baking pan. Pour boiling water into baking pan to a depth of 1 inch. Bake, uncovered, at 350° for 1 hour and 15 minutes or until set. Remove from oven; let stand 10 minutes. Spread apricot preserves over pudding.

Beat egg whites (at room temperature) at high speed just until foamy. Gradually add remaining ⅓ cup sugar, 1 tablespoon at a time, beating until stiff peaks form and sugar dissolves (2 to 4 minutes).

Spread meringue over pudding. Bake at 350° for 10 minutes or until meringue is golden brown. Serve pudding warm. Yield: 6 to 8 servings.

Evelyne Lovine

Recipes and Remembrances
The Upsala Area Historical Society
Upsala, Minnesota

Baked Pear Custard

8 medium-size, firm, ripe
  pears, peeled, cored, and
  sliced
2 tablespoons fresh lemon
  juice
1⅓ cups milk

1 cup sugar, divided
⅔ cup all-purpose flour
⅔ cup whipping cream
4 eggs
1½ teaspoons vanilla extract
2 tablespoons unsalted butter

Combine pears and lemon juice; toss well. Arrange pear slices in a buttered 13- x 9- x 2-inch baking dish.

Combine milk, ⅔ cup sugar, flour, whipping cream, eggs, and vanilla in a medium bowl; beat at low speed of an electric mixer until well blended.

Pour milk mixture over pears. Sprinkle with remaining ⅓ cup sugar; dot with butter. Bake at 375° for 55 minutes or until set. Serve warm. Yield: 8 servings.

Gourmet LA
The Junior League of Los Angeles, California

Indian Pudding

2½ cups milk
½ cup yellow cornmeal
1 egg, beaten
3 medium-size cooking
  apples, peeled, cored, and
  chopped
½ cup raisins
¼ cup molasses
3 tablespoons brown sugar

3 tablespoons maple syrup
½ teaspoon ground
  cinnamon
¼ teaspoon ground ginger
¼ teaspoon ground nutmeg
Additional ground cinnamon
Vanilla ice cream or whipped
  cream

Place milk in a large saucepan; cook over medium heat until thoroughly heated. Stir in cornmeal; cook over medium heat, stirring constantly, 2 minutes or until thickened. Remove from heat. Gradually stir about one-fourth of hot mixture into beaten egg; add to remaining hot mixture, stirring constantly. Add apple, raisins, molasses, brown sugar, maple syrup, ½ teaspoon ground cinnamon, ginger, and nutmeg; stir well.

Pour apple mixture into a well-greased 1½-quart baking dish. Bake at 325° for 1 hour and 35 minutes or until set. Sprinkle with cinnamon. Serve warm with ice cream or whipped cream. Yield: 4 to 6 servings.   Leona Pronites

From Our House to Your House
Thomson Consumer Electronics Employees, Scranton Plant
Scranton, Pennsylvania

Salzburger Nockerl

1 tablespoon plus 1 teaspoon
  unsalted butter, melted
6 egg whites
⅓ cup sugar
4 egg yolks

1 tablespoon dark rum
1½ teaspoons vanilla extract
¼ cup all-purpose flour
Powdered sugar
Sauce (recipe follows)

Grease a 13- x 9- x 2-inch baking dish with melted butter; set aside. Beat egg whites (at room temperature) in a large bowl at high speed of an electric mixer until foamy. Gradually add ⅓ cup sugar, 1 tablespoon at a time, beating until stiff peaks form and sugar dissolves (2 to 4 minutes).

Combine egg yolks, rum, and vanilla; beat at high speed until thick and lemon colored. Add flour to egg yolk mixture, stirring until blended. Fold one-fourth of egg white mixture into egg yolk mixture. Gently fold in remaining egg white mixture.

Evenly spoon 3 mounds of egg mixture into prepared dish. Bake at 425° for 7 minutes or until lightly browned. Sprinkle with powdered sugar. Serve immediately with sauce. Yield: 6 servings.

Sauce

1 cup whipping cream
2 tablespoons powdered sugar

2 tablespoons strained
  strawberry jam

Beat whipping cream at high speed of an electric mixer until foamy; gradually add powdered sugar, beating until soft peaks form. Fold in jam. Yield: 2⅓ cups.   Winifred Burnham

Bach to the Kitchen
Cappella Cantorum
Essex, Connecticut

Almond Praline Mousse with a Caramel Crown

6 egg yolks
⅓ cup sifted powdered sugar
½ cup amaretto
½ cup orange juice
1 cup whipping cream, whipped

Almond Praline
½ cup slivered almonds, toasted
1 cup sugar
½ cup light corn syrup

Beat egg yolks at medium speed of an electric mixer. Gradually add powdered sugar, beating until thick and lemon colored. Add amaretto and orange juice; beat well. Pour egg mixture into a heavy saucepan; cook over low heat until thickened, stirring constantly with a wire whisk. Remove from heat, and let cool.

Gradually stir about one-fourth of whipped cream into cooled egg yolk mixture; gently fold in remaining whipped cream. Cover and chill at least 8 hours.

Divide mousse in half. Spoon half of mousse evenly into 4 goblets; sprinkle evenly with crushed Almond Praline and slivered almonds. Top with remaining half of mousse; set aside.

Combine 1 cup sugar and corn syrup in a medium-size heavy saucepan. Cook over low heat, without stirring, to hard crack stage (310°). Remove from heat; let syrup cool slightly (about 6 to 8 minutes).

Dip fork into hot syrup; let excess drip back into pan. Repeat procedure until syrup begins to thread, and quickly move fork over mousse in a smooth, steady motion. Several layers of spun sugar will be required to achieve the desired crown effect. Top each serving with an Almond Praline flower. Yield: 4 servings.

Almond Praline

⅓ cup blanched almonds, toasted
⅓ cup sugar
⅓ cup water

Position knife blade in food processor bowl; add almonds, and process until finely chopped. Set aside. Combine sugar and water in a heavy saucepan. Cook over low heat until sugar melts. Bring to a boil; cook, without stirring, until mixture reaches hard crack stage (300°). Remove from heat, and stir in chopped almonds.

Working quickly, pour almond mixture onto a greased baking sheet, spreading with a buttered metal spatula. Immediately press a buttered 2-inch flower-shaped cutter into mixture 4 times. Let stand until hardened. Remove flowers; reserve remaining praline.

Position knife blade in food processor bowl; add reserved praline, and process until mixture resembles coarse meal. Yield: 4 flowers and about ½ cup crushed praline.   Fazol "Faz" Poursohi

A Taste of San Francisco
The Symphony of San Francisco, California

Cold Chocolate Soufflé

2 envelopes unflavored
  gelatin
2 cups milk
2 cups sugar, divided
1 (12-ounce) package
  semisweet chocolate
  morsels

8 egg yolks, beaten
1 teaspoon ground cinnamon
½ teaspoon salt
12 egg whites
1 tablespoon vanilla extract
3 cups whipping cream,
  whipped

Cut a piece of aluminum foil long enough to fit around a 3-quart soufflé dish, allowing a 1-inch overlap; fold foil lengthwise into thirds. Lightly oil one side of foil. Wrap foil around outside of dish, oiled side against dish, allowing it to extend 3 inches above rim to form a collar; secure with string.

Sprinkle gelatin over milk in a medium saucepan; let stand 1 minute. Add 1 cup sugar and next 4 ingredients, stirring with a wire whisk until blended. Cook over low heat, stirring constantly, until gelatin dissolves and chocolate melts. Remove from heat. Chill 20 minutes, stirring occasionally.

Beat egg whites (at room temperature) in a large bowl at high speed of an electric mixer until foamy. Gradually add remaining 1 cup sugar, 1 tablespoon at a time, beating until stiff peaks form and sugar dissolves (2 to 4 minutes). Fold in vanilla.

Gently fold beaten egg whites and whipped cream into chilled chocolate mixture. Pour into prepared dish. Chill 8 hours or until firm. Remove collar from dish before serving. Yield: 12 to 14 servings.   Mara Hellman

What's Cooking?
The Sisterhood of Temple Shalom
Succasunna, New Jersey

Frozen Daiquiri Soufflé

2 envelopes unflavored
  gelatin
½ cup light rum
10 eggs, separated
2 cups sugar, divided
2 tablespoons grated lime
  rind
1½ tablespoons grated lemon
  rind
½ cup lime juice
½ cup lemon juice
⅛ teaspoon salt
3 cups whipping cream,
  divided
½ cup finely chopped
  pistachios
2 tablespoons sugar
Garnish: lime slices

Cut a piece of aluminum foil long enough to fit around a 1½-quart soufflé dish, allowing a 1-inch overlap; fold foil lengthwise into thirds. Lightly oil one side of foil. Wrap foil around outside of dish, oiled side against dish, allowing it to extend 3 inches above rim to form a collar; secure with string.

Sprinkle gelatin over rum in a small saucepan; let stand 1 minute. Cook over low heat, stirring until gelatin dissolves. Remove from heat, and set aside.

Beat egg yolks at medium speed of an electric mixer until thick and lemon colored; gradually add 1 cup sugar, beating well. Add grated rinds, juices, and salt; beat until blended. Transfer egg yolk mixture to a medium-size heavy saucepan; cook over low heat, stirring constantly, 15 minutes or until thickened. Stir in reserved gelatin mixture. Remove from heat, and let cool.

Beat egg whites (at room temperature) at high speed until stiff peaks form; fold egg whites into gelatin mixture.

Beat 2 cups whipping cream at high speed until foamy. Gradually add remaining 1 cup sugar, beating until soft peaks form. Fold whipped cream into gelatin mixture; pour into prepared dish. Chill at least 8 hours.

Remove collar. Gently pat pistachios on sides of soufflé. Beat remaining 1 cup whipping cream at high speed until foamy; gradually add 2 tablespoons sugar, beating until soft peaks form. Spoon or pipe whipped cream around top of soufflé. Garnish, if desired. Yield: 12 servings.   Mrs. William P. Baxter, Jr.

Two and Company
St. Thomas' Church, Garrison Forest
Owings Mills, Maryland

English Toffee Dessert

1¼ cups coarsely crushed
  vanilla wafers, divided
1 envelope unflavored
  gelatin
1½ cups milk
2 eggs, separated
¼ cup sugar
2 tablespoons instant coffee
  granules

½ teaspoon vanilla extract
Pinch of salt
¼ cup sugar
1 cup whipping cream,
  whipped
4 (1-ounce) squares semisweet
  chocolate, grated
½ cup chopped walnuts

Sprinkle ¾ cup crushed wafers in a 9-inch square pan; set aside.

Sprinkle gelatin over milk; let stand 1 minute. Beat egg yolks at high speed of an electric mixer until thick and lemon colored. Add to milk mixture; stir well. Add ¼ cup sugar, coffee granules, vanilla, and salt; stir well.

Transfer milk mixture to top of a double boiler; bring water in bottom of double boiler to a boil. Reduce heat to low; cook until gelatin dissolves and mixture is slightly thickened, stirring occasionally. Remove from heat, and let cool.

Beat egg whites (at room temperature) at high speed just until foamy. Gradually add ¼ cup sugar, 1 tablespoon at a time, beating until stiff peaks form and sugar dissolves (2 to 4 minutes). Fold egg whites into milk mixture. Fold in whipped cream, chocolate, and walnuts. Pour mixture into prepared pan. Sprinkle with remaining ½ cup crushed vanilla wafers. Cover and chill at least 8 hours. Yield: 9 servings.

Frances Kleppin

South Dakota Centennial Cookbook
The South Dakota Historical Society
Pierre, South Dakota

The congregation of the historic St. Thomas' Church, Garrison Forest, published Two and Company *to raise funds to feed the hungry through the support of Paul's Place.*

One-Million Calorie Chocolate Frozen Dessert

1 (12-ounce) can evaporated milk
1 (6-ounce) package semisweet chocolate morsels
1 (16-ounce) package miniature marshmallows
½ cup butter
1 cup flaked coconut

1 (20-ounce) package cream-filled chocolate sandwich cookies, finely crushed
½ gallon vanilla ice cream
1 cup chopped pecans or walnuts

Place evaporated milk and chocolate morsels in top of a double boiler. Bring water to a boil; reduce heat to low, and cook until chocolate melts and mixture is smooth, stirring occasionally. Remove from heat. Stir in marshmallows. Transfer mixture to a medium bowl; cover and chill.

Melt butter in a large saucepan over medium heat; add coconut, and cook, stirring constantly, until coconut is golden brown. Remove from heat. Add crushed cookies; stir well.

Press three-fourths of cookie mixture in the bottom of a 13- x 9- x 2-inch pan. Cut ice cream into ¼- to ½-inch slices. Place half of ice cream slices on top of cookie mixture. Pour half of reserved marshmallow mixture over ice cream. Repeat layers with remaining ice cream and marshmallow mixture. Sprinkle with remaining one-fourth of cookie mixture and chopped pecans. Cover and freeze until firm. Yield: 15 servings.   Karen Bivins

Pioneers of Alaska Cookbook
The Pioneers of Alaska Auxiliary #4
Anchorage, Alaska

Frozen Champagne Cream in Chocolate Cups with Chocolate Sauce

¾ cup brut champagne, divided
½ cup sugar
5 egg yolks

1½ cups whipping cream
Chocolate Cups
Chocolate Sauce

Combine ½ cup champagne and sugar in a medium saucepan. Bring mixture to a boil, and cook, without stirring, until mixture reaches soft ball stage (238°).

Beat egg yolks in a medium bowl at high speed of an electric mixer until thick and lemon colored. Pour hot champagne mixture in a thin, steady stream over egg yolks, beating constantly at high speed. Gradually add remaining ¼ cup champagne, stirring until blended. Cover and chill.

Beat whipping cream at high speed until soft peaks form. Gently fold whipped cream into chilled champagne mixture; cover and freeze at least 8 hours.

To serve, let champagne cream stand at room temperature until slightly softened. Carefully remove paper from chocolate cups, one at a time, leaving remaining cups in freezer. Spoon champagne cream evenly into chocolate cups. Drizzle 1 teaspoon warm Chocolate Sauce over each serving. Serve with remaining Chocolate Sauce. Yield: 8 servings.

Chocolate Cups

1½ cups semisweet chocolate   **8 paper cupcake liners**
** morsels**

Place chocolate in top of a double boiler; bring water to a boil. Reduce heat to low; cook until chocolate melts, stirring occasionally.

Paint melted chocolate on inside of paper liners, using an artist brush. Place on an ungreased baking sheet; freeze 15 minutes or until chocolate is firm. Coat inside of liners with a second layer of chocolate, and freeze until firm. Yield: 8 chocolate cups.

Chocolate Sauce

¼ cup plus 2 tablespoons   **1 tablespoon sugar**
** brut champagne**   **2 tablespoons butter**
½ cup semisweet chocolate
** morsels**

Combine first 3 ingredients in top of a double boiler; bring water to a boil. Reduce heat to low; cook until chocolate melts, stirring occasionally. Add butter, stirring with a wire whisk until butter melts. Yield: about 1 cup.

Bound to Please
The Junior League of Boise, Idaho

Spumoni

⅓ cup chopped pistachios or almonds (optional)
3 cups pistachio ice cream, softened
6 maraschino cherries
¼ teaspoon rum flavoring
3 cups vanilla ice cream, softened
¾ cup whipping cream
⅓ cup instant chocolate-flavored drink mix
1 (10-ounce) package frozen raspberries, thawed and drained
½ cup whipping cream
¼ cup sifted powdered sugar
Dash of salt

Chill an 8-cup metal mold or metal bowl. Stir ⅓ cup chopped pistachios into pistachio ice cream, if desired. Spoon pistachio ice cream into mold, pressing firmly on bottom and up sides of mold. Arrange cherries around bottom of mold; press into ice cream. Freeze until firm.

Stir rum flavoring into vanilla ice cream. Spread vanilla ice cream mixture over pistachio ice cream layer, pressing firmly over bottom and up sides of mold. Freeze until firm.

Beat ¾ cup whipping cream at medium speed of an electric mixer until foamy; gradually add chocolate-flavored drink mix, beating at high speed until soft peaks form. Spread over vanilla ice cream layer. Freeze until firm.

Press raspberries through a sieve; discard seeds. Set raspberry puree aside.

Beat ½ cup whipping cream at medium speed of electric mixer until foamy; gradually add powdered sugar and salt, beating at high speed until soft peaks form. Fold in raspberry puree. Spread over frozen chocolate layer. Cover tightly with aluminum foil; freeze 8 hours or overnight.

To serve, loosen edges of ice cream from mold, using tip of a knife. Invert mold onto a chilled serving plate. Wrap a warm damp towel around mold for 30 seconds. Remove towel, and firmly hold plate and mold together. Shake gently, and slowly lift off mold. Return spumoni to freezer, and freeze until firm. Cut spumoni into wedges. Yield: 12 servings.

Ann Morris

Fiesta
The Junior Woman's Club of Pensacola, Florida

Frozen Rainbow Delight

2 cups whipping cream
3 tablespoons sugar
1 teaspoon vanilla extract
1 (13¾-ounce) package
  coconut macaroons,
  crushed

1 cup chopped walnuts
1½ quarts rainbow sherbet,
  softened

Beat whipping cream at high speed of an electric mixer until foamy; gradually add sugar and vanilla, beating until soft peaks form. Fold in macaroons and walnuts.

Spread half of whipped cream mixture in a 13- x 9- x 2-inch baking pan. Spread sherbet over whipped cream mixture. Top with remaining whipped cream mixture. Cover and freeze until firm. Yield: 15 servings.   Ruby Trow

Cal Poly Pomona 50th Anniversary
The Home Economics Alumni Association
Pomona, California

Fresh Lime Ice Cream

2 cups sugar
1 tablespoon plus 1 teaspoon
  grated lime rind
½ cup plus 1 tablespoon
  fresh lime juice

Pinch of salt
2 cups whipping cream
2 cups milk

Combine sugar, lime rind, lime juice, and salt in a large bowl; stir well. Gradually add whipping cream; stirring well. Stir in milk. Cover and chill at least 4 hours.

Stir mixture well; pour into freezer can of a 1-gallon hand-turned or electric freezer. Freeze according to manufacturer's instructions. Let ripen 1 hour before serving. Yield: 1½ quarts.

The Educated Palate
The Calhoun School Parents Association
New York, New York

Dorie's Cranberry Sherbet

1 pound fresh cranberries
3 cups hot water
2 cups sugar

½ cup orange juice
2 tablespoons lemon juice

Combine cranberries, hot water, and sugar in a large saucepan. Bring mixture to a boil; reduce heat, and simmer 15 minutes. Press cranberry mixture through a sieve; discard skins and seeds. Let cool. Stir in juices. Pour cranberry mixture into an 8-inch square pan; freeze until firm.

Position knife blade in food processor bowl; add half of frozen cranberry mixture, and process until smooth. Return mixture to pan. Repeat procedure with remaining cranberry mixture; freeze until firm. To serve, scoop sherbet into individual dessert dishes. Yield: 5 cups.   Susan Smith

RSVP: Recipes Shared Very Proudly
First Church of Christ
Simsbury, Connecticut

Winter Sherbet

1 (15¼-ounce) can crushed
   pineapple, undrained
1 (16-ounce) can sliced
   peaches, undrained

2 tablespoons lemon juice
¼ teaspoon vanilla extract

Combine pineapple and peaches in container of an electric blender; process until smooth. Pour mixture into a 9-inch square pan. Stir in lemon juice and vanilla. Freeze until almost firm, stirring occasionally.

Spoon mixture into container of an electric blender; process until mixture is smooth. Return mixture to pan, and freeze until firm. Let sherbet stand at room temperature 5 minutes before serving. Yield: 1 quart.   Scott Miller

Cooking Elementary Style
Ridgedale Elementary School PTA
Knoxville, Tennessee

Watermelon Sorbet

2 cups water
1 cup sugar
2 cups pureed watermelon

¼ cup plus 2 tablespoons
  lemon juice
Garnish: fresh mint sprigs

Combine water and sugar in a small saucepan; bring to a boil, stirring until sugar dissolves. Remove from heat, and let cool. Stir in pureed watermelon and lemon juice. Pour mixture into an 8-inch square pan; freeze until firm.

Position knife blade in food processor bowl; add half of frozen watermelon mixture, and process until fluffy but not thawed. Return mixture to pan. Repeat procedure.

To serve, scoop sorbet into individual dessert dishes. Garnish, if desired. Yield: 5 cups.   Layne Dorning

Twickenham Tables
Twickenham Historic Preservation District Association, Inc.
Huntsville, Alabama

Bananas Flambé

¼ cup butter or margarine
¾ cup firmly packed brown
  sugar
2 bananas, quartered
  lengthwise

1 tablespoon crème de
  bananes
2 tablespoons light rum
2 tablespoons brandy
Vanilla ice cream

Melt butter in a large skillet; add sugar, and cook over medium heat until bubbly. Add bananas; reduce heat, and simmer 1 minute or until bananas are thoroughly heated. Sprinkle with liqueur.

Place rum and brandy in a small long-handled saucepan; heat until warm (do not boil). Ignite with a long match, and pour over banana mixture. Baste bananas with sauce until flames die down. Serve banana mixture immediately over vanilla ice cream. Yield: 2 servings.   Mrs. Joseph Spera

100th Anniversary Cookbook
Auxiliary of Harrisburg Hospital
Harrisburg, Pennsylvania

Lychee Jubilee

1 (11½-ounce) can pitted
  lychees, undrained
1 tablespoon plus 1 teaspoon
  sugar
2 teaspoons butter or
  margarine, softened
1 teaspoon grated orange rind
¼ cup fresh orange juice
½ teaspoon grated lemon
  rind
1½ tablespoons fresh lemon
  juice
1 tablespoon cornstarch
1 tablespoon kirsch or other
  cherry-flavored brandy
2 tablespoons brandy
Vanilla ice cream

Drain lychees, reserving 1 tablespoon plus 1 teaspoon juice. Cut lychees in half; set lychees and juice aside.

Cream sugar and butter. Add orange rind and next 3 ingredients; beat well.

Transfer orange juice mixture to a small skillet; cook over medium heat 5 minutes or until sugar dissolves, stirring occasionally. Combine reserved lychee juice, cornstarch, and kirsch, stirring well. Add reserved lychees and cornstarch mixture to orange juice mixture; boil 1 minute or until thickened, stirring constantly. Remove from heat, and set aside.

Place brandy in a small, long-handled saucepan; heat until warm (do not boil). Remove from heat. Ignite with a long match; pour over lychee mixture. Stir until flames die down. Serve immediately over ice cream. Yield: 4 servings.   Jane Loomis Morse

Dining with the Daughters
The Daughters of Hawaii
Honolulu, Hawaii

Eggs & Cheese

Nestled in a dell near Blue Mounds, Wisconsin, is Little Norway's authentically reconstructed 12th-century Norwegian stavkirke, or stave church, built in Norway for the World Columbian Exposition in Chicago in 1893. The church now houses an outstanding collection of Norse antiques.

Eggs Creole

½ cup butter or margarine
3 tablespoons all-purpose
  flour
2 cups milk
2 teaspoons white wine
  Worcestershire sauce
¼ teaspoon salt
⅛ teaspoon black pepper
12 hard-cooked eggs,
  chopped
3 medium-size green peppers,
  coarsely chopped
3 medium onions, chopped
½ cup butter or margarine,
  melted

3 tablespoons all-purpose
  flour
1 (28-ounce) can whole
  tomatoes, undrained and
  chopped
¾ teaspoon ground red
  pepper
½ teaspoon salt
1 bay leaf
20 round buttery crackers,
  crushed
2 tablespoons butter or
  margarine, melted

Melt ½ cup butter in a heavy saucepan over low heat; add 3 tablespoons flour, stirring until smooth. Cook 1 minute, stirring constantly. Gradually add milk; cook over medium heat, stirring constantly, until mixture is thickened and bubbly. Stir in Worcestershire sauce, ¼ teaspoon salt, and black pepper. Add chopped eggs, stirring gently. Remove from heat, and set aside.

Sauté green pepper and onion in ½ cup melted butter in a large skillet until tender. Add 3 tablespoons flour, stirring well. Stir in tomatoes, red pepper, ½ teaspoon salt, and bay leaf; cook over medium heat until mixture is thickened and bubbly. Remove and discard bay leaf.

Grease a 13- x 9- x 2-inch baking dish with butter. Transfer egg mixture to dish; top with tomato mixture. Combine cracker crumbs and 2 tablespoons melted butter; stir well, and sprinkle over tomato mixture. Bake at 350° for 30 minutes or until bubbly and lightly browned. Yield: 10 to 12 servings.   Carolyne Bell

Twickenham Tables
Twickenham Historic Preservation District Association, Inc.
Huntsville, Alabama

Alison's Favorite Eggs

6 hard-cooked eggs
3 tablespoons mayonnaise or salad dressing
½ teaspoon salt
½ teaspoon dry mustard
¼ teaspoon pepper
2 tablespoons butter or margarine
2 tablespoons all-purpose flour
1 cup milk
½ cup (2 ounces) shredded Cheddar cheese
1 tablespoon Worcestershire sauce
½ teaspoon salt
¼ teaspoon dry mustard
⅛ teaspoon pepper
6 English muffins, split and toasted

Slice hard-cooked eggs in half lengthwise, and carefully remove yolks. Mash yolks; add mayonnaise, ½ teaspoon salt, ½ teaspoon dry mustard, and ¼ teaspoon pepper, stirring well. Spoon yolk mixture evenly into egg halves. Place egg halves together, securing with wooden picks. Place in a greased 1-quart casserole.

Melt butter in a heavy saucepan over low heat; add flour, stirring until smooth. Cook 1 minute, stirring constantly. Gradually add milk; cook over medium heat, stirring constantly, until mixture is thickened and bubbly. Add cheese and next 4 ingredients, stirring until cheese melts.

Pour cheese sauce evenly over eggs. Bake at 325° for 30 to 35 minutes or until eggs are thoroughly heated. Remove and discard wooden picks. Place 1 egg half on top of each toasted muffin half. Spoon cheese sauce over each serving, and serve immediately. Yield: 6 servings.   Karen Means

South Dakota Centennial Cookbook
The South Dakota Historical Society
Pierre, South Dakota

Crab Scramble

12 eggs
½ cup milk
1 teaspoon salt
½ teaspoon ground white pepper
½ teaspoon dried whole dillweed
1 (6-ounce) can crabmeat, drained and flaked
1 (8-ounce) package cream cheese, cut into ½-inch cubes
2 tablespoons butter, melted
Paprika

Combine eggs, milk, salt, white pepper, and dillweed in a large bowl; beat with a wire whisk until blended. Stir in crabmeat and cream cheese cubes.

Place melted butter in an 8-inch square baking dish. Pour egg mixture over butter. Sprinkle with paprika. Bake at 350° for 40 to 45 minutes or until eggs are set and top is lightly browned. Yield: 6 servings.   Joan Smart

Alaska's Cooking, Volume II
The Woman's Club of Anchorage, Alaska

Mushroom and Green Onion Omelet

½ cup sliced fresh
  mushrooms
¼ cup thinly sliced green
  onions
1 tablespoon butter or
  margarine, melted
4 eggs, beaten
1 tablespoon water

¼ teaspoon salt
Dash of freshly ground
  pepper
1 tablespoon butter or
  margarine
Garnish: fresh parsley
  sprigs

Sauté mushrooms and onions in 1 tablespoon melted butter in a small skillet until tender; set aside.

Combine eggs, water, salt, and pepper in a medium bowl, beating with a wire whisk until blended.

Heat an 8-inch omelet pan or nonstick skillet over medium heat until hot enough to sizzle a drop of water. Add 1 tablespoon butter, and rotate pan to coat bottom. Pour egg mixture into pan. As mixture starts to cook, gently lift edges of omelet with a spatula, and tilt pan so that uncooked portion flows underneath.

Spoon reserved mushroom mixture over half of omelet in pan. Loosen omelet with a spatula, and fold omelet in half. Carefully slide omelet onto a serving plate. Garnish, if desired. Yield: 1 to 2 servings.   Edith Gunderson

Feed My People
Carter-Westminster United Presbyterian Church
Skokie, Illinois

Rosemary Omelet

¼ cup butter or margarine
3 medium tomatoes, sliced
2 to 3 teaspoons chopped
 fresh rosemary or 1
 teaspoon dried whole
 rosemary

¼ teaspoon salt
¼ teaspoon pepper
8 eggs, beaten
8 slices bacon, cooked and
 crumbled

Melt butter in a 12-inch ovenproof skillet; add tomato slices. Cook over medium heat 4 to 5 minutes or until tomatoes are thoroughly heated.

Combine rosemary, salt, and pepper; sprinkle evenly over tomatoes. Pour beaten eggs over tomatoes in skillet; sprinkle crumbled bacon over egg mixture. Cover, reduce heat to medium-low, and cook 12 to 15 minutes or until eggs are almost set. Uncover and place skillet under broiler; broil 6 inches from heat 1 minute or until golden brown. Yield: 4 servings.   Aiko and Neil Fujita

You Can't be Too Rich or Too Thin
Southampton Hospital
Southampton, New York

Chinese Pancakes

4 green onions, thinly sliced
1 stalk celery, thinly sliced
2 tablespoons peanut oil
½ cup minced cooked beef,
 lamb, pork, chicken, turkey,
 or tuna
½ teaspoon salt
⅛ teaspoon freshly ground
 pepper

3 eggs, separated
¾ cup small-curd cottage
 cheese
¼ cup all-purpose flour
Melted butter (optional)
Soy sauce (optional)

Sauté onions and celery in oil in a medium skillet until vegetables are tender; set aside.

Combine meat, salt, and freshly ground pepper in a small bowl, and set aside.

Beat egg yolks at high speed of an electric mixer until thick and lemon colored. Add cottage cheese and flour, beating until smooth. Stir in reserved vegetable and meat mixtures.

Beat egg whites (at room temperature) at high speed until stiff peaks form; fold egg whites into cottage cheese mixture.

For each pancake, pour about 1 heaping tablespoon batter onto a hot, lightly greased griddle; press into 2½-inch rounds with the back of a spoon. Cook 2 minutes on each side or until golden brown. If desired, serve pancakes with melted butter and soy sauce. Yield: 20 (2½-inch) pancakes.   Helen McCarthy

Our Town Cookbook
The Historical Society of Peterborough, New Hampshire

Mustard-Brie Soufflé

¼ cup butter, softened
1 tablespoon Dijon
  mustard
½ (1-pound) loaf French
  bread, thinly sliced
1 cup milk
3 eggs

½ teaspoon salt
Pinch of ground red
  pepper
½ pound fully ripened Brie
¼ pound cooked ham, cut
  into ¼-inch cubes

Combine butter and mustard, stirring well. Spread butter mixture on one side of bread slices. Set aside.

Combine milk, eggs, salt, and red pepper in a small bowl. Beat with a wire whisk until blended; set aside.

Arrange half the bread slices, buttered side up, in a lightly greased 1½-quart soufflé dish.

Remove rind from Brie, and cut cheese into ½-inch cubes.

Top French bread slices with half the Brie cheese cubes and half the ham cubes. Repeat layers with remaining French bread slices and cheese and ham cubes. Pour reserved egg mixture over layers. Cover and chill 8 hours.

Bake at 350° for 30 minutes or until soufflé is puffed and lightly browned. Yield: 4 to 6 servings.   Gwen Couch-Edwards

RSVP: Recipes Shared Very Proudly
First Church of Christ
Simsbury, Connecticut

Eggs and Mushroom Casserole

12 slices day-old white bread
¼ cup butter or margarine,
  softened
½ pound sliced fresh
  mushrooms
2 tablespoons butter or
  margarine, melted
6 cups (24 ounces) shredded
  Cheddar cheese

6 eggs
2 cups half-and-half
1 cup whipping cream
1½ teaspoons dry mustard
¼ teaspoon salt
½ teaspoon paprika

Remove crust from bread. Spread ¼ cup butter evenly over one side of bread slices; cut into 1-inch strips. Place bread strips, buttered side up, in a 13- x 9- x 2-inch baking dish.

Sauté mushrooms in 2 tablespoons melted butter in a large skillet until tender. Remove from heat, and let cool. Add cheese to mushrooms; stir well. Sprinkle cheese mixture evenly over bread.

Combine eggs and next 4 ingredients in a bowl; beat with a wire whisk until blended. Pour egg mixture over cheese; sprinkle with paprika. Cover and bake at 350° for 30 minutes. Uncover and bake an additional 10 minutes or until set and lightly browned. Yield: 10 to 12 servings.

Stirring Performances
The Junior League of Winston-Salem, North Carolina

Stirring Performances *contains recipes from the Junior League of Winston-Salem, North Carolina. Since 1923, the league has contributed $750 thousand in support of such programs and community agencies as the Arts Council, Nature Science Center, Juvenile Justice Council, Child Guidance Clinic, and Cancer Patient Support Services.*

Zucchini Bake

1¼ pounds zucchini, cut into
   ½-inch cubes
16 ounces Monterey Jack
   cheese, cubed
½ cup milk
4 eggs, beaten

¼ cup chopped green pepper
¼ cup chopped fresh parsley
3 tablespoons all-purpose
   flour
2 teaspoons baking powder

Cook zucchini in a small amount of boiling water 5 minutes or until crisp-tender; drain. Combine zucchini and remaining ingredients; stir well.

Pour zucchini mixture into a greased 13- x 9- x 2-inch baking dish. Bake, uncovered, at 350° for 40 minutes or until zucchini mixture is set and top is lightly browned. Let stand 10 minutes before serving. Yield: 12 servings.   Beth Schwendiman

Holladay 7th Ward Cookbook
The Holladay 7th Ward Relief Society
Salt Lake City, Utah

Reuben Brunch Casserole

10 slices rye bread, cut into
   ¾-inch cubes
1½ pounds cooked corned
   beef, shredded
2½ cups (10 ounces)
   shredded Swiss cheese

6 eggs
3 cups milk
¼ teaspoon pepper

Arrange bread cubes in bottom of a greased 13- x 9- x 2-inch baking dish. Top with corned beef; sprinkle with cheese.

Combine eggs, milk, and pepper in a medium bowl; beat with a wire whisk until blended. Pour egg mixture over cheese; cover and chill at least 8 hours. Bake, covered, at 350° for 1 hour. Remove cover, and bake an additional 10 to 15 minutes or until set and lightly browned. Yield: 10 to 12 servings.   Marge Thiesse

Palate Pleasers II
Redeemer Women's Guild
Elmhurst, Illinois

Cheese-Wine Strata

⅓ cup butter, softened
1 tablespoon dry mustard
1 clove garlic, crushed
1 (1-pound) loaf French
   bread, thinly sliced
4 cups (16 ounces) shredded
   Swiss cheese, divided
3 tablespoons grated onion

1 teaspoon salt
1 teaspoon paprika
⅓ cup butter or margarine
¼ cup all-purpose flour
3 cups milk
¾ to 1 cup Chablis or other
   dry white wine
3 eggs, beaten

Cream ⅓ cup butter; add mustard and garlic, beating well. Spread butter mixture on one side of bread slices. Place one-third of bread, buttered side down, in a 13- x 9- x 2-inch baking pan.

Combine 3 cups cheese, onion, salt, and paprika; toss. Set aside.

Melt ⅓ cup butter in a saucepan over low heat; add flour, stirring until smooth. Cook 1 minute, stirring constantly. Gradually add milk and wine; cook over medium heat, stirring constantly, until mixture is thickened and bubbly. Gradually stir one-fourth of hot mixture into eggs; add to remaining hot mixture, stirring constantly. Remove from heat.

Top bread slices in pan with ⅓ cup cheese; pour half the sauce over layers. Repeat layers once; top with remaining bread slices, buttered side up. Sprinkle with remaining ⅓ cup cheese. Cover and chill at least 8 hours. Bake, uncovered, at 350° for 40 to 45 minutes or until lightly browned. Yield: 10 servings.

Hearts & Flour
The Women's Club of Pittsford, New York

Spinach Pie Parma

2 cups commercial seasoned
   croutons, crushed
¼ cup butter, melted
1 (10-ounce) package frozen
   chopped spinach, thawed
   and drained
1 cup small-curd cottage
   cheese
4 ounces Monterey Jack
   cheese, cubed

¼ cup grated Parmesan
   cheese
¼ cup chopped onion
3 eggs, beaten
2 tablespoons sour cream
1 clove garlic, minced
½ teaspoon salt
2 tablespoons grated
   Parmesan cheese

Combine crushed croutons and melted butter, stirring well. Firmly press crumb mixture evenly on bottom and up the sides of a 9-inch pieplate; set aside.

Combine spinach and next 8 ingredients, stirring well. Spoon spinach mixture into prepared crust. Bake, uncovered, at 350° for 35 minutes or until set and lightly browned. Remove from oven, and sprinkle with 2 tablespoons Parmesan cheese. Let stand 5 minutes before serving. Yield: 6 servings.   Carolyn Breeman

Land of Cotton
John T. Morgan Academy
Selma, Alabama

Mushroom Crust Quiche

¾ pound coarsely chopped fresh mushrooms

3 tablespoons butter or margarine, melted

½ cup finely crushed saltine crackers

¾ cup sliced green onions

2 tablespoons butter or margarine, melted

2 cups (8 ounces) shredded Monterey Jack cheese

1 cup small-curd cottage cheese

3 eggs, lightly beaten

¼ teaspoon pepper

¼ teaspoon paprika

Sauté mushrooms in 3 tablespoons melted butter in a large skillet over medium heat until tender. Add cracker crumbs; stir well. Press mixture evenly on bottom and up the sides of a 9-inch pieplate.

Sauté onions in 2 tablespoons melted butter in skillet 1 minute; sprinkle over mushroom crust. Sprinkle shredded cheese over onions; set aside.

Combine cottage cheese, eggs, and pepper, stirring well. Pour cottage cheese mixture over shredded cheese. Sprinkle with paprika. Bake, uncovered, at 350° for 30 to 35 minutes or until set and lightly browned. Let stand 5 minutes before serving. Yield: one 9-inch quiche.   Patrice L. Melcher

Cookin' with the Lion
The Penn State Alumni Association
University Park, Pennsylvania

Kielbasa Quiche

Pastry for one 9-inch pie
1 egg yolk
1 teaspoon water
1 cup chopped fresh broccoli
2 cups finely chopped
  kielbasa
1 small green pepper,
  chopped
½ cup chopped onion
2 teaspoons butter or
  margarine, melted

2 tablespoons all-purpose
  flour
4 eggs
⅔ cup half-and-half
2 cups (8 ounces) shredded
  Cheddar cheese, divided
2 teaspoons chopped fresh
  parsley
1 teaspoon garlic salt

Line a 9-inch pieplate with pastry; fold edges under and flute. Prick bottom and sides of pastry with a fork. Combine egg yolk and water; stir well. Brush egg yolk mixture over pastry. Bake at 400° for 10 minutes; set aside.

Cook broccoli in a small amount of boiling water until crisp-tender; set aside.

Sauté kielbasa, green pepper, and chopped onion in melted butter in a large skillet over medium heat until vegetables are tender; drain well. Add flour to kielbasa mixture, stirring well. Remove from heat.

Combine eggs and half-and-half in a medium bowl; beat well with a wire whisk until blended.

Sprinkle 1 cup shredded cheese over bottom of pastry shell; top with broccoli and kielbasa mixture. Sprinkle with remaining 1 cup cheese. Pour egg mixture over cheese; sprinkle with parsley and garlic salt. Bake, uncovered, at 375° for 30 to 40 minutes or until set and lightly browned. Let stand 5 minutes before serving. Yield: one 9-inch quiche.

Mary Dimick

State Hospital Cooks
Patient/Staff Advocacy Committee, Vermont State Hospital
Waterbury, Vermont

Fish & Shellfish

A hopeful fisherman heads out from the dock and down a river in Florida in search of a good day's catch. Over the years, the seafood industry has remained a source of fun and pleasure as well as income for many Floridians.

Thatched Fish with Cheese

2 tablespoons butter,
  divided
2 pounds orange roughy
  fillets
4 medium-size baking
  potatoes, peeled and cut
  into julienne strips
¼ cup plus 1 tablespoon
  butter, divided

3 tablespoons all-purpose
  flour
2 teaspoons dry mustard
2 cups milk
Salt and pepper to taste
1½ cups (6 ounces) shredded
  sharp Cheddar cheese

Grease a 13- x 9- x 2-inch baking dish with 2 tablespoons butter. Arrange fish in baking dish. Set aside.

Place potato strips in a large saucepan with water to cover. Bring to a boil, reduce heat, and simmer 2 minutes or until potato is almost tender. Drain well; pat dry with paper towels. Return potato strips to saucepan. Add 2 tablespoons butter, tossing gently until butter melts. Set aside.

Melt remaining 3 tablespoons butter in a heavy saucepan over low heat; add flour and mustard, stirring until smooth. Cook 1 minute, stirring constantly. Gradually add milk; cook over medium heat, stirring constantly, until mixture is thickened and bubbly. Stir in salt and pepper to taste.

Spoon sauce evenly over fish in baking dish; arrange potato strips over sauce. Sprinkle with shredded cheese. Bake at 400° for 30 minutes or until cheese melts and mixture is hot and bubbly. Serve immediately. Yield: 5 to 6 servings.   Phyllis Oddi

Ex Libris, A Treasury of Recipes
The Friends of the Wellesley Free Libraries
Wellesley, Massachusetts

Lime and Mustard Flounder Fillets

2 pounds flounder fillets
¼ cup mayonnaise

¼ cup Dijon mustard
1½ tablespoons lime juice

Place fillets on a rack in a broiler pan. Combine mayonnaise, mustard, and lime juice; spread mixture over fillets. Broil 6 inches from heat 8 to 10 minutes or until fish flakes easily when tested with a fork. Yield: 6 servings.

The Educated Palate
The Calhoun School Parents Association
New York, New York

Flounder Ravioli with Mustard-Tomato Sauce

½ pound flounder fillets, cut into 1-inch pieces
⅓ cup buttermilk
1 egg, separated
¼ teaspoon salt
⅛ teaspoon ground white pepper
2 tablespoons minced fresh parsley

1 (16-ounce) package fresh or frozen wonton skins, thawed
3 quarts water
1 teaspoon salt
Mustard-Tomato Sauce
Garnish: fresh parsley sprigs

Combine flounder, buttermilk, egg white, ¼ teaspoon salt, and pepper in container of an electric blender or food processor; process until well blended. Transfer mixture to a small bowl. Add minced parsley, stirring well.

Place 1 heaping tablespoonful of fish mixture in center of each wonton skin. Lightly beat egg yolk. Brush edges of each wonton skin with egg yolk; top with an additional wonton skin. Press edges together with a fork to seal. (Reserve any remaining wonton skins for other uses.) Place filled wontons on wax paper, and cover with plastic wrap.

Place water in a Dutch oven; add 1 teaspoon salt, and bring to a boil. Add wontons, 4 or 5 at a time, and return to a boil; reduce heat, and simmer 5 minutes or until tender. Remove ravioli with a slotted spoon; place in individual serving bowls. Spoon Mustard-Tomato Sauce over each serving. Garnish, if desired. Yield: 4 servings.

Mustard-Tomato Sauce

2 large tomatoes, seeded and cut into ½-inch cubes
2 tablespoons olive oil, divided
¼ cup minced onion
1 large clove garlic, minced
1 cup Chablis or other dry white wine

1 cup water
1½ teaspoons prepared mustard
1½ teaspoons spicy brown mustard
¼ cup butter
¼ teaspoon salt
⅛ teaspoon pepper

Sauté tomato in 1 tablespoon oil in a large skillet 3 minutes. Remove with a slotted spoon, and set aside. Add remaining 1 tablespoon oil and onion to skillet, and sauté 2 to 3 minutes or until tender. Add garlic, and sauté an additional 2 minutes. Add wine and water to skillet; cook over medium heat until liquid is reduced to about ½ cup.

Combine mustards in a small bowl. Add 1 tablespoon wine mixture, stirring well with a wire whisk. Add mustard mixture to wine mixture in skillet; stir well. Add butter, stirring until butter melts. Add sautéed tomato, salt, and pepper. Cook over medium heat until thoroughly heated. Yield: 1⅔ cups.   Susan Weisberg

Greetings from Atlantic City
The Ruth Newman Shapiro Cancer and Heart Fund
Atlantic City, New Jersey

Funds generated from the sale of Greetings from Atlantic City *will benefit the Ruth Newman Shapiro Cancer and Heart Fund, which serves the needs of the community through the diagnosis and treatment of cancer and heart disease. The comprehensive cancer care program includes state-of-the-art technology and supportive care and education.*

Halibut in Parchment with Ginger Mushrooms

4 (4-ounce) halibut fillets
Soy-Ginger Marinade
½ cup unsalted butter
1 pound fresh mushrooms,
  thinly sliced
½ pound fresh shiitake
  mushrooms, thinly sliced
2 tablespoons minced garlic
2 tablespoons peeled, minced
  fresh ginger

¼ teaspoon salt
1½ teaspoons seeded, minced
  jalapeño pepper
6 green onion tops,
  diagonally sliced
¼ cup butter
Hot cooked basmati rice

Cut four 15-inch squares of parchment paper or aluminum foil; fold squares in half, forming a triangle; crease firmly. Place on a large baking sheet; set aside.

Place fillets in a 9-inch square baking dish. Pour Soy-Ginger Marinade over fillets; cover tightly, and marinate in refrigerator 10 minutes.

Melt unsalted butter over low heat. The fat will rise to the top, and the milk solids will sink to the bottom. Skim off the white froth that appears on top. Strain off the clear, yellow butter, keeping back the sediment of milk solids.

Place clarified butter in a large skillet. Add mushrooms, garlic, and ginger, and sauté until mushrooms are tender. Add salt and jalapeño pepper, and sauté 1 additional minute.

Remove fillets from marinade; discard marinade. Place 1 fillet on half of each parchment triangle near the crease. Arrange mushroom mixture and sliced green onions evenly over fillets. Dot with ¼ cup butter. Fold over remaining halves of parchment triangles. Starting at one end of each triangle, pleat and crimp edges together to seal securely.

Bake at 375° for 7 to 8 minutes or until bags are puffed and lightly browned and fish flakes easily when tested with a fork. Serve with rice. Yield: 4 servings.

Soy-Ginger Marinade

¾ cup lemon juice
¼ cup soy sauce
¼ cup water

1 tablespoon peeled, minced
  fresh ginger
½ teaspoon minced garlic

Combine lemon juice, soy sauce, water, ginger, and garlic, and stir well. Yield: about 1⅓ cups.   Patricia Unterman

A Taste of San Francisco
The Symphony of San Francisco, California

Poached Salmon with Basil Sauce

1 teaspoon butter
3 tablespoons minced
  shallots
4 (8-ounce) salmon fillets,
  skinned
Salt and pepper
1 tablespoon butter
½ cup Chablis or other dry
  white wine

2 fresh parsley sprigs
1 bay leaf
½ cup whipping cream
½ cup chopped fresh basil
1 teaspoon fresh lemon juice
⅛ teaspoon ground red
  pepper

Melt 1 teaspoon butter in a large skillet over medium heat. Sprinkle shallots over butter. Arrange salmon fillets in a single layer over shallots; sprinkle with salt and pepper. Dot salmon fillets with 1 tablespoon butter. Add wine, parsley, and bay leaf. Bring to a boil; cover, reduce heat, and simmer 10 minutes or until fish flakes easily when tested with a fork. Remove salmon to a serving platter, and keep warm.

Bring liquid in skillet to a boil; cook until liquid is reduced to about ¼ cup. Remove from heat; remove and discard parsley sprigs and bay leaf.

Gradually add whipping cream to liquid in skillet. Return sauce to a boil; cook 2 minutes or until sauce is reduced to about ¾ cup. Add basil, lemon juice, and red pepper; stir well. Serve salmon with warm sauce. Yield: 4 servings.

Stirring Performances
The Junior League of Winston-Salem, North Carolina

Fish Cakes

½ cup finely chopped celery
½ cup finely chopped green
  pepper
½ cup finely chopped onion
2 tablespoons butter, melted
1 cup fine, dry breadcrumbs
2 tablespoons boiling water
2 (15-ounce) cans pink
  salmon, drained

2 eggs, beaten
2 teaspoons Worcestershire
  sauce
¼ teaspoon salt
⅛ teaspoon pepper
1 tablespoon vegetable oil

Sauté celery, green pepper, and onion in butter in a large skillet 2 to 3 minutes or until tender. Set aside.

Combine breadcrumbs and boiling water; stir well. Set aside.

Remove and discard skin and bones from salmon; flake salmon with a fork. Add reserved vegetable mixture, moistened breadcrumbs, eggs, Worcestershire sauce, salt, and pepper; stir well to combine. Shape salmon mixture into 8 patties. Cook in hot oil over medium heat 4 to 5 minutes on each side or until lightly browned. Yield: 8 servings.

Linda Wilson

More Memoirs of a Galley Slave
The Kodiak Fishermen's Wives Association
Kodiak, Alaska

Heart and Sole

3 or 4 tomatoes, thinly sliced
½ cup fine, dry breadcrumbs
6 (4-ounce) sole fillets
½ teaspoon salt
¼ teaspoon pepper
¾ cup Chablis or other dry
  white wine

¼ cup plus 2 tablespoons
  butter or margarine
2 teaspoons fresh lime juice
¼ cup grated Parmesan
  cheese

Arrange tomato slices evenly in the bottom of a 13- x 9- x 2-inch baking dish; sprinkle with breadcrumbs. Arrange fillets over breadcrumbs; sprinkle with salt and pepper.

Combine wine, butter, and lime juice in a saucepan; cook over medium heat until butter melts. Pour over fillets; sprinkle with cheese. Bake at 400° for 15 to 20 minutes or until fish flakes easily when tested with a fork. Remove fish to a serving platter with a slotted spoon. Serve warm. Yield: 6 servings.

Hearts and Flours
The Junior League of Waco, Texas

Sole with Pistachio Butter Sauce

1½ pounds sole fillets
¼ cup all-purpose flour
2 tablespoons vegetable oil
1 tablespoon butter, melted
¼ cup thinly sliced green
  onions
½ cup dry vermouth

½ cup canned diluted
  chicken broth
¼ cup butter
⅓ cup shelled pistachios,
  coarsely chopped and
  toasted
Garnish: lemon wedges

Dredge fillets in flour. Sauté fillets in oil and 1 tablespoon melted butter in a large nonstick skillet over medium heat 2 minutes on each side or until fish flakes easily when tested with a fork. Remove fillets from skillet, and place on a serving platter; keep warm.

Add green onions, vermouth, and chicken broth to skillet. Cook over high heat until liquid is reduced to about ½ cup. Reduce heat to low; add ¼ cup butter, and stir until butter melts. Stir in chopped pistachios. Spoon sauce over fish. Garnish, if desired. Yield: 4 to 6 servings.   Adelle Gross

Delectable Edibles from the Livable Forest
The Women's Club of Kingwood, Texas

Monies earned from the sale of the Junior League of Waco's **Hearts and Flours** *will benefit programs such as GATE (Gain Awareness through Education) which educates fourth-grade students on the effects of drugs and alcohol.*

Grilled Swordfish with Tomato-Feta Relish

1 medium tomato, seeded and chopped
1 green onion, sliced
¼ cup extra-virgin olive oil
¼ cup crumbled feta cheese
1 tablespoon fresh lemon juice
2 teaspoons chopped fresh dillweed
Freshly ground pepper to taste

¼ cup extra-virgin olive oil
¼ cup Dijon mustard
2½ tablespoons red wine vinegar
1 teaspoon garlic powder
1 teaspoon ground oregano
½ teaspoon salt
4 (6- to 8-ounce) swordfish steaks

Combine first 7 ingredients in a medium bowl; stir well, and set Tomato-Feta Relish aside.

Combine ¼ cup olive oil, mustard, vinegar, garlic powder, oregano, and salt; stir well. Brush both sides of swordfish steaks with half of mustard mixture.

Grill fish over hot coals 6 to 8 minutes on each side or until fish flakes easily when tested with a fork, basting frequently with remaining mustard mixture. Serve fish with relish. Yield: 4 servings.

One Magnificent Cookbook
The Junior League of Chicago, Illinois

Trout with Almonds

1 cup coarsely chopped blanched almonds
¼ cup plus 2 tablespoons butter, melted
1½ tablespoons fresh lemon juice
1 cup all-purpose flour

1 teaspoon salt
8 (8- to 10-ounce) trout fillets
¾ cup butter, divided
Garnish: lemon wedges dipped in minced fresh parsley

Sauté almonds in ¼ cup plus 2 tablespoons melted butter in a large skillet over medium heat until golden brown. Stir in lemon juice. Remove from heat, and set aside.

Combine flour and salt; dredge fillets in flour mixture. Melt ¼ cup plus 2 tablespoons butter in a large skillet over medium-high heat. Add half of fillets; cook 5 minutes on each side or until fish flakes easily when tested with a fork. Remove to a serving platter, and keep warm. Repeat procedure with remaining ¼ cup plus 2 tablespoons butter and fillets. Sprinkle with reserved almond mixture. Garnish, if desired. Yield: 8 servings.   Amy Williams

The Scott & White Collection
The Scott and White Memorial Hospital Auxiliary
Temple, Texas

Whitefish-Kiwi Stir-Fry

¼ cup all-purpose flour
¼ teaspoon salt
¼ teaspoon pepper
1 pound whitefish, sole, or orange roughy fillets, cut into 1-inch pieces
¼ cup vegetable oil, divided
1 cup chopped green pepper
1 cup chopped sweet red pepper
1 cup peeled, sliced jicama or scraped, sliced carrot
1 (8-ounce) can sliced water chestnuts, drained
6 green onions, diagonally sliced
1 clove garlic, crushed
¼ cup dry sherry or water
2 tablespoons brown sugar
2 tablespoons vinegar
1 tablespoon teriyaki sauce
⅛ teaspoon ground allspice
4 kiwifruit, peeled and sliced
Hot cooked rice

Combine flour, salt, and pepper; add fish to flour mixture, tossing gently to coat evenly. Sauté fish in 2 tablespoons oil in a large skillet until fish flakes easily when tested with a fork. Remove fish from skillet with a slotted spoon; set aside, and keep warm.

Sauté green pepper and next 5 ingredients in remaining 2 tablespoons oil in skillet until crisp-tender. Stir in sherry, brown sugar, vinegar, teriyaki sauce, and allspice. Cook over medium heat, stirring occasionally, until mixture is slightly thickened. Add reserved fish and kiwifruit; cook just until thoroughly heated. Serve over rice. Yield: 4 servings.   Patty Hoffman

The Mark Twain Library Cookbook, Volume III
The Mark Twain Library Association
Redding, Connecticut

Fried Soft-Shell Crabs with Figaro Sauce

12 fresh soft-shell crabs
¼ teaspoon salt
⅛ teaspoon pepper
½ teaspoon dried whole tarragon
½ teaspoon dried whole thyme
¼ teaspoon ground nutmeg
4 cups milk
1 small clove garlic, crushed
2 tablespoons chopped onion
2 tablespoons chopped leek
2 tablespoons chopped celery leaves
2 tablespoons chopped fresh chives
2 tablespoons chopped fresh parsley
1 cup all-purpose flour
¼ teaspoon salt
⅛ teaspoon pepper
1 cup butter, melted
Figaro Sauce

To clean crabs, remove spongy substance (gills) that lies under the tapering points on either side of back shell. Place crabs on back, and remove the small piece at lower part of shell that terminates in a point (the apron). Wash crabs thoroughly; drain well. Place crabs in a large shallow dish.

Combine ¼ teaspoon salt, ⅛ teaspoon pepper, tarragon, thyme, and nutmeg; stir well. Sprinkle herb mixture evenly over both sides of crabs.

Combine milk, garlic, onion, leek, celery leaves, chives, and parsley in a medium bowl; stir well, and pour over crabs. Cover and chill 30 minutes.

Combine flour, ¼ teaspoon salt, and ⅛ teaspoon pepper in a small bowl; stir well.

Remove crabs from milk mixture, and dredge in flour mixture. Sauté crabs in melted butter in a large skillet over medium heat until golden brown on both sides. Drain well on paper towels. Serve fried crabs immediately with Figaro Sauce. Yield: 4 to 6 servings.

Figaro Sauce

1½ cups commercial hollandaise sauce
3 tablespoons tomato puree
1 tablespoon tomato paste
1 tablespoon chopped fresh parsley
⅛ teaspoon salt
⅛ teaspoon ground red pepper

Combine first 3 ingredients in a medium bowl; beat with a wire whisk until smooth. Add parsley, salt, and pepper; stir well. Yield: 1¾ cups.   Lynda Kimbrough Beneke

A Grand Heritage
The Heritage Academy
Columbus, Mississippi

Oysters Tetrazzini

5 (10-ounce) containers fresh Standard oysters, undrained	4 cups fine egg noodles, uncooked
¼ cup butter or margarine	½ teaspoon salt
¼ cup all-purpose flour	⅛ teaspoon pepper
2 teaspoons salt	½ teaspoon paprika
2 teaspoons Worcestershire sauce	1 cup soft breadcrumbs
⅛ teaspoon pepper	¼ cup grated Parmesan cheese
3 cups milk	3 tablespoons butter or margarine, melted
¼ cup dry sherry	

Drain oysters, reserving ½ cup liquid. Chill oysters, and set oyster liquid aside.

Place ¼ cup butter in top of a double boiler; bring water to a boil. Reduce heat to low, and cook until butter melts. Add flour, 2 teaspoons salt, Worcestershire sauce, and ⅛ teaspoon pepper, stirring until smooth. Gradually add reserved oyster liquid and milk; cook, stirring occasionally, until mixture is thickened. Remove from heat; stir in sherry. Cover and chill 1 hour.

Cook noodles according to package directions; drain. Place noodles in a 13- x 9- x 2-inch baking dish; top with chilled oysters. Sprinkle with ½ teaspoon salt, ⅛ teaspoon pepper, and paprika. Pour chilled sauce over oysters. Combine breadcrumbs, Parmesan cheese, and 3 tablespoons melted butter in a small bowl; sprinkle evenly over sauce. Bake at 350° for 30 minutes or until hot and bubbly. Yield: 8 servings.   Pat Hill

Bach to the Kitchen
Cappella Cantorum
Essex, Connecticut

Oyster-Artichoke Pan Roast

1 (14-ounce) can quartered
  artichoke hearts, drained
3 (10-ounce) containers fresh
  Standard oysters, undrained
1 cup chopped green onions
½ cup chopped onion
1 clove garlic, minced
¼ cup butter, melted
3 tablespoons all-purpose
  flour

½ cup chopped fresh parsley
1 tablespoon lemon juice
1 teaspoon Worcestershire
  sauce
½ teaspoon salt
¼ teaspoon hot sauce
1 cup soft breadcrumbs
2 tablespoons butter, melted

Place artichoke hearts in a medium saucepan; add water to cover. Cook over medium heat until thoroughly heated. Set aside, and keep warm.

Place oysters and oyster liquid in a large saucepan. Bring to a boil; reduce heat, and cook 3 minutes or until edges of oysters curl. Drain oysters, reserving 1 cup liquid. Set oysters and liquid aside.

Sauté onions and garlic in ¼ cup butter in a skillet until tender. Add flour, and cook 3 minutes, stirring constantly. Gradually add oyster liquid, stirring constantly. Add parsley, lemon juice, Worcestershire sauce, salt, and hot sauce. Cook over medium heat until thickened and bubbly, stirring constantly. Set aside.

Drain artichoke hearts. Place artichoke hearts and reserved oysters in the bottom of a 1½-quart casserole; pour sauce over oyster mixture. Combine breadcrumbs and 2 tablespoons melted butter. Sprinkle over sauce. Bake at 350° for 15 to 20 minutes or until hot and bubbly. Yield: 4 servings.

From a Lighthouse Window
The Chesapeake Bay Maritime Museum
St. Michaels, Maryland

Bacon-Wrapped Scallops with Lemon-Chive Sauce

3 dozen fresh sea scallops
  (about 2 pounds)

1 pound sliced bacon
Lemon-Chive Sauce

Cut bacon in half crosswise. Wrap each scallop in a piece of bacon, and secure with a wooden pick.

Place scallops on a rack in a broiler pan; brush with Lemon-Chive Sauce. Broil 6 inches from heat 10 to 15 minutes or until scallops are opaque and bacon is done, turning occasionally. Serve immediately. Yield: 6 servings.

Lemon-Chive Sauce

2 tablespoons chopped fresh chives	1 clove garlic, minced
2 tablespoons fresh lemon juice	¼ teaspoon salt
1 tablespoon olive oil	⅛ teaspoon freshly ground pepper

Combine all ingredients in a small bowl; stir well with a wire whisk until blended. Yield: ¼ cup.

Honest to Goodness
The Junior League of Springfield, Illinois

Speared Shrimp

2 pounds unpeeled large fresh shrimp	¼ cup chopped fresh parsley
½ cup chili sauce	2 cloves garlic
¼ cup olive oil	¼ teaspoon salt
2 tablespoons dark corn syrup	¼ teaspoon pepper
2 tablespoons red wine vinegar	2 lemons, cut into wedges

Peel and devein shrimp; set aside.
Position knife blade in food processor bowl. Add chili sauce and next 7 ingredients, and process until smooth. Set aside.
Loosely thread shrimp and lemon wedges onto 6 (12-inch) metal skewers. Place kabobs in a 13- x 9- x 2-inch baking dish; spoon marinade mixture over kabobs. Cover and marinate in refrigerator 1 hour. Remove kabobs from marinade, and discard marinade. Grill kabobs over medium-hot coals 3 minutes on each side or until shrimp turn pink. To serve, squeeze lemon wedges over grilled shrimp. Yield: 6 servings.   Gaylen Millard

Out of This World
Wood Acres Elementary School
Bethesda, Maryland

Shrimp Pilau

1 pound unpeeled
  medium-size fresh shrimp
3 slices bacon
1 cup chopped green pepper
¼ cup chopped onion
1 (16-ounce) can whole
  tomatoes, undrained and
  chopped
¾ cup water
¾ cup long-grain rice,
  uncooked
1 teaspoon salt
⅛ teaspoon pepper
⅛ teaspoon dried whole
  thyme

Peel and devein shrimp; set aside.

Cook bacon in a skillet until crisp; remove bacon, reserving drippings in skillet. Crumble bacon, and set aside.

Sauté green pepper and onion in reserved bacon drippings in skillet 2 to 3 minutes or until vegetables are tender. Add tomatoes and water; bring mixture to a boil. Add rice, salt, pepper, and thyme. Cover, reduce heat, and simmer 18 to 20 minutes. Add shrimp; cover and cook an additional 10 to 12 minutes or until shrimp turn pink and liquid is absorbed. Sprinkle with bacon just before serving. Yield: 6 to 8 servings.   Robin Anderson

Fiesta
The Junior Woman's Club of Pensacola, Florida

Shrimp Scampi

2 pounds unpeeled large
  fresh shrimp
2 tablespoons butter or
  margarine, melted
½ cup butter or margarine
1 tablespoon minced celery
1 tablespoon minced onion
2 teaspoons chopped fresh
  chives
2 teaspoons chopped fresh
  parsley
½ teaspoon garlic powder
½ teaspoon dried whole
  basil
½ teaspoon dried whole
  marjoram
½ teaspoon dried whole
  thyme
Hot cooked rice

Peel, devein, and butterfly shrimp. Sauté shrimp in 2 tablespoons melted butter in a large skillet 3 to 5 minutes over medium heat or until shrimp turn pink. Remove shrimp with a slotted spoon; set aside, and keep warm.

Combine ½ cup butter and next 8 ingredients in a skillet. Cook over medium heat 3 to 4 minutes or until butter melts and mixture is thoroughly heated. Add shrimp; cook 1 minute. Serve over rice. Yield: 6 servings.   The Family of Melanie Jessup

Symphony of Tastes
The Youth Symphony of Anchorage, Alaska

Shrimp Stroganoff

4 pounds unpeeled
  medium-size fresh shrimp
½ pound sliced fresh
  mushrooms
¼ cup chopped green onions
¼ cup butter or margarine,
  melted
1 teaspoon salt

¼ teaspoon pepper
4 cups canned diluted
  chicken broth
4 ounces vermicelli or thin
  spaghetti, uncooked
1 (8-ounce) carton sour cream
¼ cup dry sherry

Peel and devein shrimp; set aside.

Sauté sliced mushrooms and chopped green onions in melted butter in a large skillet until vegetables are tender. Add shrimp, and sauté 3 to 5 minutes or until shrimp turn pink. Sprinkle mixture with salt and pepper. Remove from heat. Set aside, and keep shrimp and vegetable mixture warm.

Place chicken broth in a large Dutch oven; bring to a boil. Add vermicelli, and return to a boil. Boil 6 to 8 minutes or until vermicelli is al dente; drain well.

Place vermicelli in a large serving bowl. Add shrimp and vegetable mixture, sour cream, and sherry; toss gently to combine. Serve immediately. Yield: 4 to 6 servings.   Helen Moore

Critics' Choice
The Corinth Theatre Arts Guild
Corinth, Mississippi

Seafood Risotto

½ pound unpeeled
medium-size fresh shrimp
1½ cups long-grain rice,
uncooked
1 small onion, chopped
2 tablespoons butter or
margarine, melted
5 cups canned diluted
chicken broth
½ teaspoon salt
¼ teaspoon pepper

⅛ teaspoon saffron threads,
crushed
½ pound sliced fresh
mushrooms
3 green onions, sliced
2 tablespoons butter or
margarine, melted
¼ pound bay scallops
½ cup peeled, seeded, and
chopped tomato

Peel and devein shrimp; set aside.

Sauté rice and chopped onion in 2 tablespoons melted butter in a large skillet until rice is opaque and onion is tender.

Bring broth to a boil in a large saucepan. Transfer 1½ cups hot chicken broth to a skillet; add rice mixture, salt, pepper, and saffron. Bring to a boil; cover, reduce heat, and simmer until liquid is absorbed. Remove cover; add remaining hot broth, ½ cup at a time, stirring after each addition until liquid is absorbed. Continue adding hot broth until mixture is creamy and rice is tender.

Sauté mushrooms and green onions in 2 tablespoons melted butter in a large skillet until vegetables are tender. Add reserved shrimp, scallops, and tomato; cover, reduce heat, and simmer 5 minutes or until shrimp turn pink and scallops are opaque.

Add shrimp mixture to rice mixture; toss gently to combine. Cook over low heat 3 minutes or until thoroughly heated. Yield: 6 to 8 servings.

Cal Poly Pomona 50th Anniversary
The Home Economics Alumni Association
Pomona, California

Meats

Located in the Baltimore and Ohio Transportation Museum in Maryland, the Mount Clare roundhouse serves as a display area for historic locomotives. In 1828, the launching of the Baltimore and Ohio Railroad began what became the most influential transportation system in America. The transcontinental railroad was completed by 1869.

Roast Tenderloin Diane

¼ cup Chablis or other dry
  white wine
¼ cup brandy
3 tablespoons lemon juice
1 teaspoon Worcestershire
  sauce
2 tablespoons minced fresh
  chives
1½ teaspoons salt
¼ teaspoon freshly ground
  pepper

1 (2-pound) beef tenderloin,
  trimmed
½ pound fresh mushrooms,
  sliced
1 tablespoon butter or
  margarine, melted
2 tablespoons water
2 tablespoons butter or
  margarine

Combine first 7 ingredients in a small bowl; stir well.

Place tenderloin in a large shallow dish; pour marinade mixture over tenderloin. Cover and marinate in refrigerator 8 hours, turning occasionally.

Remove tenderloin from marinade, reserving marinade. Place marinade in a small saucepan. Bring to a boil; reduce heat, and simmer 3 minutes. Set aside.

Place tenderloin on a rack in a shallow roasting pan; insert meat thermometer, making sure it does not touch fat. Bake at 425° for 45 to 55 minutes or until thermometer registers 140° (rare), 150° (medium rare), or 160° (medium), basting occasionally with marinade. Let tenderloin stand 10 minutes before serving.

Sauté mushrooms in 1 tablespoon melted butter in a skillet until tender; set aside, and keep warm.

Place any remaining marinade in a small saucepan; add water and 2 tablespoons butter. Bring to a boil; reduce heat, and simmer 3 minutes. Slice tenderloin; spoon sauce over tenderloin. Top with sautéed mushrooms. Yield: 6 servings.   Diane Bertsch

Gingerbread . . . and all the trimmings
The Junior Service League of Waxahachie, Texas

Brisket with Fruit

1 (2- to 3-pound) beef brisket
2 onions, sliced and divided
1 (12-ounce) can beer
1 cup dried apricots
1 cup pitted prunes
3 tablespoons brown sugar
2 tablespoons orange
  marmalade
1 tablespoon brandy

1 tablespoon grated lemon
  rind
Juice of 1 lemon
¾ teaspoon ground ginger
½ teaspoon ground cinnamon
½ teaspoon pepper
½ teaspoon Worcestershire
  sauce

Trim excess fat from brisket. Place half of onion slices on a large piece of heavy-duty aluminum foil. Place brisket on top of onion slices; top with remaining half of onion slices. Wrap brisket and onion in foil; seal tightly. Place in a greased large shallow baking dish. Bake at 350° for 3 hours.

Combine beer and remaining ingredients in a medium saucepan; stir well. Bring fruit mixture to a boil over medium heat. Remove brisket from foil, and place in baking dish. Pour fruit mixture over brisket. Reduce oven temperature to 300°; cover brisket, and bake 1 hour. Yield: 4 to 6 servings.   Shirley Miller

A Taste of Hope
The Camarillo Chapter of City of Hope
Camarillo, California

Pot Roast with Pomegranates

1 (6-pound) beef brisket
2 cloves garlic, slivered
¼ cup plus 2 tablespoons
  olive oil
3 tablespoons red wine
  vinegar
1 tablespoon lemon juice
15 fresh sage leaves or 2
  tablespoons dried whole
  sage
6 cloves garlic
1 teaspoon coarse salt

¼ teaspoon pepper
1 large onion, sliced
2 tablespoons vegetable oil
4 cups canned diluted
  chicken broth
2 cups water
2 tablespoons soy sauce
¼ teaspoon salt
¼ teaspoon pepper
2 pomegranates or 2 pounds
  small seedless grapes
Garnish: fresh parsley sprigs

Trim fat from brisket. Make several slits in brisket, inserting garlic slivers into slits. Place brisket in a large roasting pan; set aside.

Position knife blade in food processor bowl; add olive oil and next 6 ingredients, and process until well blended. Spread marinade mixture over brisket. Cover and marinate in refrigerator 8 hours.

Sauté onion in 2 tablespoons vegetable oil in a Dutch oven until tender. Add brisket; cook until browned on all sides. Add broth, water, soy sauce, ¼ teaspoon salt, and ¼ teaspoon pepper. Bring to a boil; cover, reduce heat, and simmer 2½ hours. Remove brisket from pan, reserving pan juices. Set brisket aside, and keep warm. Skim fat from pan juices.

Remove seeds from pomegranates; add seeds to pan juices. Slice meat across grain into thin slices, and serve with pan juices. Garnish, if desired. Yield: 12 servings.   Barbara Sasson

Deal Delights II
Sephardic Women's Organization
Deal, New Jersey

New England Boiled Dinner

1 (4-pound) corned beef brisket, trimmed	1 cabbage, cut into 6 wedges
6 carrots, scraped	6 small fresh beets, unpeeled
4 small turnips, peeled	8 medium-size baking potatoes, peeled

Place brisket in a large Dutch oven; add water to cover. Bring to a boil; cover, reduce heat, and simmer 2 hours and 45 minutes.

Add carrots, turnips, and cabbage. (Add additional water to cover, if necessary.) Cover and simmer 30 minutes.

Leave root and 1 inch of stem on beets; scrub with a vegetable brush. Place beets in a saucepan; add water to cover. Bring to a boil; cover, reduce heat, and simmer 35 to 40 minutes or until tender. Drain; pour cold water over beets, and drain. Trim off roots and stems, and rub off skins. Set aside, and keep warm.

Add potatoes to corned beef mixture in Dutch oven. Cover and simmer 30 minutes or until potatoes are tender.

Transfer brisket to a serving platter; place vegetables around brisket. Place beets around brisket. Yield: 8 servings.

Our Town Cookbook
The Historical Society of Peterborough, New Hampshire

Stuffed Flank Steak

1 (1½-pound) flank steak
1 clove garlic, crushed
2 tablespoons soy sauce
½ teaspoon pepper
½ cup chopped onion
1 clove garlic, crushed
¼ cup butter or margarine, melted
1½ cups cooked long-grain rice

½ cup grated Parmesan cheese
½ cup chopped fresh parsley
¼ teaspoon pepper
½ cup canned undiluted beef broth
½ cup water
1 tablespoon chopped crystallized ginger

Trim fat from steak. Cut steak lengthwise to within ½ inch of outer edge, leaving one long side connected; flip cut piece over to enlarge steak. Rub steak with 1 crushed garlic clove. Brush soy sauce over steak; sprinkle with ½ teaspoon pepper. Set aside.

Sauté onion and 1 crushed garlic clove in butter in a saucepan until tender. Remove from heat; stir in rice and next 3 ingredients.

Spread rice mixture down center of steak to within 1½ inches of outside edges. Roll up jellyroll fashion, starting with long side. Tie with heavy string at 2-inch intervals. Place in a shallow baking dish.

Combine beef broth and water; pour over steak. Sprinkle with crystallized ginger. Bake at 350° for 45 to 50 minutes or to desired degree of doneness, basting occasionally with pan juices. Yield: 6 servings.   The Family of Cecilia M. Valentine

Symphony of Tastes
The Youth Symphony of Anchorage, Alaska

The Anchorage Youth Symphony Orchestra is supported by the Anchorage Youth Symphony Association, Inc., which provides student scholarships and sponsors national and international tours, in part, through the sale of Symphony of Tastes.

Southwestern Flank Steak with Fresh Fruit Salsa

1 (1½-pound) flank steak
¼ cup fresh orange juice
2 tablespoons chili sauce
2 tablespoons soy sauce
2 tablespoons vegetable oil
1 teaspoon honey
2 cloves garlic, minced
1 teaspoon grated orange rind
½ teaspoon grated lemon rind
2 tablespoons chili powder
½ teaspoon salt
¼ teaspoon ground red pepper
1 medium-size orange, thinly sliced
Fresh Fruit Salsa
Garnishes: orange wedges and fresh cilantro sprigs

Place steak in a large shallow dish, and set aside.

Combine orange juice and next 10 ingredients in a small bowl; stir well. Pour marinade mixture over steak. Place orange slices over steak. Cover and marinate in refrigerator 8 hours, turning steak occasionally.

Remove steak from marinade, and discard marinade. Grill steak over hot coals 4 to 6 minutes on each side or to desired degree of doneness. To serve, slice steak diagonally across grain into thin slices. Serve with Fresh Fruit Salsa. Garnish, if desired. Yield: 4 servings.

Fresh Fruit Salsa

1 cup diced fresh pineapple
1 cup chopped fresh papaya
1 kiwifruit, sliced
½ cup diced sweet red pepper
¼ cup diced green pepper
2½ tablespoons white wine vinegar
1½ tablespoons minced fresh cilantro
1 tablespoon plus 1 teaspoon sugar
½ teaspoon crushed red pepper

Combine all ingredients in a small bowl, tossing gently. Cover and chill 8 hours. Let stand at room temperature before serving. Yield: about 3 cups.

Gourmet LA
The Junior League of Los Angeles, California

Grilled Flank Steak with Sherry-Mustard Sauce

1 (1½-pound) flank steak
⅓ cup dry sherry
⅓ cup soy sauce
2 tablespoons chopped green onions
1 tablespoon cracked pepper

2 teaspoons coarse-grained Dijon mustard
1 teaspoon peeled, chopped fresh ginger
Sherry-Mustard Sauce

Score steak ¼-inch deep on both sides; place in a large shallow dish. Combine sherry and next 5 ingredients in a small bowl; stir well. Pour marinade mixture over steak; cover and marinate in refrigerator 8 hours.

Remove steak from marinade; discard marinade. Grill steak over medium coals or broil 6 inches from heat 6 to 8 minutes on each side or to desired degree of doneness. To serve, slice diagonally across grain into thin slices. Serve with Sherry-Mustard Sauce. Yield: 4 to 6 servings.

Sherry-Mustard Sauce

1 (8-ounce) carton plain low-fat yogurt
2 tablespoons chopped green onions

2 tablespoons dry sherry
2 teaspoons coarse-grained Dijon mustard
Pinch of salt

Combine all ingredients in a small bowl; stir well. Cover and chill 1 hour. Yield: 1 cup.   Sandy Maslowski Kuchta

Hudson Cooks
The Community Playground of Hudson, Ohio

Miller's Beef Jerky

1½ pounds flank steak
1 small onion, sliced
¾ cup water
¾ cup Burgundy or other dry red wine
½ cup soy sauce

⅓ cup Worcestershire sauce
1 teaspoon salt or seasoned salt (optional)
1 teaspoon onion powder
½ teaspoon garlic powder
¼ teaspoon pepper

Trim fat from steak. Partially freeze steak, and cut with the grain into ¼-inch-thick strips. Combine sliced onion and remaining ingredients in a medium bowl. Add steak strips, and toss to coat. Cover and chill 8 hours.

Drain steak; discard marinade mixture. Place steak strips in a single layer on 2 broiler racks in 2 shallow roasting pans. Bake at 150° for 8 hours (do not allow temperature to go above 150°). Turn oven off. Let sit in oven 2 hours or until dry. Store in an airtight container. Yield: 1 pound.   Mason C. Miller, Jr.

Wilderness Ranger Cookbook
San Juan National Forest Association
Durango, Colorado

Medaillons of Beef in Cognac Cream

4 (4-ounce) beef tenderloin steaks
Salt and cracked pepper
2 tablespoons olive oil
2 tablespoons butter
2 shallots or 1 small onion, chopped
¼ cup cognac
½ cup whipping cream
Garnish: fresh parsley sprigs

Sprinkle beef tenderloin steaks with salt and cracked pepper.

Combine olive oil and butter in a large skillet, and cook over medium heat until butter melts. Add steaks to mixture in skillet, and cook 5 minutes on each side. Remove steaks to a serving platter, and keep warm.

Drain drippings from skillet, reserving 2 tablespoons drippings in skillet. Sauté shallots in drippings until tender. Add cognac, and cook over medium heat, deglazing skillet by scraping particles that cling to bottom. Gradually stir in whipping cream, and cook until thoroughly heated. Pour sauce over steaks. Garnish, if desired. Yield: 4 servings.

Twickenham Tables
Twickenham Historic Preservation District Association, Inc.
Huntsville, Alabama

Elegant Beef Wellingtons

4 (4-ounce) beef tenderloin
   steaks
1½ teaspoons garlic salt
⅛ teaspoon pepper
2 tablespoons butter or
   margarine, melted
½ pound finely chopped
   fresh mushrooms
¼ cup chopped onion
¼ cup dry sherry
2 tablespoons minced fresh
   parsley
4 commercial frozen puff
   pastry patty shells, thawed
1 egg, lightly beaten

⅓ cup chopped onion
6 fresh mushrooms, sliced
2 tablespoons butter or
   margarine, melted
2 tablespoons all-purpose
   flour
1 (10½-ounce) can beef broth,
   undiluted
½ cup Burgundy or other dry
   red wine
¼ teaspoon Worcestershire
   sauce
¼ teaspoon salt
Dash of pepper
1 bay leaf

Sprinkle steaks with garlic salt and ⅛ teaspoon pepper. Sauté steaks in 2 tablespoons melted butter in a large skillet 2 to 4 minutes on each side. Remove steaks from skillet, reserving drippings in skillet. Drain steaks on paper towels. Cover and chill.

Add chopped mushrooms, ¼ cup chopped onion, sherry, and parsley to drippings in skillet. Sauté over medium heat until onion is tender and liquid evaporates. Spread mushroom mixture evenly over top of chilled steaks.

Roll out each patty shell to a 6-inch square on a lightly floured surface. Place steaks, mushroom side down, on pastry squares. Brush edges of pastry with beaten egg. Fold pastry over meat, pinching seams and ends to seal. Place seam side down in a greased 15- x 10- x 1-inch jellyroll pan. Brush with any remaining beaten egg. Bake at 425° for 15 to 20 minutes or until golden brown.

Sauté ⅓ cup onion and sliced mushrooms in 2 tablespoons melted butter in a medium skillet until vegetables are tender. Add flour, stirring until smooth. Cook 1 minute, stirring constantly. Gradually add broth and wine. Cook over medium heat, stirring constantly, until mixture is thickened and bubbly. Stir in Worcestershire sauce, salt, and pepper. Add bay leaf. Reduce heat to low; simmer 10 minutes. Remove and discard bay leaf. Serve beef Wellingtons with sauce. Yield: 4 servings.

Nancy Schorr

Delectable Edibles from the Livable Forest
The Women's Club of Kingwood, Texas

Beef Bavarian on Rice

1 pound sirloin steak
1½ tablespoons cornstarch
1½ teaspoons salt
¼ teaspoon garlic powder
¼ teaspoon pepper
1½ tablespoons vegetable oil
1 medium onion, sliced
1 (12-ounce) can beer
½ cup canned diluted beef
  broth

2 teaspoons brown sugar
⅛ teaspoon hot sauce
3 large carrots, scraped and
  sliced
2 tablespoons cold water
2 tablespoons cornstarch
Hot cooked rice

Trim fat from steak; pound to ½-inch thickness, using a meat mallet. Slice steak diagonally across grain into 2- x 1-inch strips.

Combine 1½ tablespoons cornstarch, salt, garlic powder, and pepper; stir well. Dredge steak strips in cornstarch mixture. Cook in oil in a large skillet until browned. Add onion, and cook 3 minutes. Stir in beer and next 3 ingredients. Bring to a boil; cover, reduce heat, and simmer 15 minutes. Add carrot; cover and simmer 15 minutes or until carrot is tender.

Combine water and 2 tablespoons cornstarch; gradually stir into beef mixture. Cook, stirring constantly, until mixture thickens. Serve over rice. Yield: 4 servings.   Martha Thibodeau

Favorite Recipes from Fishers Island
The Island Bowling Center
Fishers Island, New York

Funds from the sale of Favorite Recipes from Fishers Island *will be used to improve the Island Bowling Center and Snack Bar. During the winter, the center provides the only organized recreation area for residents of the island.*

Barbecued Short Ribs

3 to 3½ pounds beef short
  ribs
1 cup catsup
½ cup water
1 medium onion, chopped
1 lemon, sliced
¼ cup firmly packed brown
  sugar

2 tablespoons Worcestershire
  sauce
2 teaspoons garlic salt
2 teaspoons prepared mustard
¼ teaspoon dried whole
  thyme

Place short ribs in a 13- x 9- x 2-inch baking pan. Bake at 450° for 20 minutes; drain. Return ribs to baking pan.

Combine catsup and remaining ingredients in a small bowl; stir well. Pour sauce over ribs. Reduce heat to 350°, and bake for 1½ hours or until ribs are tender, basting occasionally with sauce.

Place any remaining sauce in a small saucepan. Bring to a boil; reduce heat, and simmer 3 minutes. Serve ribs with sauce. Yield: 4 to 6 servings.

Kasey Henley

Crossroads Cuisine
The Winona Manor Christmas Fund
Kilmichael, Mississippi

German Beef Supper

2 tablespoons shortening
1½ pounds lean beef for
  stewing, cut into 1-inch
  pieces
1 large cooking apple, peeled,
  cored, and shredded
1 medium carrot, scraped and
  shredded
½ medium onion, sliced
1 clove garlic, minced
1 (12-ounce) can beer

½ cup water
2 beef-flavored bouillon cubes
1 teaspoon salt
1 small bay leaf
⅛ teaspoon dried whole
  thyme
1 teaspoon cornstarch
1 tablespoon cold water
4 cups hot cooked medium
  egg noodles
¼ teaspoon poppy seeds

Melt shortening in a large Dutch oven over medium heat. Add meat, and cook until meat is browned on all sides. Add shredded apple and next 9 ingredients to Dutch oven, stirring well. Cover, reduce heat, and simmer 2 hours or until beef is tender. Remove and discard bay leaf.

Combine cornstarch and water, stirring well. Add to beef mixture, and cook, stirring constantly, until mixture thickens.

Combine noodles and poppy seeds; toss gently. Serve beef mixture over noodles. Yield: 4 servings.

The Children of Tikvah's Special Cookbook, Volume 3
Tikvah Institute for Childhood Learning Disabilities
Chicago, Illinois

Beef Bonaparte

1 pound ground beef
1 (16-ounce) can tomatoes, undrained and chopped
1 (8-ounce) can tomato sauce
2 teaspoons garlic juice
2 teaspoons sugar
½ teaspoon salt
¼ teaspoon cracked pepper
Hot sauce to taste
1 bay leaf (optional)
1 (5-ounce) package fine egg noodles
1 (8-ounce) carton sour cream
1 (3-ounce) package cream cheese, softened
6 green onions, chopped
1 cup (4 ounces) shredded Cheddar cheese
2 cups (8 ounces) shredded mozzarella cheese

Cook ground beef in a large skillet over medium heat until browned, stirring to crumble meat; drain well. Add tomato, next 6 ingredients, and, if desired, bay leaf. Bring to a boil; reduce heat, and simmer, uncovered, 25 minutes, stirring occasionally. Remove and discard bay leaf. Set aside.

Cook noodles according to package directions. Drain; set aside.

Combine sour cream and cream cheese in a medium bowl; beat at low speed of an electric mixer until smooth. Gently stir in noodles and green onions.

Place half the noodle mixture in a greased 11- x 7- x 1½-inch baking dish; top with half the beef mixture. Sprinkle with ½ cup Cheddar cheese. Repeat layers with remaining noodle mixture, beef mixture, and Cheddar cheese. Cover and bake at 350° for 20 minutes. Remove from oven; sprinkle with mozzarella cheese. Bake 3 minutes or until cheese melts and mixture is hot and bubbly. Yield: 6 to 8 servings.   Pam Carpenter

Rebel Recipes
Department of Home Economics, University of Mississippi
Oxford, Mississippi

Meat Loaf Soufflé

1½ pounds ground beef
½ cup fine, dry breadcrumbs
1 egg, beaten
½ cup milk
½ cup chopped onion
1½ teaspoons salt
⅛ teaspoon pepper
1 cup (4 ounces) shredded
  Cheddar cheese

2 medium tomatoes, sliced
1 (8-ounce) carton sour cream
¾ cup instant-blending flour
3 eggs, separated
½ teaspoon salt
⅛ teaspoon pepper

Combine first 7 ingredients; mix well. Press mixture into an ungreased 9-inch square baking pan. Bake at 350° for 25 minutes. Drain and discard pan drippings. Sprinkle cheese over meat. Layer tomato slices over cheese; set aside.

Beat sour cream, flour, egg yolks, salt, and pepper at low speed of an electric mixer until smooth. Beat egg whites (at room temperature) at high speed until stiff peaks form. Gently fold egg whites into sour cream mixture. Spread over tomato slices. Bake at 350° for 40 minutes or until golden brown. Let stand 5 minutes before serving. Yield: 8 servings.   Lois Russell

The Mark Twain Library Cookbook, Volume III
The Mark Twain Library Association
Redding, Connecticut

Shepherd's Pie

2 pounds lean ground beef or
  ground lamb
½ cup Burgundy or other dry
  red wine
2 tablespoons commercial
  steak sauce
1 tablespoon Worcestershire
  sauce
1 bay leaf
½ teaspoon dried whole
  marjoram

Dash of ground cloves
Dash of ground red pepper
Salt and pepper to taste
2 large onions, thinly sliced
5 cups cooked mashed
  potatoes
3 tablespoons grated
  Parmesan cheese
Dash of paprika
1 tablespoon butter or
  margarine

Cook meat in a large skillet over medium heat until browned, stirring to crumble meat. Add wine and next 7 ingredients; stir well.

Cook over medium-high heat 3 minutes. Transfer meat mixture to a 3-quart casserole, reserving drippings in skillet. Remove and discard bay leaf.

Sauté onion in pan drippings until tender; drain. Add onion to meat mixture, stirring well. Spread potatoes over meat mixture. Sprinkle with Parmesan cheese and paprika; dot with butter. Bake at 350° for 15 minutes or until potatoes are browned and mixture is thoroughly heated. Yield: 6 servings.   Betsy Weedon

The Educated Palate
The Calhoun School Parents Association
New York, New York

Pastor Pete's Enchiladas

1 pound ground beef or turkey
2 cups (8 ounces) shredded Cheddar cheese, divided
¼ cup sliced green onions
1 (8-ounce) carton sour cream
1 teaspoon dried parsley flakes
½ teaspoon salt
⅛ teaspoon pepper
3 (8-ounce) cans tomato sauce
1 cup water
2 cloves garlic, crushed
1 teaspoon chili powder
½ teaspoon dried whole oregano
⅛ teaspoon ground cumin
8 (8-inch) flour tortillas

Cook ground beef in a large skillet until browned, stirring to crumble meat; drain. Add ¾ cup cheese, green onions, sour cream, parsley, salt, and pepper, stirring well. Remove from heat; cover and set aside.

Combine tomato sauce and next 5 ingredients in a medium saucepan. Bring to a boil; reduce heat, and simmer, uncovered, 5 minutes.

Spoon about ¼ cup reserved beef mixture over tortillas; roll up tightly. Place seam side down in a 13- x 9- x 2-inch baking dish. Pour tomato sauce mixture over tortillas. Sprinkle with remaining 1¼ cups cheese. Bake, uncovered, at 350° for 20 to 30 minutes or until thoroughly heated. Yield: 4 servings.   Peter Thomson

Sharing Recipes
St. John's Women of the Evangelical Lutheran Church in America
Springfield, Illinois

Crispy Corn Dogs

1 cup all-purpose flour
¾ cup yellow cornmeal
2 tablespoons sugar
1 tablespoon dry mustard
2 teaspoons baking powder
½ teaspoon salt
1 cup milk
1 egg, lightly beaten
2 tablespoons shortening, melted
15 wooden skewers
15 all-beef frankfurters (about 1½ pounds)
Vegetable oil

Combine first 6 ingredients in a bowl; stir well. Add milk, egg, and shortening; stir well.

Insert a wooden skewer in one end of each frankfurter. Dip frankfurters into batter, and fry in deep hot oil (375°) for 2 to 3 minutes or until browned. Drain corn dogs well on paper towels. Yield: 15 servings.   Phyllis Mayo

State Hospital Cooks
Patient/Staff Advocacy Committee, Vermont State Hospital
Waterbury, Vermont

Veal Bauletto

8 (2- to 3-ounce) veal cutlets
4 thin slices prosciutto
4 (1-ounce) slices Monterey Jack cheese
Salt and pepper
⅓ cup all-purpose flour
3 tablespoons olive oil
1 pound fresh mushrooms, sliced
¼ cup chopped shallots or onion
1 cup canned diluted chicken broth
½ cup Chablis or other dry white wine
2 tablespoons chopped fresh parsley
¼ cup butter or margarine, softened

Place cutlets between 2 sheets of wax paper; flatten to ⅛-inch thickness, using a meat mallet or rolling pin.

Place a slice of prosciutto and a slice of cheese on 4 veal cutlets; top with remaining cutlets. Place between 2 sheets of wax paper; flatten slightly, using a meat mallet or rolling pin. Sprinkle with salt and pepper; dredge in flour.

Cook cutlets in oil in a large skillet until browned on both sides. Remove cutlets to a serving platter, reserving drippings in skillet. Set cutlets aside, and keep warm.

Sauté sliced mushrooms and chopped shallots in drippings in skillet until vegetables are tender. Add chicken broth, wine, and chopped fresh parsley. Bring to a boil; cook 5 minutes or until mixture is reduced by half. Add butter, stirring with a wire whisk until sauce is blended. Spoon warm sauce over cutlets on serving platter. Yield: 4 servings.   Modesto Lanzone

A Taste of San Francisco
The Symphony of San Francisco, California

Bavarian Schnitzel

4 veal cutlets (about 1 pound)
½ teaspoon salt
¼ teaspoon pepper
2 eggs
2 tablespoons water
¾ cup fine, dry breadcrumbs
1 tablespoon chopped fresh parsley
2 teaspoons grated lemon rind
½ cup all-purpose flour
3 tablespoons butter or margarine, melted
3 tablespoons vegetable oil
Garnish: lemon slices

Place cutlets between 2 sheets of wax paper; flatten to ¼-inch thickness, using a meat mallet or rolling pin. Sprinkle with salt and pepper.

Combine eggs and water in a small bowl; beat well with a wire whisk. Set aside.

Combine breadcrumbs, chopped parsley, and lemon rind in a shallow bowl; set aside.

Dredge cutlets in flour; dip in egg mixture, and coat with breadcrumb mixture. Chill at least 15 minutes.

Cook cutlets in melted butter and vegetable oil in a large skillet over medium heat until browned on both sides. Garnish, if desired. Yield: 4 servings.   Winifred Burnham

Bach to the Kitchen
Cappella Cantorum
Essex, Connecticut

Grillades

2 pounds veal cutlets
½ cup all-purpose flour
1 teaspoon salt
1 teaspoon freshly ground
white pepper
2 tablespoons butter, melted
2 tablespoons vegetable oil
½ pound fresh mushrooms,
thinly sliced
1 cup finely chopped green
onions
½ cup finely chopped green
pepper

1 clove garlic, minced
2 tablespoons butter, melted
3 cups peeled, chopped
tomatoes
1½ cups water
½ cup Burgundy or other dry
red wine
2 tablespoons tomato paste
2 tablespoons finely chopped
fresh parsley
1 bay leaf
½ teaspoon ground thyme
Hot cooked, buttered grits

Place veal between 2 sheets of wax paper; flatten to ¼-inch thickness, using a meat mallet. Cut veal into 1½-inch pieces. Combine flour, salt, and white pepper. Dredge veal in flour mixture. Cook veal in 2 tablespoons butter and oil in a Dutch oven over medium-high heat until browned. Remove veal from Dutch oven; set aside.

Sauté mushrooms, green onions, green pepper, and garlic in 2 tablespoons butter in Dutch oven until tender. Add chopped tomato and next 6 ingredients. Add reserved veal; stir gently. Bring to a boil; cover, reduce heat, and simmer 40 minutes. Remove cover, and cook 20 minutes. Remove bay leaf. Serve over grits. Yield: 4 to 6 servings.   Lisa Thomas

Fiesta
The Junior Woman's Club of Pensacola, Florida

*The Pensacola Junior Woman's Club provides means whereby young women may be of service to their community. Proceeds from the sale of **Fiesta** will help support a suicide prevention hot line for teenagers.*

Braised Herb-Flavored Veal Tidbits with Mushrooms

1½ pounds boneless veal
  shoulder roast, cut into
  1½-inch cubes
3 tablespoons butter, melted
2 tablespoons vegetable oil
1 medium onion, finely
  chopped
1 clove garlic, minced
2 tablespoons all-purpose
  flour
½ cup Chablis or other dry
  white wine
½ cup canned Italian-style
  tomatoes, undrained and
  chopped

1 cup water
1 teaspoon dried whole
  rosemary, crushed
⅛ teaspoon dried whole sage,
  crushed
1 teaspoon salt
⅛ teaspoon freshly ground
  pepper
½ pound fresh mushrooms,
  sliced
1 tablespoon butter, melted
1 tablespoon vegetable oil
Hot cooked rice (optional)

Sauté veal in 3 tablespoons melted butter and 2 tablespoons vegetable oil in a large Dutch oven over medium heat until veal is browned on all sides.

Add chopped onion and minced garlic to veal in Dutch oven, and sauté until onion is golden brown, stirring constantly. Add flour, stirring until smooth. Cook 1 minute, stirring constantly. Gradually add wine; cook over medium heat, stirring constantly, until mixture is thickened and bubbly. Add tomatoes, water, rosemary, sage, salt, and freshly ground pepper. Cover, reduce heat, and simmer 55 minutes, stirring occasionally.

Sauté sliced mushrooms in 1 tablespoon melted butter and 1 tablespoon oil in a large skillet over medium heat until mushrooms are tender and liquid evaporates. Add sautéed mushrooms to veal mixture, and cook 5 minutes. Serve over rice, if desired. Yield: 4 to 6 servings.   Mrs. D. Ryan Cook

Three Rivers Cookbook, Volume III
Child Health Association of Sewickley, Pennsylvania

Garlic-Crusted Leg of Lamb

1 (5- to 6-pound) leg of lamb
2 slices bacon, finely
   chopped
¼ cup minced fresh parsley
2 tablespoons butter or
   margarine, softened

1 tablespoon vinegar
4 cloves garlic, minced
1 teaspoon salt
1 teaspoon paprika
Freshly ground pepper

Score fat on lamb in a diamond design. Combine bacon and remaining ingredients; stir well. Rub mixture into scored slits and over entire surface of lamb. Cover and chill 1 hour.

Place lamb, fat side up, on a rack in a shallow roasting pan; insert meat thermometer, making sure it does not touch fat or bone. Bake at 325° for 2½ hours or until meat thermometer registers 160°. Yield: 8 servings.   Jane Koehler

What's Cooking in Philadelphia
The Rotary Club of Philadelphia, Pennsylvania

Mustard-Rosemary Barbecued Leg of Lamb

1 (5- to 6-pound) leg
   of lamb, boned and
   butterflied
¼ cup olive oil
¼ cup tarragon vinegar
¼ cup Dijon mustard
1 clove garlic, minced

2 teaspoons minced fresh
   rosemary
¼ teaspoon seasoned salt
⅛ teaspoon pepper
Commercial mint jelly
   (optional)

Trim fat from lamb. Place lamb in a large shallow dish.

Combine olive oil, vinegar, mustard, garlic, rosemary, seasoned salt, and pepper in a small bowl; stir well. Pour marinade mixture over lamb. Cover and marinate in refrigerator 8 hours, turning occasionally.

Remove lamb from marinade, reserving marinade. Set lamb aside. Place marinade in a small saucepan. Bring to a boil; reduce heat, and simmer 3 minutes.

Grill lamb over medium coals 20 minutes, basting occasionally with marinade. Turn lamb, and insert meat thermometer. Grill an additional 20 minutes or until meat thermometer registers 160°, basting occasionally with marinade. Let stand 10 minutes.

Slice lamb diagonally across grain into thin slices. Serve with mint jelly, if desired. Yield: 8 servings.

Only in California
The Children's Home Society of California
Los Angeles, California

Lamb with Artichokes and Lemon

3 pounds boneless leg of lamb, cut into 2-inch pieces
1 teaspoon dried whole oregano
½ teaspoon salt
¼ teaspoon pepper
2 tablespoons olive oil
2 (9-ounce) packages frozen artichoke hearts, thawed

1 cup canned diluted beef broth
2 tablespoons fresh lemon juice
4 cloves garlic, minced
¼ cup unsalted butter

Sprinkle leg of lamb with oregano, salt, and pepper.

Sauté lamb in olive oil in a large skillet 10 to 12 minutes or until browned on all sides and to desired degree of doneness. Remove lamb to a serving platter, reserving drippings in skillet. Set lamb aside, and keep warm.

Add artichoke hearts, beef broth, fresh lemon juice, and minced garlic to drippings in skillet. Bring artichoke mixture to a boil; reduce heat, and simmer, uncovered, until liquid is reduced and slightly thickened.

Add reserved lamb to artichoke mixture in skillet, and stir well. Add butter, stirring gently until butter melts. Serve immediately. Yield: 8 servings.   Iris Cosnow

Hemi-demi-semi Flavors
The Chamber Music Society of the North Shore
Glencoe, Illinois

Roast Pork Calypso

1 (5- to 6-pound) pork loin
  roast
2 cloves garlic, crushed
1 teaspoon salt
1 teaspoon ground ginger
½ teaspoon ground cloves
½ teaspoon freshly ground
  pepper
2 bay leaves, broken into
  pieces

1½ cups canned diluted
  chicken broth, divided
1 cup dark rum, divided
½ cup firmly packed brown
  sugar
¼ cup lime juice
1 tablespoon cold water
2 teaspoons arrowroot

Score fat on pork loin roast in a diamond design.

Combine crushed garlic, salt, ginger, cloves, and freshly ground pepper in a small bowl. Rub spice mixture into scored fat on roast; sprinkle with bay leaves.

Pour ½ cup chicken broth and ½ cup rum into a shallow roasting pan. Place roast, fat side up, on a rack in roasting pan. Insert meat thermometer into thickest part of roast, making sure it does not touch fat or bone. Bake at 325° for 1 hour and 15 minutes.

Combine remaining ½ cup rum, brown sugar, and lime juice in a small bowl; stir well. Baste roast with rum mixture, reserving any remaining rum mixture. Bake an additional 1 hour and 15 minutes.

Remove and discard bay leaves. Transfer roast to a serving platter. Set aside, and keep warm.

Add enough remaining 1 cup chicken broth to remaining rum mixture to make 1½ cups. Pour liquid into a small heavy saucepan, and cook over medium heat until thoroughly heated. Combine cold water and arrowroot; stir well. Stir arrowroot mixture into broth mixture, stirring constantly; cook over medium heat, stirring constantly, until mixture is thickened and bubbly. Serve roast with sauce. Yield: 12 to 14 servings.   Marlene Taylor

Southern California Style
The Assistance League® of Anaheim, California

Roast Pork with Applejack

1 (5-pound) pork loin roast
¾ cup applejack or other
  apple-flavored brandy
1 tablespoon coarse salt
¼ teaspoon ground cloves
¼ teaspoon freshly grated
  nutmeg
¼ teaspoon freshly ground
  pepper

Dash of allspice
6 medium-size red potatoes,
  peeled
6 Granny Smith apples, cored
  and sliced
½ cup firmly packed brown
  sugar
¼ teaspoon ground cinnamon

When buying roast, ask the butcher to saw across the rib bones at the base of the backbone, to separate the ribs from the backbone.

Place roast in a large, zip-top heavy-duty plastic bag. Pour brandy over roast; seal bag. Place in a large bowl; marinate in refrigerator 4 hours, turning occasionally.

Remove roast from marinade, reserving marinade. Set marinade aside. Combine salt and next 4 ingredients; rub spice mixture over entire surface of roast. Place roast, fat side up, on a rack in a shallow roasting pan; insert meat thermometer, making sure it does not touch fat or bone. Bake at 325° for 2 hours.

Place potatoes in a large saucepan; add water to cover. Bring to a boil; cover, reduce heat, and simmer 5 minutes. Drain; quarter potatoes, and set aside.

Remove roast and rack from roasting pan; set aside. Discard pan drippings. Place apple slices in center of roasting pan; sprinkle with brown sugar and cinnamon.

Strain reserved marinade through several layers of cheesecloth. Place marinade in a small, long-handled saucepan. Bring to a boil; reduce heat, and simmer 3 minutes. Remove from heat and ignite; pour over apples. Let flames die down.

Place reserved potatoes around apples in roasting pan. Place roast on top of apples. Bake at 325° for 45 minutes or until meat thermometer registers 160°, turning potatoes after 30 minutes. Remove roast and apples from pan; place on a serving platter. Increase oven temperature to 500°; bake potatoes 5 minutes. Arrange potatoes around roast. Let roast stand 10 minutes before serving. Yield: 10 to 12 servings.   Donna Hammerbacker

A Collection of Recipes
Worcester Country School Development Office
Berlin, Maryland

Pork with Rosemary

3 (¾- to 1-pound) pork
  tenderloins
Salt and pepper
3 cloves garlic, minced
4 small onions, quartered
1 tablespoon butter or
  margarine, melted
1 tablespoon vegetable oil
2 teaspoons dried whole
  rosemary

1½ cups water
½ cup Madeira wine
3 tablespoons butter or
  margarine, melted
3 tablespoons all-purpose
  flour
Salt and pepper to taste

Rub tenderloins with salt and pepper; place in a 13- x 9- x 2-inch dish. Sprinkle with garlic. Arrange onion around tenderloins.

Combine 1 tablespoon butter, oil, and rosemary; drizzle over tenderloins and onion. Insert meat thermometer into thickest part of 1 tenderloin. Bake at 325° for 45 to 60 minutes or until thermometer registers 170°. Transfer tenderloins and onion to a serving platter, reserving drippings in dish. Set aside, and keep warm.

Add water to drippings; cook over high heat, deglazing pan by scraping particles that cling to bottom. Stir in wine. Combine 3 tablespoons melted butter and flour; stir well. Add flour mixture to pan; cook over medium heat, stirring constantly, until mixture is thickened and bubbly. Add salt and pepper to taste. Serve tenderloins with sauce. Yield: 8 servings.

Lasting Impressions
The St. Joseph's Hospital of Atlanta Auxiliary
Atlanta, Georgia

Iowa Stuffed Pork Chops

⅓ cup chopped celery
¼ cup chopped onion
3 tablespoons butter or
  margarine, melted
1 cup fine, dry breadcrumbs
2 tablespoons chopped fresh
  parsley

⅛ teaspoon salt
⅛ teaspoon paprika
⅓ cup milk
6 (1½-inch-thick) pork chops,
  cut with pockets
1½ cups milk

Sauté chopped celery and onion in melted butter in a large skillet until vegetables are tender. Transfer sautéed celery and onion to a medium mixing bowl, using a slotted spoon and reserving butter in skillet.

Add breadcrumbs, chopped parsley, salt, and paprika to celery mixture, and stir well. Add ⅓ cup milk, stirring well. Stuff breadcrumb mixture into pockets of chops, and secure openings with wooden picks.

Cook chops in reserved butter in skillet over medium heat until chops are browned on both sides.

Pour 1½ cups milk in bottom of a 13- x 9- x 2-inch baking dish; place chops in dish. Cover and bake at 350° for 45 minutes to 1 hour or until chops are tender. Remove and discard wooden picks before serving. Yield: 6 servings.

Recipes & Recollections from Terrace Hill
The Terrace Hill Society
Des Moines, Iowa

Pork with Cider

1½ pounds lean boneless
   pork, cut into 2-inch cubes
⅓ cup all-purpose flour
⅓ cup vegetable oil
1½ cups apple cider
2 carrots, scraped and sliced
1 medium onion, sliced
1 bay leaf

1 teaspoon salt
½ teaspoon pepper
½ teaspoon dried whole
   rosemary
Cooked mashed potatoes, hot
   cooked noodles, or hot
   cooked rice

Dredge pork in flour; cook in oil in a large ovenproof skillet until browned on all sides. Remove pork; set pork aside. Discard drippings. Add apple cider to skillet; cook over medium-high heat, deglazing skillet by scraping particles that cling to bottom.

Return pork to skillet; add carrot and next 5 ingredients. Cover and bake at 325° for 2 hours. Remove and discard bay leaf. Serve pork immediately over mashed potatoes, noodles, or rice. Yield: 4 to 6 servings.   Fran McCole

Port's Galley
The Port Council of Port of Portland, Oregon

Festive Holiday Ham

1 (9- to 10-pound) smoked, fully cooked ham
Whole cloves
½ cup Triple Sec or other orange-flavored liqueur
1½ cups firmly packed brown sugar
1 cup cranberry juice cocktail
½ cup honey
⅓ cup Triple Sec or other orange-flavored liqueur
3½ tablespoons prepared mustard
3 tablespoons butter or margarine
2 tablespoons cider vinegar
1½ tablespoons all-purpose flour
2 oranges, peeled and sliced
Maraschino cherries, halved

Slice skin from ham. Score fat on ham in a diamond design, and stud with cloves.

Inject ½ cup liqueur into ham at 3-inch intervals, using a bulb baster with a food injecting syringe attachment.

Combine brown sugar and next 7 ingredients in a medium saucepan; stir well. Bring to a boil; reduce heat, and simmer 2 minutes. Set glaze aside.

Place ham, fat side up, on a rack in a shallow roasting pan; pour brown sugar mixture over ham. Insert meat thermometer, making sure it does not touch fat or bone. Cover and bake at 325° for 2½ hours, basting frequently with glaze.

Arrange orange slices over exposed portion of ham; secure with wooden picks. Place a cherry half in center of each orange slice. Bake, uncovered, an additional 30 minutes or until thermometer registers 140°. Yield: 15 to 20 servings.

Hearts & Flour
The Women's Club of Pittsford, New York

Pasta, Rice & Grains

A farmer in the Skyrocket Hills of southeastern Washington state guides his combine over the contours of the field on a steep slope in a pattern that fits the land.

Angel Hair with Broccoli

1½ pounds fresh broccoli
2 green onions, sliced
1 clove garlic, crushed
1 tablespoon unsalted butter or margarine, melted
2 tablespoons Chablis or other dry white wine
¼ cup olive oil
3 tablespoons unsalted butter or margarine, melted
1 (8-ounce) package angel hair pasta
Grated Parmesan cheese

Trim off large leaves of broccoli; remove and discard tough ends of lower stalks. Wash broccoli thoroughly. Cut broccoli into flowerets; cut stalks into ½-inch pieces. Cook broccoli in a small amount of boiling water 10 to 12 minutes or until crisp-tender; drain well. Set aside.

Sauté sliced green onions and garlic in 1 tablespoon melted butter in a skillet over medium heat until tender. Add wine; reduce heat, and simmer, uncovered, 5 minutes. Add olive oil, 3 tablespoons melted butter, and broccoli; cook over medium heat until thoroughly heated.

Cook pasta according to package directions, and drain well. Combine cooked pasta and broccoli mixture in a large serving bowl, tossing gently to combine. Sprinkle with Parmesan cheese, and serve immediately. Yield: 4 servings.   Maylien Woodside Grosjean

Dining with the Daughters
The Daughters of Hawaii
Honolulu, Hawaii

Baked Fettuccine Mold

1 cup fine, dry breadcrumbs, divided
2 eggs, beaten
1 (16-ounce) package fettuccine
4 cups (16 ounces) shredded Muenster cheese
1 cup small-curd cottage cheese
1 cup whipping cream
¼ cup plus 1 tablespoon butter or margarine, cut into small pieces
¼ cup grated Parmesan cheese
½ teaspoon salt
¼ teaspoon pepper
Garnish: fresh parsley sprigs

Grease a shallow 3½-quart oval baking dish with butter. Sprinkle ½ cup breadcrumbs in bottom and up sides of dish. Drizzle beaten eggs over breadcrumbs; sprinkle with remaining ½ cup breadcrumbs. Set dish aside.

Cook fettuccine according to package directions. Drain; place in a bowl. Add Muenster cheese and next 6 ingredients; stir well. Pour into prepared dish. Bake, uncovered, at 350° for 30 to 35 minutes. Let stand 10 minutes. Invert onto a serving platter. Garnish, if desired. Yield: 8 to 10 servings.   Moselle Tobias

Deal Delights II
Sephardic Women's Organization
Deal, New Jersey

Fettuccine with Sausage and Vegetables

1 (8-ounce) package fettuccine
1 pound Italian sausage, cut into 1-inch pieces
¾ cup sliced green onions
2 cloves garlic, minced
3 tablespoons butter or margarine, melted
2 tablespoons vegetable oil
3 cups sliced zucchini
2 cups broccoli flowerets
2 cups sliced fresh mushrooms
2 medium tomatoes, cut into wedges
½ cup chopped fresh parsley
1 tablespoon lemon juice
1 teaspoon dried whole basil
1 teaspoon dried whole oregano
¼ teaspoon pepper
Dash of ground red pepper
¾ cup (3 ounces) shredded mozzarella cheese
½ cup grated Romano cheese

Cook fettuccine according to package directions; drain well. Set fettuccine aside.

Cook sausage in a large skillet over medium heat until browned on all sides; drain well, discarding drippings. Set sausage aside.

Sauté green onions and garlic in butter and oil in a large skillet over medium heat 3 minutes. Add zucchini, broccoli, and mushrooms, and sauté 3 to 5 minutes. Add reserved sausage, tomato, and next 6 ingredients; cook 3 minutes.

Combine cooked fettuccine and vegetable mixture; toss gently. Sprinkle with mozzarella and Romano cheese; toss well. Serve immediately. Yield: 6 to 8 servings.   Martha Bonhus

Black-Eyed Susan Country
The Saint Agnes Hospital Auxiliary
Baltimore, Maryland

One-Pot Pasta

2 quarts water
1 (12-ounce) package linguine
2 cups broccoli flowerets
½ pound fresh asparagus spears, cut into 1-inch pieces
½ cup scraped, thinly sliced carrot
2 cups sliced zucchini
½ cup frozen English peas, thawed
½ cup fresh snow pea pods
½ cup half-and-half
½ cup grated Parmesan cheese
2 tablespoons butter or margarine, melted
Salt and pepper to taste

Bring water to a boil in a large Dutch oven; add linguine, and return to a boil. Cook 7 minutes. Add broccoli, asparagus, and carrot; cook 2 minutes. Add zucchini, English peas, and snow peas; cook 3 minutes. Drain well, and place linguine mixture in a large serving bowl.

Combine half-and-half and remaining ingredients in a small bowl; stir well. Pour over linguine mixture; toss gently to combine. Serve immediately. Yield: 6 to 8 servings.

Merrymeeting Merry Eating
The Regional Memorial Hospital Auxiliary
Brunswick, Maine

Linguine Medley

4 ounces linguine, uncooked
4 ounces spinach linguine, uncooked
4 ounces tomato linguine, uncooked
1 pound fresh asparagus spears
1 pound chicken breast halves, skinned, boned, and cut into 1-inch pieces
2 tablespoons butter or margarine, melted
1 medium-size sweet red pepper, cut into ¼-inch strips
3 tablespoons finely chopped shallots or onion
1 cup whipping cream
½ teaspoon crushed red pepper
1 (4-ounce) package blue cheese, crumbled
½ teaspoon dried whole tarragon, crushed
Freshly ground pepper to taste
½ cup freshly grated Parmesan cheese

Cook linguine, separately, according to package directions. Drain well, and set aside.

Snap off tough ends of asparagus. Remove scales from stalks with a knife or vegetable peeler, if desired. Cut spears into 1½-inch pieces. Cook asparagus, covered, in a small amount of boiling water 6 to 8 minutes or until crisp-tender. Drain.

Sauté chicken in butter in a large skillet until lightly browned. Add red pepper strips and shallots, and sauté 1 minute. Add asparagus, and cook until thoroughly heated. Stir in cream and crushed red pepper. Add blue cheese, tarragon, and freshly ground pepper; cook until cheese melts, stirring frequently.

Combine chicken mixture and linguine; toss gently. Sprinkle with Parmesan cheese. Serve immediately. Yield: 6 to 8 servings.

A Matter of Taste
The Junior League of Morristown, New Jersey

Swordfish with Greek Olives and Pasta

½ pound (1-inch-thick) swordfish steaks
¾ cup chopped Greek olives
1 small onion, thinly sliced
2 cloves garlic, minced
¼ cup olive oil
1 tablespoon capers
1 teaspoon dried whole oregano
1 (8-ounce) package spaghetti

Place swordfish steaks on a lightly greased rack in a shallow roasting pan; broil 6 inches from heat 3 minutes. Turn swordfish; broil 4 to 5 minutes or until fish flakes easily when tested with a fork. Cut swordfish steaks into thin strips. Set aside.

Sauté olives, onion, and garlic in oil in a large skillet over medium heat until tender. Stir in capers and oregano; remove from heat.

Cook pasta according to package directions; drain well. Place in a large bowl. Add olive mixture; toss gently to combine. Add swordfish strips to pasta mixture, and toss gently. Serve immediately. Yield: 4 servings.

More Than a Tea Party
The Junior League of Boston, Massachusetts

Fiesta Spaghetti

3 cups chopped onion
½ cup chopped celery
2 cloves garlic, crushed
½ cup vegetable oil
1 pound lean ground beef
1 (4-ounce) can mushroom
  stems and pieces,
  undrained
3 (6-ounce) cans tomato paste

1 cup water
2½ tablespoons chili powder
2 teaspoons salt
1 (16-ounce) package thin
  spaghetti
2 cups (8 ounces) shredded
  Cheddar cheese, divided
¾ cup evaporated milk

Sauté onion, celery, and garlic in oil in a large skillet until vegetables are tender. Add ground beef, and cook until browned, stirring to crumble meat; drain well. Add mushrooms and next 4 ingredients; stir well. Reduce heat, and simmer, uncovered, 15 minutes.

Cook spaghetti according to package directions; drain well. Place spaghetti in a greased 13- x 9- x 2-inch baking dish. Top with sauce, and sprinkle with 1 cup cheese. Pour milk over cheese, and sprinkle with remaining 1 cup cheese. Bake, uncovered, at 350° for 20 to 30 minutes or until cheese melts and mixture is thoroughly heated. Yield: 12 servings.   Diane S. Thompson

Aggies, Moms, and Apple Pie
The Federation of Texas A&M University Mothers' Clubs
College Station, Texas

Lemon Pasta with Chicken and Zucchini

5 small zucchini, cut into
  julienne strips
¼ cup plus 1 tablespoon
  olive oil
2 (6-ounce) chicken breast
  halves, skinned, boned, and
  cut into 1-inch pieces
3 cups chopped onion

1 clove garlic, crushed
⅔ cup whipping cream
¾ cup freshly grated
  Parmesan cheese, divided
¼ teaspoon salt
⅛ teaspoon pepper
Lemon Pasta

Sauté zucchini in olive oil in a large skillet until tender. Remove zucchini with a slotted spoon, and drain well on paper towels.

Add chicken, onion, and garlic to oil in skillet; cook over medium heat, stirring frequently, 8 to 10 minutes or until chicken is done. Add whipping cream; bring to a boil, reduce heat, and simmer 5 minutes or until liquid is reduced by about one third. Add reserved zucchini, ½ cup Parmesan cheese, salt, pepper, and cooked Lemon Pasta; cook until thoroughly heated. Sprinkle with remaining ¼ cup Parmesan cheese. Yield: 6 to 8 servings.

Lemon Pasta

3 to 3½ cups all-purpose
  flour, divided
1 teaspoon salt
3 eggs, lightly beaten
2 teaspoons grated lemon rind

½ cup lemon juice
1 tablespoon vegetable oil
4 quarts water
1 tablespoon salt

Combine 3 cups flour and 1 teaspoon salt in a large bowl; stir well. Make a well in center of mixture. Combine eggs and next 3 ingredients; stir well. Add to flour mixture; stir well to combine.

Turn dough out onto a lightly floured surface; shape into a ball. Knead until smooth and elastic (about 10 to 15 minutes). Add enough remaining ½ cup flour, 1 tablespoon at a time, to keep dough from sticking to hands. Dust dough lightly with flour, and wrap in plastic wrap; let rest 10 minutes.

Divide dough into 4 equal portions. Working with 1 portion at a time, pass dough through smooth rollers of pasta machine on widest setting. Continue moving width gauge to narrower settings, passing dough through rollers once at each setting until about 1/16-inch thick. (Dust dough with flour to prevent sticking, if necessary.)

Pass each sheet of pasta through the linguine cutting rollers of machine. Hang pasta on a wooden drying rack (dry no longer than 30 minutes). Repeat procedure with remaining portions of dough.

Combine water and 1 tablespoon salt in a large Dutch oven. Bring to a boil; add pasta, and cook 2 to 3 minutes or until al dente. Yield: about 8 cups.

Recipes & Recollections from Terrace Hill
The Terrace Hill Society
Des Moines, Iowa

Thick and Rich Macaroni and Cheese

1 (12-ounce) package elbow macaroni
1 cup finely chopped green pepper
¾ cup finely chopped onion
½ cup butter or margarine, melted
2 tablespoons all-purpose flour
1 (12-ounce) can evaporated milk

½ cup milk
4 cups (16 ounces) shredded sharp Cheddar cheese, divided
1 (8-ounce) package process American cheese, cubed
⅛ teaspoon pepper
1 (2-ounce) jar diced pimiento, drained
Paprika

Cook macaroni according to package directions; drain well, and set aside.

Sauté green pepper and onion in butter in a saucepan until vegetables are tender. Add flour, stirring well. Cook 1 minute, stirring constantly. Gradually add milks; cook over medium heat, stirring constantly, until mixture is thickened and bubbly. Add 3 cups Cheddar cheese, process American cheese, and pepper; stir until cheeses melt. Add reserved macaroni to cheese sauce; stir well.

Pour macaroni mixture into a greased 3-quart baking dish. Bake, uncovered, at 350° for 20 minutes. Sprinkle with remaining 1 cup Cheddar cheese, pimiento, and paprika. Bake 5 minutes or until cheese melts and mixture is hot and bubbly. Yield: 8 to 10 servings.

Wild about Texas
The Cypress-Woodlands Junior Forum
Houston, Texas

Tortellini con Prosciutto

2 cloves garlic, crushed
¼ cup olive oil
1 tablespoon butter or
  margarine, melted
½ pound prosciutto, chopped
1 (16-ounce) can whole
  tomatoes, undrained and
  chopped
1 (10¾-ounce) can tomato
  puree
1 cup canned undiluted
  chicken broth
½ cup grated Romano cheese

1 teaspoon dried whole
  oregano
1 teaspoon pepper
¼ cup Marsala wine
2 (8-ounce) packages fresh
  cheese- or meat-filled
  tortellini
¼ cup grated Romano cheese
1 tablespoon butter or
  margarine, melted
2 tablespoons chopped fresh
  parsley

Sauté garlic in olive oil and 1 tablespoon melted butter in a large saucepan until golden brown. Add prosciutto and next 6 ingredients; bring to a boil. Reduce heat, and simmer 15 to 20 minutes or until mixture thickens. Add wine, and cook 1 to 2 minutes.

Cook tortellini according to package directions. Drain; place in a bowl. Add ¼ cup Romano cheese and 1 tablespoon butter; toss. Pour prosciutto mixture over tortellini; toss. Sprinkle with parsley. Yield: 4 to 6 servings.   Creighton Brittell

Capital Connoisseur
The Lawrence Center Independence House
Schenectady, New York

Orzo Gratin

3 quarts water
1 (16-ounce) package orzo
6 cloves garlic, unpeeled
1 cup whipping cream
1 cup canned diluted chicken
  broth
1¼ cups minced fresh
  parsley, divided

1 cup freshly grated
  Parmesan cheese, divided
Salt and pepper to taste
¼ cup fine, dry breadcrumbs
3 tablespoons unsalted butter
  or margarine

Bring water to a boil in a large Dutch oven. Add orzo and garlic, and return to a boil; cook 10 minutes. Drain; rinse in cold water, and drain again. Remove garlic; peel and crush garlic. Set orzo aside.

Combine garlic and whipping cream in a large bowl; beat with a wire whisk until blended. Add orzo, chicken broth, 1 cup minced parsley, ¾ cup Parmesan cheese, and salt and pepper to taste; stir well.

Place mixture in a greased 2-quart baking dish. Combine breadcrumbs, remaining ¼ cup parsley, and remaining ¼ cup Parmesan cheese; stir well. Sprinkle crumb mixture over orzo mixture. Dot with butter. Bake at 325° for 1 hour and 15 minutes or until golden brown. Yield: 10 to 12 servings.

Cardinal Cuisine
The Mount Vernon Hospital Auxiliary
Alexandria, Virginia

Arancini (Italian Rice Balls)

2⅔ cups water
1⅓ cups long-grain rice, uncooked
2 cloves garlic
1 bay leaf
¾ teaspoon salt
Freshly ground pepper to taste
1 cup (4 ounces) diced mozzarella cheese
4 ounces prosciutto, finely chopped
¼ cup chopped fresh basil
2 teaspoons olive oil
5 egg whites, divided
3 tablespoons grated Parmesan cheese
1 teaspoon olive oil
1 cup fine, dry breadcrumbs
Vegetable oil

Bring water to a boil in a medium saucepan; add rice and next 4 ingredients. Cover, reduce heat, and simmer 20 minutes or until rice is tender and liquid is absorbed. Remove from heat. Remove and discard bay leaf and garlic cloves. Let cool.

Combine mozzarella cheese, prosciutto, basil, and 2 teaspoons olive oil, tossing gently; set aside. Stir 3 egg whites and Parmesan cheese into reserved rice. Add prosciutto mixture; stir well. With wet hands, shape rice mixture into 12 balls; set aside.

Combine remaining 2 egg whites and 1 teaspoon olive oil. Dip rice balls into egg white mixture; roll in breadcrumbs. Fry rice balls in deep hot vegetable oil (375°) 4 minutes or until golden; drain. Serve immediately. Yield: 1 dozen.   Rose Caravello Verbeski

A Taste of Memories from the Old "Bush"
The Italian-American Women's Mutual Aid Society
Madison, Wisconsin

Fried Rice

3 cups water
1 pound unpeeled
  medium-size fresh shrimp
3 cups water
1½ teaspoons salt
1½ cups long-grain rice,
  uncooked
4 slices bacon, chopped
3 eggs, lightly beaten
⅛ teaspoon pepper

2 tablespoons vegetable oil
2 teaspoons peeled, grated
  fresh ginger
½ pound cooked lean pork,
  cut into thin strips
8 green onions, finely
  chopped
2 to 3 tablespoons soy
  sauce

Bring 3 cups water to a boil; add shrimp, and cook 3 to 5 minutes. Drain well; rinse with cold water. Chill. Peel and devein shrimp. Coarsely chop shrimp, and set aside.

Combine 3 cups water and salt in a heavy saucepan; bring to a boil. Gradually add rice, stirring constantly. Cover, reduce heat, and simmer 25 minutes or until rice is tender and liquid is absorbed. Remove from heat, and set aside.

Cook bacon in a wok or electric skillet until crisp; remove bacon, reserving 1 tablespoon drippings. Crumble bacon, and set aside. Set aside 1½ teaspoons drippings, and return 1½ teaspoons drippings to wok.

Combine beaten eggs and pepper in a medium bowl; stir well with a wire whisk.

Pour half of egg mixture into wok, and cook until eggs are set, tilting wok so that uncooked portion covers bottom of wok. Remove egg "pancake" from wok, and let cool. Roll up egg, and cut into thin strips; set aside. Repeat procedure with remaining 1½ teaspoons drippings and remaining egg mixture.

Add oil and ginger to wok, and sauté just until ginger is golden brown. Add reserved cooked rice, and stir-fry 5 minutes. Add reserved shrimp, bacon, egg strips, pork, green onions, and soy sauce; stir-fry 4 to 5 minutes or until mixture is thoroughly heated. Yield: 6 to 8 servings.   Jun Seen

Recipes to Cherish
Women's Missionary and Service Commission
Harrisonburg, Virginia

Peas and Rice Casserole

¼ cup chopped onion
2 tablespoons chopped fresh
  parsley
¼ cup butter or margarine,
  melted
1 cup long-grain rice,
  uncooked

2 cups water
1 (10-ounce) package frozen
  English peas
1 teaspoon salt
¼ cup grated Parmesan
  cheese

Sauté onion and parsley in melted butter in a large skillet until tender. Add rice, and sauté 5 minutes, stirring frequently. Add water; bring to a boil. Cover, reduce heat, and simmer 15 minutes or until rice is tender and liquid is absorbed.

Cook peas according to package directions; drain. Add peas and salt to rice; stir well. Transfer rice mixture to a serving dish; sprinkle with Parmesan cheese. Yield: 6 to 8 servings.

Hearts & Flour
The Women's Club of Pittsford, New York

Chile Rice Casserole

1 cup long-grain rice,
  uncooked
2 tablespoons butter or
  margarine
1 (8-ounce) carton sour cream

1 (4-ounce) can chopped
  green chiles, drained
3 cups (12 ounces) shredded
  Monterey Jack cheese

Cook rice according to package directions; add butter, stirring until butter melts. Combine sour cream and chiles; add to rice mixture, stirring well.

Place half of rice mixture in a greased 1½-quart casserole; sprinkle with 1½ cups cheese. Repeat layers with remaining rice mixture and 1½ cups cheese.

Cover and bake at 350° for 30 to 35 minutes or until cheese melts and mixture is thoroughly heated. Serve immediately. Yield: 4 to 6 servings.
Ruby Trow

Cal Poly Pomona 50th Anniversary
The Home Economics Alumni Association
Pomona, California

Charleston Rice

2 cups sliced fresh
  mushrooms
¾ cup chopped onion
½ cup chopped celery
⅓ cup chopped green pepper
1½ tablespoons butter or
  margarine, melted

1 pound bulk pork sausage
1 cup long-grain rice,
  uncooked
2 cups canned diluted
  chicken broth
2 tablespoons minced fresh
  parsley

Sauté first 4 ingredients in melted butter in a large skillet until vegetables are tender. Transfer vegetable mixture to a large bowl; set aside.

Cook sausage in a large heavy skillet over medium-high heat until browned, stirring to crumble meat; drain well. Add sausage, rice, chicken broth, and parsley to vegetable mixture; stir well. Transfer rice mixture to a greased 11- x 7- x 1½-inch baking dish. Cover and bake at 350° for 30 minutes. Remove cover, and stir gently. Cover and bake an additional 30 minutes or until rice is tender and liquid is absorbed. Yield: 8 servings.   Lyn Kennedy

Cookin' with the Lion
The Penn State Alumni Association
University Park, Pennsylvania

Rice Indienne

2 tablespoons butter or
  margarine
1 cup long-grain rice,
  uncooked
2 teaspoons curry powder
2 cups canned diluted
  chicken broth
⅔ cup raisins
⅓ cup chopped celery
⅓ cup chopped green onions
⅓ cup chopped green pepper

1 tablespoon butter or
  margarine, melted
2 tablespoons commercial
  chutney
2 tablespoons diced pimiento
2 tablespoons chopped
  blanched almonds
1 tablespoon brown sugar
1 tablespoon cider vinegar
½ teaspoon salt

Melt 2 tablespoons butter in a medium saucepan. Add rice and curry powder; cook over low heat 5 minutes, stirring occasionally.

Add chicken broth; bring to a boil. Cover, reduce heat, and simmer 13 to 15 minutes or until rice is tender and liquid is absorbed.

Sauté raisins, celery, green onions, and green pepper in 1 tablespoon melted butter in a small skillet until vegetables are tender. Add chutney and remaining ingredients; stir well.

Transfer rice to a serving dish; top with raisin mixture. Yield: 6 to 8 servings.

Capital Classics
The Junior League of Washington, DC

Rice Soufflé

2 tablespoons butter or margarine
2 tablespoons all-purpose flour
1½ cups milk
2 cups cooked long-grain rice
1½ cups (6 ounces) shredded sharp Cheddar cheese
1 tablespoon minced green onions
1 tablespoon minced fresh parsley
1 teaspoon salt
1 teaspoon Worcestershire sauce
¼ teaspoon hot sauce
3 eggs, separated

Melt butter in a heavy saucepan over low heat; add flour, stirring until smooth. Cook 1 minute, stirring constantly. Gradually add milk; cook over medium heat, stirring constantly, until mixture is thickened and bubbly. Add rice and next 6 ingredients; stir well. Remove from heat, and let cool completely.

Beat egg yolks at high speed of an electric mixer until thick and lemon colored. Add egg yolks to rice mixture; stir well.

Beat egg whites (at room temperature) at high speed until stiff peaks form. Fold one-third of beaten egg whites into rice mixture; gently fold in remaining egg whites.

Spoon rice mixture into an ungreased 1½-quart casserole. Bake, uncovered, at 325° for 45 minutes to 1 hour or until a knife inserted in center of soufflé comes out clean. Serve immediately. Yield: 6 servings.   Vivian Covey

Musical Tastes
Chancel and Bell Choirs, First United Methodist Church
Charlottesville, Virginia

Mexican Rice

1 cup chopped onion
¼ cup butter or margarine,
  melted
4 cups cooked long-grain rice
1 (12-ounce) carton
  small-curd cottage cheese
1 large bay leaf, crushed

½ teaspoon salt
⅛ teaspoon pepper
2 (4-ounce) cans chopped
  green chiles, drained
2 cups (8 ounces) shredded
  sharp Cheddar cheese
Chopped fresh parsley

Sauté onion in butter in a skillet 3 minutes or until tender.
Combine sautéed onion, rice, and next 4 ingredients; stir well.

Layer rice mixture and chiles in an 11- x 7- x 1½-inch dish;
sprinkle with cheese and parsley. Bake, uncovered, at 375° for 25
minutes or until cheese melts. Yield: 6 servings.   Beth Lilleston

641.5 "Show Me" Recipes
The Missouri Association of School Librarians
Glen Carbon, Illinois

Creole Rice Pilaf

2¼ cups canned diluted
  chicken broth
¼ cup Chablis or other dry
  white wine
¼ cup plus 2 tablespoons
  butter
1 cup long-grain brown rice,
  uncooked
¼ cup finely chopped onion
¼ teaspoon salt
1¼ cups sliced fresh
  mushrooms

2 tablespoons butter, melted
2 medium tomatoes, peeled,
  seeded, and diced
1 clove garlic, crushed
½ teaspoon dried whole
  oregano
¼ teaspoon pepper
1 ripe avocado, peeled and
  diced
1 tablespoon lemon juice
½ teaspoon dried parsley
  flakes

Combine chicken broth, wine, and ¼ cup plus 2 tablespoons
butter in a medium saucepan. Bring to a boil; add rice, onion, and ¼
teaspoon salt. Cover, reduce heat, and simmer 45 to 50 minutes or
until rice is tender and liquid is absorbed.

Sauté mushrooms in 2 tablespoons melted butter in a medium
skillet 3 minutes or until tender. Add tomato, garlic, oregano, and
pepper; reduce heat, and simmer 5 minutes.

Combine avocado and lemon juice in a small bowl; toss gently. Add avocado to rice mixture, tossing gently to combine. Sprinkle with parsley; toss gently. Serve immediately. Yield: 6 to 8 servings.

Celebrations on the Bayou
The Junior League of Monroe, Louisiana

Rice and Pecan Casserole

1 pound sliced fresh mushrooms
4 green onions, sliced
1 clove garlic, minced
½ cup unsalted butter or margarine, melted
2 cups long-grain brown rice, uncooked
1 teaspoon salt
½ teaspoon dried whole thyme

¼ teaspoon freshly ground pepper
¼ teaspoon ground turmeric
3 (10½-ounce) cans beef broth, undiluted
2¼ cups water
1½ cups chopped pecans
Garnishes: whole pecans and sliced green onion tops

Sauté mushrooms, sliced green onions, and garlic in melted butter in a Dutch oven until vegetables are tender. Add rice; cook over medium heat 3 minutes, stirring constantly. Add salt and next 3 ingredients; stir well. Add broth, water, and chopped pecans; bring to a boil. Remove from heat. Cover and bake at 325° for 1 hour and 20 minutes or until rice is tender and liquid is absorbed. Garnish, if desired. Yield: 12 to 14 servings.

Marblehead Cooks
Tower School Associates
Marblehead, Massachusetts

The Junior League of Monroe will use funds generated from the sale of Celebrations on the Bayou *to support programs concerning child advocacy, historical preservation, and substance abuse prevention.*

Summer Wild Rice

1 (4-ounce) package wild rice
Lemon Vinaigrette, divided
⅓ cup currants
⅓ cup orange juice
½ cup peeled, seeded, and
  sliced cucumber
¼ cup chopped purple onion
  or green onions
¼ cup chopped fresh
  parsley

1 tablespoon grated orange
  rind
Freshly ground pepper to
  taste
1 ripe avocado, peeled and
  coarsely chopped
½ cup chopped pecans or
  walnuts (optional)
¼ cup chopped fresh mint
  (optional)

Cook rice according to package directions; drain. Combine rice and ½ cup Lemon Vinaigrette; let cool to room temperature.

Combine currants and orange juice; let stand 15 minutes. Drain well, discarding orange juice. Combine rice mixture, currants, cucumber, and next 4 ingredients. Add remaining ¼ cup Lemon Vinaigrette; toss gently to combine. Add avocado and, if desired, pecans and mint; toss well. Yield: 4 to 6 servings.

Lemon Vinaigrette

⅓ cup lemon juice
1 teaspoon salt
½ teaspoon sugar

¼ teaspoon pepper
⅔ cup olive oil

Position knife blade in food processor bowl; add first 4 ingredients, and process until blended. With processor running, pour olive oil through food chute in a slow, steady stream, processing until blended. Yield: ¾ cup.

Stirring Performances
The Junior League of Winston-Salem, North Carolina

Cracked Wheat-Lentil Casserole

6 cups tomato juice, divided
1 cup dried lentils
1 cup cracked wheat,
  uncooked
1 pound ground beef or lamb

1 onion, chopped
1½ teaspoons salt
1 teaspoon chili powder
¼ teaspoon dried whole
  oregano

Combine 4 cups tomato juice, lentils, and cracked wheat in a 13- x 9- x 2-inch baking dish; cover tightly, and let stand at room temperature 6 to 8 hours. Bake lentil mixture at 300° for 1 hour, stirring occasionally.

Cook ground beef in a large skillet over medium heat until browned, stirring to crumble meat. Add chopped onion, and cook over medium-high heat until onion is tender; drain.

Add ground beef mixture, remaining 2 cups tomato juice, salt, chili powder, and oregano to lentil mixture in baking dish, stirring well. Cover tightly, and bake at 300° for 30 minutes. Remove cover, and bake an additional 30 minutes or until lentils are tender. Yield: 8 to 10 servings.   Barbara Coan Houghton

Friends Come in All Flavors
Buckingham Friends School
Lahaska, Pennsylvania

Bulgur Pilaf with Green Peppercorns

2 tablespoons whole green
  peppercorns
1 small onion, diced
¼ cup plus 2 tablespoons
  butter or margarine,
  melted
4 cups canned diluted
  chicken broth

2 cups bulgur wheat,
  uncooked
1 teaspoon salt
½ cup chopped fresh
  parsley

Place peppercorns in a small bowl; add water to cover. Let stand at least 10 minutes. Drain; discard water. Set peppercorns aside.

Sauté diced onion in melted butter in a large saucepan 5 minutes or until tender. Add peppercorns, chicken broth, bulgur, and salt. Bring to a boil; cover, reduce heat, and simmer 15 minutes or until bulgur is tender. Drain and let cool slightly. Stir in parsley. Yield: 8 servings.   Elaine W. Hoppe Mueller

Palate Pleasers II
Redeemer Women's Guild
Elmhurst, Illinois

Cajun Golden Garlic Cheese Grits

4 cups water
1 teaspoon salt
1 cup regular grits, uncooked
½ cup butter or margarine
1 (6-ounce) roll process
  cheese spread with garlic
2 tablespoons Worcestershire
  sauce

Freshly ground pepper to
  taste
Ground red pepper to taste
2 eggs, separated
Paprika

Combine water and salt in a large saucepan; bring to a boil. Stir in grits. Cover, reduce heat, and simmer 10 minutes, stirring occasionally. Remove from heat. Add butter and next 4 ingredients, stirring until cheese melts.

Beat egg yolks at high speed of an electric mixer. Stir a small amount of hot grits into beaten yolks; add to remaining hot grits, stirring constantly.

Beat egg whites (at room temperature) at high speed of electric mixer until stiff peaks form. Gently fold egg whites into grits. Pour mixture into a greased 2-quart casserole; sprinkle with paprika. Bake at 350° for 45 minutes or until lightly browned. Yield: 6 to 8 servings.   Charlotte Dix

Heavenly Delights
United Methodist Women, First United Methodist Church
Noblesville, Indiana

Pies & Pastries

Located in Woodstock, Vermont, this inviting porch is at the home of George Perkins Marsh, a noted diplomat, scholar, and pioneer conservationist in the fields of resource management and ecology.

Apple Crisp Pie

¾ cup (3 ounces) finely
  shredded Cheddar cheese
⅓ cup sugar
2 tablespoons all-purpose
  flour
½ teaspoon ground cinnamon
¾ teaspoon grated lemon
  rind

4 large cooking apples,
  peeled, cored, and thinly
  sliced (about 5½ cups)
2 tablespoons lemon juice
1 unbaked 9-inch pastry shell
Topping (recipe follows)

Combine shredded cheese, sugar, flour, cinnamon, and lemon
rind in a small bowl; stir well, and set aside.

Combine apple slices and lemon juice in a large bowl; toss gently
to coat well. Sprinkle cheese mixture over apple mixture; toss gently
to combine.

Arrange apple mixture in pastry shell; sprinkle with topping.
Bake at 375° for 30 minutes. Cover edges of pastry with strips of
aluminum foil to prevent excessive browning. Bake an additional 20
to 25 minutes. Yield: one 9-inch pie.

Topping

⅓ cup all-purpose flour
⅓ cup firmly packed brown
  sugar
½ teaspoon ground
  cinnamon
¼ teaspoon ground allspice

⅛ teaspoon ground mace
¼ cup butter or margarine
⅓ cup regular oats,
  uncooked
⅓ cup chopped walnuts

Combine first 5 ingredients in a small bowl; cut in butter with a
pastry blender until mixture resembles coarse meal. Stir in oats and
walnuts. Yield: about 1⅓ cups.   Kathy Lickiss

Crème de la Congregation
Our Saviors Lutheran Church
Lafayette, California

Calico Apple Pie

½ cup raisins
½ cup Burgundy or other dry
  red wine
4 large cooking apples,
  peeled, cored, and sliced

1 unbaked 9-inch pastry shell
1 cup sugar, divided
1 teaspoon ground cinnamon
¾ cup all-purpose flour
⅓ cup butter or margarine

Combine raisins and wine in a small bowl; let stand at least 8 hours. Drain well; discard wine.

Combine raisins and apple slices; place in pastry shell. Combine ½ cup sugar and cinnamon in a small bowl; stir well. Sprinkle over apple mixture.

Combine remaining ½ cup sugar and flour; stir well. Cut in butter with a pastry blender until mixture resembles coarse meal. Sprinkle crumb mixture evenly over apple mixture. Bake at 400° for 20 minutes. Cover edges of pastry with strips of aluminum foil to prevent excessive browning. Bake an additional 30 minutes. Yield: one 9-inch pie.   Sara Danforth Aasland

South Dakota Centennial Cookbook
The South Dakota Historical Society
Pierre, South Dakota

Fresh Peach 'n' Praline Pie

1 teaspoon all-purpose flour
1 unbaked 9-inch pastry shell
½ cup light corn syrup
3 eggs
¼ cup sugar
3 tablespoons all-purpose
  flour
¼ teaspoon salt
¼ teaspoon freshly grated
  nutmeg
3 cups peeled, cubed fresh
  peaches

½ cup butter or margarine,
  melted
½ cup coarsely chopped
  pecans
¼ cup all-purpose flour
¼ cup firmly packed brown
  sugar
2 tablespoons butter or
  margarine, softened
Whipped cream (optional)
Vanilla ice cream (optional)

Sprinkle 1 teaspoon flour over unbaked pastry shell; set aside.

Combine syrup, eggs, ¼ cup sugar, 3 tablespoons flour, salt, and nutmeg in a large bowl; beat at medium speed of an electric mixer 1 minute. Stir in peaches and ½ cup melted butter. Pour peach mixture into prepared pastry shell.

Combine pecans, ¼ cup flour, and ¼ cup brown sugar in a medium bowl, stirring well. Cut in 2 tablespoons butter with a pastry blender until mixture resembles coarse meal. Sprinkle pecan mixture evenly over peach mixture.

Bake at 350° for 45 to 50 minutes or until pie is set. Let cool completely. If desired, serve pie with whipped cream or vanilla ice cream. Yield: one 9-inch pie.

More Than a Tea Party
The Junior League of Boston, Massachusetts

Pear Crunch Pie

6 medium-size ripe pears, peeled, cored, and sliced
2 tablespoons lemon juice
½ cup sugar
¼ cup all-purpose flour
1 teaspoon grated lemon rind
1 unbaked 10-inch pastry shell

1 cup all-purpose flour
½ cup firmly packed brown sugar
¼ teaspoon ground cinnamon
¼ teaspoon ground nutmeg
½ cup butter or margarine
½ cup chopped pecans

Combine pears and lemon juice in a large bowl; toss gently. Sprinkle with ½ cup sugar, ¼ cup flour, and lemon rind; toss well. Arrange pear mixture in pastry shell. Set aside.

Combine 1 cup flour, brown sugar, cinnamon, and nutmeg in a medium bowl; stir well. Cut in butter with a pastry blender until mixture resembles coarse meal. Stir in chopped pecans; sprinkle pecan mixture evenly over pear mixture. Bake at 400° for 25 to 30 minutes or until pears are tender and crust is golden brown. Yield: one 10-inch pie.   JoAnn Copeland

Rosemalers' Recipes
The Vesterheim-Norwegian American Museum
Decorah, Iowa

Macadamia Nut Pie

7 eggs, lightly beaten
¾ cup sugar
¾ cup butter or margarine,
  melted
¾ cup honey
1 cup flaked coconut

1 unbaked 9-inch pastry shell
1½ cups chopped macadamia
  nuts
1 cup whipping cream,
  whipped

Combine eggs, sugar, butter, and honey in a large bowl; stir with a wire whisk until well blended.

Sprinkle coconut in pastry shell. Gently pour egg mixture over coconut; sprinkle with nuts. Bake at 325° for 50 minutes or until a knife inserted in center comes out clean. Let cool completely. Top with whipped cream. Yield: one 9-inch pie.   Helen Paulson

The Village Gourmet
The Historical Society of Bedford, Ohio

Holiday Walnut Pie

½ cup sugar
½ cup firmly packed brown
  sugar
¼ cup butter or margarine,
  melted
¼ teaspoon salt
3 eggs, beaten

½ cup evaporated milk
¼ cup light corn syrup
½ teaspoon vanilla extract
1 cup coarsely chopped
  walnuts
1 unbaked 9-inch pastry shell

Combine sugars, butter, and salt in a large bowl; stir well. Add eggs and next 4 ingredients; stir well. Pour filling into pastry shell. Bake at 400° for 25 to 30 minutes or until a knife inserted in center comes out clean. (Cover edges of pastry with strips of aluminum foil to prevent excessive browning, if necessary.) Let cool completely. Yield: one 9-inch pie.   Callie Pritchett

In the Pink of Things
The Muskogee Regional Medical Center Auxiliary
Muskogee, Oklahoma

Colonial Innkeeper's Pie

1 cup all-purpose flour
½ teaspoon salt
⅓ cup plus 1 tablespoon
  shortening
2 tablespoons cold water
1½ (1-ounce) squares
  unsweetened chocolate
½ cup water
⅔ cup sugar
¼ cup butter or margarine
1½ teaspoons vanilla extract
¼ cup shortening
1 cup all-purpose flour

¾ cup sugar
1 teaspoon baking powder
½ teaspoon salt
½ cup milk
1 egg
½ teaspoon vanilla
  extract
½ cup chopped pecans or
  walnuts
Garnishes: whipped cream
  and grated semisweet
  chocolate

Combine 1 cup flour and ½ teaspoon salt; cut in ⅓ cup plus 1 tablespoon shortening with a pastry blender until mixture resembles coarse meal. Sprinkle 2 tablespoons cold water (1 tablespoon at a time) over surface; stir with a fork until dry ingredients are moistened. Shape into a ball; chill.

Roll pastry to ⅛-inch thickness on a lightly floured surface. Place in a 9-inch pieplate; trim off excess pastry along edges. Fold edges under and flute; set aside.

Combine unsweetened chocolate and ½ cup water in a small saucepan. Cook over low heat, stirring until chocolate melts. Add ⅔ cup sugar; stir well. Bring to a boil, stirring constantly. Remove from heat; add butter and 1½ teaspoons vanilla, stirring until butter melts. Set aside.

Cream ¼ cup shortening. Combine 1 cup flour, ¾ cup sugar, baking powder, and ½ teaspoon salt. Add flour mixture to creamed shortening alternately with milk, beginning and ending with flour mixture. Mix just until blended after each addition. Add egg; beat well. Stir in ½ teaspoon vanilla.

Pour filling into pastry shell. Drizzle reserved chocolate mixture over filling. Sprinkle with pecans. Bake at 350° for 45 to 50 minutes or until a wooden pick inserted in center comes out clean. Garnish, if desired. Serve warm or cool. Yield: one 9-inch pie.

Concertos for Cooks
North Group, Symphony Women's Committee
Indianapolis, Indiana

Famous Buttermilk Pie

½ cup butter or margarine,
  softened
1¼ cups sugar
1 tablespoon cornstarch
½ teaspoon salt

3 eggs
½ cup buttermilk
1 teaspoon vanilla extract
1 unbaked 9-inch pastry shell

Cream butter; gradually add sugar, cornstarch, and salt, beating well at medium speed of an electric mixer. Add eggs, one at a time, beating well after each addition. Stir in buttermilk and vanilla.

Pour filling into pastry shell. Place in a preheated 425° oven. Reduce heat to 350°, and bake 50 minutes or until pie is set. Yield: one 9-inch pie.   Dr. Frances Riley

Gracious Goodness: The Taste of Memphis
The Symphony League of Memphis, Tennessee

Maple Syrup Pie

1 cup pure maple syrup
½ cup water
3 tablespoons cornstarch
3 tablespoons cold water
2 tablespoons butter

¼ cup chopped pecans or
  walnuts
Pastry for double-crust
  9-inch pie

Combine maple syrup and ½ cup water in a small saucepan. Bring to a boil, and boil 5 minutes. Combine cornstarch and 3 tablespoons cold water, stirring well. Add cornstarch mixture to syrup mixture, stirring well. Cook over medium heat, stirring constantly, until mixture thickens and comes to a boil. Remove from heat. Add butter and pecans, stirring until butter melts. Let cool slightly.

Divide pastry in half. Roll one half of pastry to ⅛-inch thickness on a lightly floured surface, and place in a 9-inch pieplate. Spoon filling into pastry shell. Roll remaining half of pastry to ⅛-inch thickness; transfer to top of pie. Trim off excess pastry along edges. Fold edges under and flute. Cut slits in top crust to allow steam to escape. Bake at 400° for 25 to 30 minutes or until crust is golden brown. Yield: one 9-inch pie.   Roxanne Menard

Cuisine à la Mode
Les Dames Richelieu du Rhode Island
Woonsocket, Rhode Island

Fresh Blueberry Pie

¾ cup sugar
2 tablespoons cornstarch
⅛ teaspoon salt
¼ cup water
4½ cups fresh blueberries, divided
1 tablespoon butter or margarine

1 tablespoon lemon juice
1 baked 9-inch pastry shell
Garnishes: whipped cream, grated lemon rind, and fresh blueberries

Combine first 3 ingredients in a medium saucepan; add water, and stir well. Add 2¼ cups blueberries. Cook over medium heat, stirring constantly, until mixture thickens and comes to a boil; boil 1 minute. Remove from heat; add butter and lemon juice, stirring until butter melts. Let cool.

Place remaining 2¼ cups blueberries in bottom of prepared pastry shell. Pour cooled blueberry mixture over blueberries. Cover and chill at least 4 hours. Garnish, if desired. Yield: one 9-inch pie.

A Matter of Taste
The Junior League of Morristown, New Jersey

Published by the Memphis Symphony League, **Gracious Goodness: The Taste of Memphis** *explores Memphis, Tennessee, and its people. The publishers went behind the scenes to homes, places of business, and community events to provide a glimpse of the city's history and way of life. The Memphis Symphony League is dedicated to supporting the orchestra by raising funds, increasing concert subscriptions, and sponsoring educational programs in the field of music.*

Coconut-Pineapple Pie

9 coconut macaroons,
  crushed
1 cup shredded coconut
3 tablespoons butter or
  margarine, melted
1 (20-ounce) can unsweetened
  crushed pineapple,
  undrained
¾ cup sugar

1 tablespoon lemon juice
½ teaspoon salt
1 envelope unflavored
  gelatin
½ cup cold water
3 eggs, separated
1 cup whipping cream,
  whipped and divided

Reserve 2 tablespoons crushed macaroons for garnish; set aside. Combine remaining crushed macaroons, shredded coconut, and melted butter in a medium bowl; stir well. Firmly press crumb mixture evenly in bottom and up the sides of a buttered 9-inch pieplate. Bake at 300° for 20 minutes; let cool.

Press pineapple through a sieve, reserving 1 cup juice.

Combine pineapple juice, pineapple, sugar, lemon juice, and salt in a medium saucepan. Cook over medium heat, stirring constantly, until sugar dissolves.

Sprinkle gelatin over cold water in a small bowl; let stand 1 minute. Add gelatin mixture to pineapple mixture; cook over low heat, stirring until gelatin dissolves.

Beat egg yolks at high speed of an electric mixer until thick and lemon colored. Gradually stir about one-fourth of hot mixture into yolks; add to remaining hot mixture, stirring constantly. Cook over medium heat, stirring constantly, until mixture thickens slightly and comes to a boil. Transfer to a medium bowl, and chill until the consistency of unbeaten egg white.

Beat egg whites (at room temperature) at high speed until stiff peaks form. Gently fold beaten egg whites into chilled pineapple mixture. Fold in half of whipped cream. Pour into prepared crust; chill until firm. Pipe or spoon remaining half of whipped cream over chilled pie. Sprinkle with reserved 2 tablespoons crushed macaroons. Yield: one 9-inch pie.   Diane Hill

Cal Poly Pomona 50th Anniversary
The Home Economics Alumni Association
Pomona, California

Piña Colada Chiffon Pie

1 cup graham cracker
crumbs
⅓ cup flaked coconut
¼ cup butter or margarine,
melted
1 (20-ounce) can unsweetened
crushed pineapple,
undrained
2 envelopes unflavored
gelatin

1 (15-ounce) can cream of
coconut
2 eggs, separated
⅓ cup orange juice
1 cup whipping cream,
whipped
¼ cup sugar
Garnishes: pineapple chunks
and toasted flaked coconut

Combine graham cracker crumbs, ⅓ cup flaked coconut, and melted butter in a small bowl; stir well. Firmly press crumb mixture evenly in bottom and up the sides of a 9-inch pieplate. Cover and freeze at least 30 minutes.

Drain crushed pineapple, reserving juice. Set crushed pineapple aside. Sprinkle gelatin over pineapple juice in a small saucepan; let stand 1 minute. Cook over low heat, stirring until gelatin dissolves. Remove from heat, and set side.

Combine cream of coconut and egg yolks in a medium saucepan, stirring well. Cook over low heat 5 minutes, stirring constantly. Remove from heat; add gelatin mixture, stirring well. Stir in reserved crushed pineapple and orange juice. Pour mixture into a large bowl; let cool 15 minutes. Cover and chill 45 minutes or until the consistency of unbeaten egg white.

Beat chilled gelatin mixture at high speed of an electric mixer just until foamy. Fold whipped cream into gelatin mixture.

Beat egg whites (at room temperature) at high speed of electric mixer until foamy. Gradually add sugar, 1 tablespoon at a time, beating until stiff peaks form and sugar dissolves (2 to 4 minutes). Gently fold beaten egg whites into gelatin mixture. Spoon filling into prepared crust. Chill pie at least 1 hour. Garnish, if desired. Yield: one 9-inch pie.   Connie DeWell

Indiana University Northwest Staff Cookbook
Indiana University Northwest Staff Council
Gary, Indiana

Sour Cream-Lime Pie

1½ cups graham cracker
  crumbs
½ cup sugar
¼ cup plus 2 tablespoons
  butter or margarine, melted
1 cup sugar
3 tablespoons cornstarch
1 tablespoon grated lime or
  lemon rind

1 cup whipping cream
⅓ cup fresh lime juice
¼ cup butter or margarine
1 (8-ounce) carton sour cream
1 cup whipping cream
¼ cup sugar
¾ cup sour cream
1½ teaspoons vanilla extract

Combine crumbs, ½ cup sugar, and ¼ cup plus 2 tablespoons butter; stir well. Firmly press crumb mixture evenly in bottom and up the sides of a 9-inch pieplate. Bake at 350° for 10 to 12 minutes or until lightly browned. Remove from oven; let cool.

Combine 1 cup sugar, cornstarch, and lime rind in a medium saucepan. Gradually add 1 cup whipping cream, stirring until smooth. Add lime juice and ¼ cup butter; cook over medium heat, stirring constantly, until butter melts and mixture thickens and comes to a boil. Remove from heat; let cool. Add sour cream, stirring well. Pour lime mixture into prepared crust.

Beat 1 cup whipping cream at high speed of an electric mixer until foamy; gradually add ¼ cup sugar, beating until soft peaks form. Fold in ¾ cup sour cream and vanilla. Spread whipped cream mixture over filling. Chill at least 4 hours. Yield: one 9-inch pie.

Seasoned with Sun
The Junior League of El Paso, Texas

Baked Chocolate Pie

1½ cups sugar
3 tablespoons cornstarch
¼ teaspoon salt
2 eggs, lightly beaten
1 teaspoon vanilla extract
4 (1-ounce) squares
  unsweetened chocolate

¼ cup butter
1 (12-ounce) can evaporated
  milk
1 unbaked 9-inch pastry shell
Garnish: whipped cream

Combine first 3 ingredients in a medium bowl; add eggs and vanilla, stirring well. Set aside.

Combine chocolate and butter in top of a double boiler; bring water to a boil. Reduce heat to low; cook until chocolate and butter melt, stirring occasionally. Gradually add milk, beating with a wire whisk until well blended. Add egg mixture, stirring well to combine.

Pour chocolate mixture into pastry shell. Bake at 375° for 45 minutes. Let cool slightly. Chill at least 4 hours. Garnish, if desired. Yield: one 9-inch pie.   JoAnn Gregory

Calling All Cooks Two
The Telephone Pioneers of America
Birmingham, Alabama

German Chocolate Pie

⅓ cup sugar
3 tablespoons cornstarch
1½ cups milk
1 (4-ounce) bar sweet baking chocolate, broken into pieces
1 tablespoon butter or margarine
2 egg yolks, beaten

1 teaspoon vanilla extract
1 baked 9-inch pastry shell
1 egg, beaten
½ cup sugar
¼ cup butter or margarine
1 (5.3-ounce) can evaporated milk
1⅓ cups flaked coconut
⅔ cup chopped pecans

Combine ⅓ cup sugar and cornstarch in a medium saucepan. Gradually add 1½ cups milk, stirring well. Add chocolate and 1 tablespoon butter; cook over medium heat, stirring constantly, until chocolate and butter melt and mixture thickens. Reduce heat, and cook 2 minutes, stirring constantly. Gradually stir about one-fourth of hot mixture into 2 egg yolks. Add to remaining hot mixture, stirring constantly. Cook over medium heat until mixture thickens; cook an additional 2 minutes. Remove from heat, and stir in vanilla. Pour chocolate mixture into pastry shell.

Combine egg, ½ cup sugar, ¼ cup butter, and evaporated milk in a saucepan. Cook over medium heat, stirring until mixture thickens. Remove from heat; add coconut and pecans, stirring well. Spread coconut mixture over filling. Let cool slightly. Cover and chill 4 hours. Yield: one 9-inch pie.   Renee Greene

A Taste of Hope
The Camarillo Chapter of City of Hope
Camarillo, California

Black Bottom Pie

1¼ cups chocolate wafer
   crumbs
¼ cup butter or margarine,
   melted
2 (1-ounce) squares
   unsweetened chocolate
⅓ cup sugar
1 tablespoon cornstarch
4 eggs, separated
2 cups whipping cream

1 teaspoon vanilla extract
1 envelope unflavored gelatin
¼ cup cold water
¼ cup light rum
¼ teaspoon cream of tartar
¼ cup sugar
Garnishes: whipped cream
   and grated semisweet
   chocolate

Combine chocolate wafer crumbs and melted butter in a medium bowl; stir well. Firmly press crumb mixture evenly in bottom and up the sides of a 10-inch pieplate. Bake at 350° for 8 minutes. Set aside, and let cool.

Place unsweetened chocolate in top of a double boiler; bring water to a boil. Reduce heat to low; cook until chocolate melts, stirring occasionally. Set aside.

Combine ⅓ cup sugar and cornstarch in top of double boiler. Add egg yolks; beat at medium speed of an electric mixer until thick and lemon colored. Stir in 2 cups whipping cream. Place over boiling water. Reduce heat to low; cook, stirring constantly, 35 minutes or until mixture coats the back of a metal spoon (do not boil). Remove from heat.

Combine 1 cup custard mixture and melted chocolate in a small bowl; stir in vanilla. Pour into prepared crust. Chill until set.

Sprinkle gelatin over cold water; let stand 1 minute. Add softened gelatin to remaining custard mixture. Place in top of double boiler; cook, stirring constantly, until gelatin dissolves. Pour into a large bowl. Chill 20 minutes or until the consistency of unbeaten egg white, stirring occasionally. Stir in rum.

Beat egg whites (at room temperature) and cream of tartar at high speed just until foamy. Gradually add ¼ cup sugar, 1 tablespoon at a time, beating until stiff peaks form and sugar dissolves (2 to 4 minutes). Fold beaten egg whites into thickened gelatin mixture. Spoon over chocolate layer in crust. Chill 4 hours. Garnish, if desired. Yield: one 10-inch pie.

Terry Home Presents Food & Fun from Celebrities & Us
Terry Home, Inc.
Sumner, Washington

Lemon Ribbon Layered Meringue Pie

¼ cup plus 2 tablespoons
   butter or margarine
1 cup sugar
Grated rind of 1 lemon
⅓ cup fresh lemon juice
⅛ teaspoon salt
2 eggs

2 egg yolks
1 quart vanilla ice cream,
   softened
1 baked 9-inch pastry shell
3 egg whites
¼ cup plus 2 tablespoons
   sugar

Melt butter in a saucepan over low heat. Add next 4 ingredients; cook over medium heat, stirring until sugar dissolves.

Combine eggs and egg yolks; beat at high speed of an electric mixer until thick and lemon colored. Gradually stir about one-fourth of hot mixture into eggs; add to remaining hot mixture, stirring constantly. Cook over medium heat, stirring constantly, 6 to 8 minutes or until thickened. Let cool completely.

Spread half of ice cream in bottom of pastry shell, and freeze until firm. Spread half of lemon mixture over ice cream; freeze until firm. Repeat layers and freezing procedure.

Beat 3 egg whites (at room temperature) at high speed just until foamy. Gradually add ¼ cup plus 2 tablespoons sugar, 1 tablespoon at a time, beating until stiff peaks form and sugar dissolves (2 to 4 minutes). Spread meringue over frozen pie, sealing to edge of pastry. Bake at 475° for 3 to 4 minutes or until golden brown. Serve immediately. Yield: one 9-inch pie.   Gretchen Beyers

100th Anniversary Cookbook
Auxiliary of Harrisburg Hospital
Harrisburg, Pennsylvania

Pumpkin Ice Cream Pie

1½ cups graham cracker
 crumbs
⅓ cup butter or margarine,
 melted
1 cup cooked, mashed
 pumpkin
½ cup firmly packed brown
 sugar

½ teaspoon salt
½ teaspoon ground cinnamon
½ teaspoon ground ginger
¼ teaspoon ground nutmeg
1 quart vanilla ice cream,
 softened

Combine graham cracker crumbs and butter; stir well. Firmly press crumb mixture evenly in bottom and up the sides of a 9-inch pieplate. Chill 1 hour.

Combine pumpkin and next 5 ingredients in a medium bowl; stir well. Add ice cream, stirring until well blended.

Spoon ice cream mixture into chilled crust; freeze until firm. Let stand at room temperature 5 minutes before serving. Yield: one 9-inch pie.   Louise J. Nichols

Pioneers of Alaska Cookbook
The Pioneers of Alaska Auxiliary #4
Anchorage, Alaska

Frozen Praline Pie

4 egg whites
½ teaspoon cream of tartar
1 cup sugar
2 cups sugar
2 cups whipping cream,
 divided
1¾ cups light corn syrup

1 cup butter
1 teaspoon vanilla extract
2 quarts vanilla ice cream,
 softened
1 cup pecan halves
1 cup ground pecans

Beat egg whites (at room temperature) and cream of tartar at high speed of an electric mixer just until foamy. Gradually add 1 cup sugar, 1 tablespoon at a time, beating until stiff peaks form and sugar dissolves (2 to 4 minutes). Spread meringue in bottom and up the sides of a 10-inch springform pan. Bake at 275° for 1 hour. Let cool completely.

Combine 2 cups sugar, 1 cup whipping cream, syrup, and butter in a large saucepan. Cook over medium heat, stirring until sugar dissolves. Continue to cook, without stirring, to soft ball stage (238°). Add remaining 1 cup whipping cream; stir well. Cook over medium heat until mixture reaches 218°. Remove from heat; stir in vanilla. Set aside, and let cool completely.

Spread 1 quart softened ice cream in meringue shell; freeze until firm. Pour 2 cups sauce over ice cream. Arrange pecan halves over sauce; freeze until firm. Spread remaining 1 quart ice cream over pecan halves; freeze until firm. Pour 2 cups sauce over ice cream. Sprinkle ground pecans over sauce; cover and freeze until firm.

To serve, carefully remove sides of springform pan. Serve with remaining sauce. Yield: 12 to 14 servings.

RSVP: Fortress Monroe
The Officers' and Civilians' Wives' Club
Fort Monroe, Virginia

Festival Cranberry Torte

1 cup graham cracker crumbs
⅓ cup chopped walnuts
¼ cup butter or margarine, melted
3 tablespoons sugar
1½ cups finely chopped fresh cranberries
1 cup sugar

2 egg whites
1 tablespoon orange juice
1 teaspoon vanilla extract
½ teaspoon salt
1 cup whipping cream, whipped
Garnish: sweetened whipped cream

Combine first 4 ingredients in a small bowl; stir well. Firmly press crumb mixture on bottom of a 9-inch springform pan. Chill.

Combine cranberries and 1 cup sugar in a large mixing bowl; let stand 5 minutes. Add egg whites (at room temperature), orange juice, vanilla, and salt. Beat at low speed of an electric mixer until foamy. Beat at high speed until stiff peaks form. Fold whipped cream into cranberry mixture. Pour into prepared crust. Cover and freeze 8 hours or until firm. Garnish, if desired. Yield: 8 to 10 servings.

Albertina's II
The Albertina Kerr Centers for Children
Portland, Oregon

Mocha Nut Tarts

1¾ cups all-purpose flour
⅓ cup cocoa
¼ cup sugar
¾ cup butter
¼ cup strong brewed coffee, chilled
1 (12-ounce) package semisweet chocolate morsels
2 tablespoons butter or margarine
⅔ cup sugar
2 tablespoons milk
1 tablespoon Kahlúa or other coffee-flavored liqueur
2 eggs
½ cup finely chopped walnuts

Combine flour, cocoa, and ¼ cup sugar; stir well. Cut in ¾ cup butter with a pastry blender until mixture resembles coarse meal. Sprinkle chilled coffee (1 tablespoon at a time) evenly over surface; stir with a fork just until dry ingredients are moistened. Shape pastry into a ball, and chill at least 1 hour. Press pastry into miniature (1¾-inch) muffin pans; set aside.

Place chocolate morsels and butter in top of a double boiler; bring water to a boil. Reduce heat to low; cook until chocolate and butter melt, stirring occasionally. Combine melted chocolate mixture, ⅔ cup sugar, milk, and liqueur; beat at low speed of an electric mixer until well blended. Add eggs, beating until smooth. Stir in walnuts.

Spoon about 2 teaspoons chocolate mixture into each prepared tart shell. Bake at 350° for 20 minutes or until filling is set. Let cool in pans 15 minutes. Remove from pans, and let cool completely on wire racks. Yield: 4 dozen.

Merrymeeting Merry Eating
The Regional Memorial Hospital Auxiliary
Brunswick, Maine

Maids of Honor

1 cup all-purpose flour
1 tablespoon sugar
¼ teaspoon salt
¼ cup butter or margarine
¼ cup milk, chilled
2 eggs, lightly beaten
2 tablespoons dry sherry
¾ cup sugar
1 tablespoon plus 1 teaspoon all-purpose flour
¼ teaspoon ground nutmeg
¾ cup finely chopped blanched almonds
¼ cup plus 2 tablespoons fruit jam

Combine 1 cup flour, 1 tablespoon sugar, and salt; stir well. Cut in butter with a pastry blender until mixture resembles coarse meal. Sprinkle chilled milk (1 tablespoon at a time) evenly over surface; stir with a fork just until dry ingredients are moistened. Shape into a ball; chill.

Roll pastry to ⅛-inch thickness on a lightly floured surface; cut into 24 circles, using a 2½-inch cutter. Place pastry circles in greased miniature (1¾-inch) muffin pans; set aside.

Combine eggs and sherry; stir well. Combine ¾ cup sugar, 1 tablespoon plus 1 teaspoon flour, and nutmeg; stir well. Add flour mixture to egg mixture, stirring well. Stir in almonds. Set aside.

Spoon ¾ teaspoon jam into each pastry shell; spoon almond mixture over jam. Bake at 350° for 20 to 25 minutes or until lightly browned. Yield: 2 dozen.   Lynn Belluscio

A Taste of Generations
The Granger Homestead Society, Inc., Women's Council
Canandaigua, New York

Creeping Crust Cobbler

½ cup butter or margarine, melted	½ cup milk
1 cup all-purpose flour	2 cups fresh blueberries, blackberries, or raspberries
1 cup sugar	1 cup sugar
1 teaspoon baking powder	Vanilla ice cream

Place melted butter in a 10-inch pieplate; set aside.

Combine flour, 1 cup sugar, and baking powder; stir well. Add milk, stirring until blended. Spoon batter over melted butter in pieplate (do not stir).

Combine fruit and 1 cup sugar in a medium saucepan. Cook over low heat 5 minutes; spoon over batter (do not stir). Bake at 350° for 30 to 35 minutes or until golden brown. Serve warm with ice cream. Yield: 4 to 6 servings.   Carol Miller

This Side of the River Cookbook
The Hatfield Book Club
Hatfield, Massachusetts

Peach Cobbler

1 cup sugar
3 tablespoons all-purpose
  flour
¼ teaspoon ground cinnamon
Dash of salt
5 cups peeled, sliced fresh
  peaches
2 tablespoons butter or
  margarine
1 cup all-purpose flour

1 cup sugar
1 teaspoon baking powder
¾ teaspoon salt
1 egg
⅓ cup butter or margarine,
  melted
Additional ground cinnamon
Whipped cream or vanilla ice
  cream

Combine first 4 ingredients in a large bowl, stirring well. Add peaches; toss gently.

Arrange peach mixture in bottom of an ungreased 13- x 9- x 2-inch baking pan. Dot with 2 tablespoons butter.

Combine 1 cup flour, 1 cup sugar, baking powder, and salt; stir well. Add egg, and stir well. Sprinkle crumb mixture evenly over peaches. Drizzle ⅓ cup melted butter evenly over crumb mixture. Sprinkle with cinnamon.

Bake, uncovered, at 350° for 35 to 40 minutes or until golden brown. Serve with whipped cream or vanilla ice cream. Yield: 8 servings.   Adam Harshbarger, Mary Harshbarger

Cookin' with the Crusaders
Most Holy Redeemer School
Tampa, Florida

Poultry

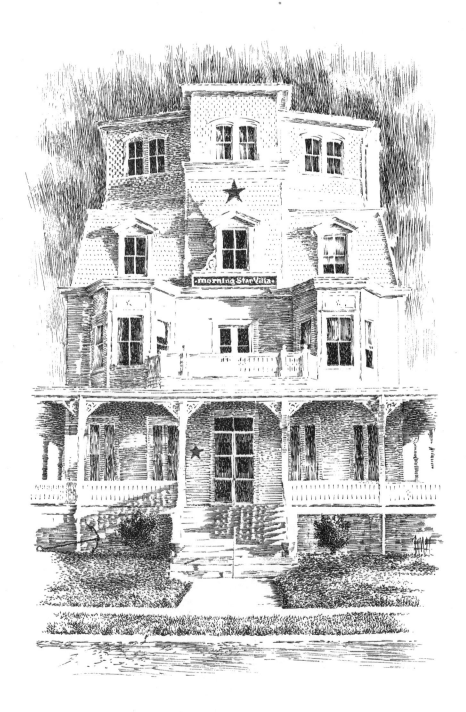

Morning Star Villa is located in Cape May, New Jersey, a picturesque seaside resort community. Renovated during a 1967 urban renewal project, Morning Star Villa is an example of the eccentric design of many Cape May houses. Visitors can relax in rocking chairs and enjoy the ocean breezes on the villa's wide veranda.

Zabar's Lemon-Garlic Chicken

2 (3½-pound) broiler-fryers
8 cups water
1 cup chopped fresh dillweed
¾ cup vinegar
½ cup lemon juice

13 large cloves garlic, minced
5 bay leaves
2 lemons, thinly sliced
¾ cup vegetable oil
1 tablespoon paprika

Place chickens in a 2-gallon zip-top heavy-duty plastic bag. Combine next 7 ingredients; pour over chickens. Seal bag securely. Marinate chickens in refrigerator 12 hours, turning occasionally.

Remove chickens from marinade, reserving lemon slices. Discard marinade. Place chickens, breast side up, in a large roasting pan. Combine oil and paprika; pour over chickens. Place lemon slices over chickens. Bake, uncovered, at 450° for 10 minutes. Reduce heat to 350°; cover and bake 1 hour and 10 minutes or until done. Yield: 8 to 10 servings.   Sheila Gould

The Educated Palate
The Calhoun School Parents Association
New York, New York

Chicken Rosemary

1 large onion, chopped
1 medium zucchini, chopped
2 tablespoons minced fresh
   rosemary
2 tablespoons vegetable oil
1 (3- to 3½-pound)
   broiler-fryer, cut up

3 tablespoons lemon juice
¼ teaspoon salt
⅛ teaspoon pepper
1½ cups sour cream
Hot cooked rice or noodles

Sauté first 3 ingredients in oil in a skillet over medium heat until vegetables are tender. Add chicken, juice, salt, and pepper. Cover, reduce heat, and simmer 45 minutes or until chicken is done.

Remove chicken; keep warm. Add sour cream to mixture in skillet; cook over low heat until thoroughly heated. Pour sauce over chicken; serve with rice. Yield: 4 to 6 servings.   Wendy Friefeld

Home on the Range
West Marin Health Project and Dance Palace Community Center
Point Reyes, California

Chicken à l'Orange

1 (3- to 3½-pound)
    broiler-fryer, cut up
2 tablespoons butter or
    margarine, melted
1 teaspoon salt
⅛ teaspoon ground ginger
⅛ teaspoon pepper
3 large carrots, scraped and
    cut into julienne strips

1 small onion, thinly sliced
    and separated into rings
⅔ cup orange juice
1 tablespoon cornstarch
⅓ cup orange marmalade
3 tablespoons brown sugar
1 tablespoon lemon juice

Brown chicken pieces in melted butter in a large skillet over medium heat. Combine salt, ginger, and pepper in a small bowl; stir well, and sprinkle over chicken. Add carrot strips and onion rings to chicken.

Combine orange juice and cornstarch in a medium bowl, stirring well. Add orange marmalade, brown sugar, and lemon juice to orange juice mixture; stir well.

Pour orange juice mixture over chicken and vegetables. Bring to a boil; cover, reduce heat, and simmer 45 to 50 minutes or until chicken is done. Yield: 4 to 6 servings.   Rose Brusinski

From Our House to Your House
Thomson Consumer Electronics Employees, Scranton Plant
Scranton, Pennsylvania

From Our House to Your House *is an employee-sponsored cookbook by the Thomson Consumer Electronics, Inc., Scranton Plant. Donations for the cookbook will help support the Scranton Plant's Clothe-a-Child Campaign which provides new school clothes and food during the Christmas season to over 141 children in need.*

Coq au Vin

1 (3- to 3½-pound)
broiler-fryer, cut up
1 (4-ounce) can sliced
mushrooms, undrained
1 cup Burgundy or other dry
red wine
¼ cup soy sauce
1 tablespoon brown sugar

1 tablespoon olive oil
1 teaspoon ground ginger
¼ teaspoon garlic powder
¼ teaspoon onion powder
¼ teaspoon dried whole
oregano
Hot cooked rice

Place chicken in a 13- x 9- x 2-inch baking dish. Drain mushrooms, reserving liquid. Add enough water to liquid to equal ¼ cup. Combine mushrooms, liquid, wine, and next 7 ingredients in a jar. Cover tightly, and shake vigorously. Pour mushroom mixture over chicken. Bake, uncovered, at 375° for 1 hour or until chicken is done. Serve with rice. Yield: 4 servings.   Lynn Budnick

What's Cooking?
The Sisterhood of Temple Shalom
Succasunna, New Jersey

Honey-Baked Chicken

⅓ cup honey
¼ cup vegetable oil
2 tablespoons prepared
mustard
1 tablespoon curry powder

1 teaspoon salt
3 pounds assorted chicken
pieces (breasts, drumsticks,
and thighs)

Combine honey, oil, mustard, curry powder, and salt in a small bowl; stir well. Place chicken in a lightly greased 13- x 9- x 2-inch baking dish. Bake at 350° for 45 to 50 minutes or until chicken is done, basting with honey mixture every 15 minutes. Yield: 4 to 6 servings.   Grace Sloan

Bethany Christian Community, A Recipe Collection
Bethany Christian Community
Anchorage, Alaska

Memphis Outdoor Barbecued Chicken

1 cup catsup
½ cup butter or margarine
½ cup vinegar
¼ cup cola-flavored beverage
¼ cup prepared mustard
1 lemon, sliced
1 tablespoon hot sauce
1 tablespoon commercial
  steak sauce
1 tablespoon Worcestershire
  sauce
¼ teaspoon pepper
18 assorted chicken pieces
  (breasts, drumsticks, and
  thighs)

Combine all ingredients except chicken in a medium saucepan. Bring to a boil; reduce heat, and simmer, uncovered, 1 hour, stirring occasionally.

Grill chicken over medium-low coals 35 minutes, turning occasionally. Baste with sauce; grill an additional 25 minutes or until chicken is done, basting frequently with remaining sauce. Yield: 8 servings.

Stirring Performances
The Junior League of Winston-Salem, North Carolina

Barbecue Chicken

6 chicken breast halves,
  skinned
3 cups water
1 cup vegetable oil
1 cup lemon juice
1 cup vinegar
2 teaspoons seasoned salt
2 cloves garlic, crushed

Place chicken in a large Dutch oven. Combine water and remaining ingredients, stirring well; pour over chicken. Bring to a boil; cover, reduce heat, and simmer 10 minutes. Remove from heat; let stand 30 minutes. Remove chicken from liquid; discard liquid. Grill chicken over medium coals 5 to 6 minutes on each side or until chicken is done. Yield: 6 servings.   Donnie Erwin-Brown

The Cookbook
East Lake United Methodist Church
Birmingham, Alabama

Jamaican Chicken Calypso

1 (8-ounce) can unsweetened pineapple chunks, undrained
½ cup rum
3 tablespoons lime juice
2 tablespoons soy sauce
1 tablespoon brown sugar
2 cloves garlic, minced
2 teaspoons curry powder
½ teaspoon ground ginger
¼ teaspoon ground cloves
¼ teaspoon ground red pepper
4 chicken breast halves
1 (11-ounce) can mandarin orange segments, drained
Garnish: lime wedges

Drain pineapple, reserving juice. Store pineapple chunks in refrigerator. Combine pineapple juice, rum, lime juice, soy sauce, brown sugar, garlic, curry powder, ginger, cloves, and red pepper in a medium bowl; stir well.

Place chicken in a 13- x 9- x 2-inch baking dish. Pour marinade mixture over chicken; cover tightly, and marinate in refrigerator at least 8 hours.

Drain chicken, reserving marinade. Place marinade in a small saucepan. Bring to a boil; reduce heat, and simmer 3 minutes. Set marinade aside.

Bake chicken, uncovered, at 375° for 40 minutes, basting occasionally with reserved marinade. Add reserved pineapple chunks and orange segments to chicken. Bake an additional 10 to 15 minutes or until chicken is done. Garnish, if desired. Yield: 4 servings.   Debbie Balk

What's Cooking in Chagrin Falls
Chagrin Falls Parent Teacher Organization
Chagrin Falls, Ohio

Country-Style Chicken Kiev

½ cup fine, dry breadcrumbs
2 tablespoons grated
   Parmesan cheese
1 teaspoon dried whole basil
1 teaspoon dried whole
   oregano
½ teaspoon garlic salt
¼ teaspoon salt
4 chicken breast halves

¼ cup butter or margarine,
   melted
½ cup butter or margarine,
   melted
¼ cup Chablis or other dry
   white wine
¼ cup chopped green onions
¼ cup chopped fresh parsley

Combine breadcrumbs, Parmesan cheese, basil, oregano, garlic salt, and salt in a small bowl; stir well. Dip chicken in ¼ cup melted butter; dredge in breadcrumb mixture. Place chicken, skin side up, in an ungreased 9-inch square baking dish. Bake, uncovered, at 375° for 50 to 60 minutes or until chicken is done.

Combine ½ cup melted butter, wine, green onions, and chopped parsley in a small bowl; stir well. Pour wine mixture over chicken. Bake an additional 5 minutes or until sauce is thoroughly heated. Yield: 4 servings.   Darlene Hanson

South Dakota Centennial Cookbook
The South Dakota Historical Society
Pierre, South Dakota

Chicken in Balsamic Vinegar

2 tablespoons all-purpose
   flour
⅛ teaspoon salt
⅛ teaspoon freshly ground
   pepper
4 chicken breast halves,
   skinned and boned
3 tablespoons virgin olive oil
6 cloves garlic
¾ pound small fresh
   mushrooms

¾ cup canned diluted
   chicken broth
¼ cup balsamic vinegar
1 bay leaf
¼ teaspoon dried whole
   thyme
1 tablespoon butter or
   margarine
Garnishes: sliced ripe olives
   and chopped fresh parsley

Combine flour, salt, and pepper. Dredge chicken in flour mixture. Sauté chicken in oil in a large skillet 4 minutes. Add garlic, and sauté

2 minutes. Turn chicken; add mushrooms, and sauté 3 minutes. Add broth and next 3 ingredients; cover, reduce heat, and simmer 10 minutes, turning chicken occasionally.

Remove chicken to a serving platter; keep warm. Cook mushroom mixture over medium heat 7 minutes. Remove and discard garlic and bay leaf. Add butter, stirring until butter melts. Spoon mushroom mixture evenly over chicken. Garnish, if desired. Yield: 4 servings.

A Matter of Taste
The Junior League of Morristown, New Jersey

Chicken and Avocados in Cognac Cream

6 chicken breast halves, skinned and boned
½ teaspoon salt
½ teaspoon pepper
3 tablespoons butter or margarine
¼ pound fresh mushrooms, sliced

1 tablespoon finely chopped shallots or onion
½ cup cognac
1½ cups whipping cream
1 ripe avocado, peeled and cut into ½-inch slices

Cut each chicken breast half into 3 strips; sprinkle evenly with salt and pepper.

Melt butter in a large heavy skillet over high heat. Add chicken, and cook 3 to 4 minutes or until browned. Remove chicken from skillet; set aside. Reduce heat to medium. Add mushrooms and shallots to skillet, and sauté until tender. Add cognac; stir well. Gradually add whipping cream, stirring constantly. Cook, stirring occasionally, 30 minutes or until mixture is thickened. Return chicken to skillet. Add avocado, and cook until thoroughly heated. Yield: 6 servings.

Gourmet LA
The Junior League of Los Angeles, California

Orange-Tarragon Chicken

8 chicken breast halves,
 skinned and boned
1 tablespoon grated orange
 rind
1 cup fresh orange juice
⅓ cup honey
¼ cup fresh lemon juice
1 tablespoon Worcestershire
 sauce
1 tablespoon chopped fresh
 tarragon or 1 teaspoon
 dried whole tarragon

1 teaspoon dry mustard
¼ teaspoon salt
⅛ teaspoon pepper
2 tablespoons cornstarch
2 tablespoons Grand Marnier
 or other orange-flavored
 liqueur
Garnishes: orange slices and
 fresh tarragon sprigs

Place chicken breast halves in a 13- x 9- x 2-inch baking dish. Combine orange rind and next 8 ingredients; stir well. Pour orange juice mixture over chicken; cover and marinate in refrigerator 2 hours.

Bake chicken, covered, at 350° for 40 to 50 minutes or until chicken is done. Remove chicken to a serving platter; keep warm.

Place remaining liquid in a saucepan. Bring to a boil; reduce heat, and simmer, uncovered, 2 minutes. Combine cornstarch and Grand Marnier, stirring well. Add cornstarch mixture to liquid in saucepan; cook 1 minute or until mixture is slightly thickened. Pour sauce over chicken. Garnish, if desired. Yield: 8 servings.

From Scratch Cookbook
The Assistance League® of Glendale, California

Hot Tomato Vinaigrette Chicken

4 chicken breast halves,
 skinned and boned
1 tablespoon butter, melted
1 tablespoon olive oil

Tomato Vinaigrette
1 tablespoon chopped fresh
 parsley

Place chicken between 2 sheets of wax paper; flatten to ¼-inch thickness, using a meat mallet or rolling pin.

Cook chicken in butter and oil in a large skillet over medium heat 3 minutes on each side or until chicken is done. Remove chicken to a serving platter, and keep warm. Add Tomato Vinaigrette to skillet; cook, stirring constantly, 2 minutes or until thoroughly heated. Pour over chicken, and sprinkle with parsley. Serve immediately. Yield: 4 servings.

Tomato Vinaigrette

1 tablespoon olive oil
1 clove garlic, crushed
½ teaspoon dried whole
  basil
¼ teaspoon crushed red
  pepper
1 (14½-ounce) can whole
  tomatoes, undrained and
  chopped

1 (3-inch) strip lemon rind
½ teaspoon sugar
½ teaspoon salt
1 tablespoon chopped fresh
  parsley
1 tablespoon red wine
  vinegar

Heat oil in a skillet over medium heat. Add garlic, basil, and pepper; cook 1 minute, stirring constantly. Add tomatoes, rind, and sugar. Bring to a boil; reduce heat, and simmer, uncovered, 20 minutes.

Remove from heat; stir in salt, parsley, and vinegar. Remove lemon rind. Yield: 1¾ cups.   Vernon D. Schauble

Three Rivers Cookbook, Volume III
Child Health Association of Sewickley, Pennsylvania

The **Three Rivers Cookbook, Volume III** *was created in an effort to raise funds to support the child-oriented agencies and projects of the Child Health Association of Sewickley, Inc. Since 1946, the association has awarded grants totaling over $1.5 million to 174 child-related agencies and has contributed more than 75,000 volunteer hours.*

Herbed Chicken Paillards

⅓ cup olive oil
3 tablespoons minced fresh parsley or 1 tablespoon dried parsley flakes
1 tablespoon minced fresh thyme or 1 teaspoon dried whole thyme
1½ teaspoons minced fresh rosemary or ½ teaspoon dried whole rosemary
1½ teaspoons minced fresh sage or ½ teaspoon dried whole sage
1 teaspoon grated lemon rind

¾ teaspoon minced fresh marjoram or ¼ teaspoon dried whole marjoram
¾ teaspoon minced fresh savory or ¼ teaspoon dried whole savory
Pinch of ground allspice
Pinch of ground red pepper
4 chicken breast halves, skinned and boned
¼ teaspoon salt
⅛ teaspoon pepper
Garnish: lemon wedges

Combine first 10 ingredients; stir well. Place chicken between 2 sheets of wax paper; flatten to ¼-inch thickness, using a meat mallet. Rub herb mixture on chicken; place in a 13- x 9- x 2-inch dish. Cover; chill 8 hours. Sprinkle chicken with salt and pepper. Grill over medium coals 2 minutes on each side or until done. Garnish, if desired. Yield: 4 servings.   Mrs. Theodore A. Eastman

Two and Company
St. Thomas' Church, Garrison Forest
Owings Mills, Maryland

Chicken Breasts Olé

6 chicken breast halves, skinned and boned
¾ cup (3 ounces) shredded Cheddar cheese
¾ cup (3 ounces) shredded Monterey Jack cheese
1 (4-ounce) can chopped green chiles, drained
1 (2½-ounce) can chopped ripe olives, drained
3 tablespoons chopped onion

2 to 4 tablespoons chopped fresh cilantro
⅓ cup butter or margarine, melted
¼ teaspoon chili powder
¼ teaspoon ground cumin
1 cup crushed tortilla chips
Sour cream
Commercial taco sauce
Garnishes: chopped fresh cilantro and lemon or lime wedges

Place chicken between 2 sheets of wax paper; flatten to ¼-inch thickness, using a meat mallet or rolling pin.

Combine cheeses, chiles, olives, onion, and 2 to 4 tablespoons chopped cilantro; stir well. Place cheese mixture evenly in center of each chicken breast. Fold long sides of chicken over cheese mixture; fold ends over, and secure with wooden picks.

Combine butter, chili powder, and cumin; stir well. Dip chicken in butter mixture, and dredge in crushed tortilla chips. Place chicken in an 11- x 7- x 1½-inch baking dish. Bake, uncovered, at 375° for 40 to 45 minutes or until chicken is done. Serve with sour cream and taco sauce. Garnish, if desired. Yield: 6 servings.

Only in California
The Children's Home Society of California
Los Angeles, California

Chicken Guadalajara

½ cup all-purpose flour
¼ teaspoon salt
⅛ teaspoon pepper
10 chicken breast halves, skinned, boned, and cut into strips
¼ cup plus 3 tablespoons butter or margarine, divided

2 to 3 poblano chiles, seeded and cut into rings
1 medium onion, halved and sliced
½ cup whipping cream
1 cup (4 ounces) shredded Monterey Jack cheese

Combine flour, salt, and pepper; stir well. Dredge chicken in flour mixture.

Melt ¼ cup plus 1 tablespoon butter in a large Dutch oven over medium-high heat. Add chicken, and cook 5 to 6 minutes or until done, stirring occasionally. Remove chicken from Dutch oven. Set aside, and keep warm.

Melt remaining 2 tablespoons butter in Dutch oven over medium heat. Add chiles and onion, and sauté until tender. Gradually stir in whipping cream. Add reserved chicken, and cook until thoroughly heated. Remove from heat. Sprinkle cheese over chicken mixture. Cover and let stand until cheese melts. Yield: 8 servings.

Seasoned with Sun
The Junior League of El Paso, Texas

Chicken Kiwi

1 pound boneless, skinless
chicken breast halves, cut
into strips
3 tablespoons vegetable oil,
divided
1 onion, chopped
1 cup scraped, thinly sliced
carrot
1 cup sliced fresh
mushrooms
1 cup diagonally sliced
celery
1 (13¾-ounce) can chicken
broth, undiluted

1 tablespoon plus 2 teaspoons
cornstarch
1 tablespoon soy sauce
1 teaspoon hot sauce
½ teaspoon grated lemon or
lime rind
½ teaspoon salt
Dash of pepper
2 or 3 kiwifruit, peeled and
sliced
Hot cooked rice

Brown chicken in 1 tablespoon oil in a skillet. Remove chicken from skillet; set aside, and keep warm. Add remaining 2 tablespoons oil to skillet. Add vegetables; sauté until carrot is crisp-tender. Return chicken to skillet. Combine chicken broth and next 6 ingredients. Add to chicken mixture; cook, stirring constantly, until mixture is thickened. Add kiwifruit; stir gently. Serve over rice. Yield: 4 to 6 servings.   Betsy Lee McNair Holladay

Georgia on My Menu
The Junior League of Cobb-Marietta, Georgia

Savory Chicken Pies

8 ounces bulk pork sausage
¼ cup butter or margarine
½ cup all-purpose flour
1¾ cups canned diluted
chicken broth
⅔ cup milk
¼ teaspoon salt

⅛ teaspoon pepper
2½ cups cubed cooked
chicken
1 (10-ounce) package frozen
mixed vegetables, thawed
Savory Pastry

Cook sausage in a heavy saucepan over medium-high heat 10 minutes or until browned, stirring to crumble meat; drain and discard drippings. Set sausage aside.

Add butter to saucepan, and cook over low heat until butter melts; add flour, stirring until smooth. Cook 1 minute, stirring constantly.

Gradually add broth and milk; cook over medium heat, stirring constantly, until mixture is thickened and bubbly. Add salt and pepper; stir well. Add reserved sausage, chicken, and vegetables; stir well. Cook until thoroughly heated. Spoon chicken mixture into six 1-cup casseroles.

Roll Savory Pastry to ⅛-inch thickness on a lightly floured surface. Cut six 6½-inch circles; place 1 pastry circle over chicken filling in each casserole. Trim off excess pastry along edges. Fold edges under and flute. Cut slits in top of pastry to allow steam to escape. Bake at 425° for 20 to 25 minutes or until pastry is lightly browned. Yield: 6 servings.

Savory Pastry

1 cup all-purpose flour	½ teaspoon paprika
1 teaspoon celery seeds	⅓ cup shortening
½ teaspoon salt	2 tablespoons cold water

Combine first 4 ingredients in a medium bowl; cut in shortening with a pastry blender until mixture resembles coarse meal. Sprinkle cold water (1 teaspoon at a time) evenly over surface; stir with a fork until dry ingredients are moistened. Shape into a ball; chill. Yield: pastry for six 6½-inch pies.   Regis Engelhardt

Historic Lexington Cooks: *Rockbridge Regional Recipes*
Historic Lexington Foundation
Lexington, Virginia

Historic Lexington Cooks: Rockbridge Regional Recipes *features recipes compiled by the Stonewall Jackson House Cookbook Committee. Proceeds will benefit the preservation of General Stonewall Jackson's House by the Historic Lexington Foundation, an organization whose purpose is to preserve the history of the city of Lexington and Rockbridge County.*

Elegant Chicken Livers

6 slices bacon
1 (2½-ounce) can mushroom
  stems and pieces, drained
½ cup chopped green onions
1 pound chicken livers

½ cup Chablis or other dry
  white wine
½ cup water
1 beef-flavored bouillon cube
Hot cooked rice

Cook bacon in a large skillet until crisp; remove bacon, reserving drippings in skillet. Crumble bacon, and set aside.

Sauté mushrooms and green onions in bacon drippings 2 to 3 minutes or until tender. Remove from skillet; set aside, and keep warm. Add livers to skillet, and sauté 12 to 15 minutes or until tender. Add reserved bacon, reserved mushroom mixture, wine, water, and bouillon cube; cook 5 minutes or until bouillon cube dissolves and mixture is thoroughly heated, stirring occasionally. Serve over rice. Yield: 4 servings.

Hearts and Flours
The Junior League of Waco, Texas

Andre Soltner's Chicken Livers Provençal

1 pound chicken livers
2 teaspoons butter or
  margarine, melted
2 teaspoons vegetable oil
2 tablespoons minced shallots
  or green onions

1 large tomato, peeled,
  seeded, and chopped
½ teaspoon minced garlic
½ teaspoon salt
⅛ teaspoon pepper
¼ cup chopped fresh parsley

Sauté livers in butter and oil in a medium skillet 8 to 10 minutes or until livers are tender. Add shallots, and cook 1 minute, stirring constantly. Add tomato and next 3 ingredients; cook 2 minutes, stirring occasionally. Remove from heat, and stir in parsley. Yield: 4 servings.   Sue Critz

Central Texas Style
The Junior Service League of Killeen, Texas

Apricot-Cashew Cornish Hens

4 (1½- to 2-pound) Cornish
  hens
½ teaspoon paprika
⅔ cup apricot preserves
2 teaspoons grated orange
  rind
2 tablespoons orange
  juice
2⅓ cups canned diluted
  chicken broth

1 (6-ounce) package
  long-grain and wild rice
  mix
2 tablespoons butter or
  margarine
¾ cup roasted cashews
¾ cup sliced green
  onions

Remove giblets from hens; reserve for other uses. Rinse hens with cold water, and pat dry. Close cavities, and secure with wooden picks; truss. Place hens, breast side up, in a lightly greased shallow roasting pan. Sprinkle hens with paprika. Bake, uncovered, at 350° for 1 hour.

Combine apricot preserves, orange rind, and orange juice in a small bowl; stir well. Set aside ⅓ cup apricot mixture. Brush hens with remaining ⅓ cup apricot mixture. Bake 30 minutes or until hens are done, basting occasionally with apricot mixture.

Bring broth to a boil in a medium saucepan; add rice mix. Return to a boil; cover, reduce heat, and simmer 25 minutes or until rice is tender and liquid is absorbed.

Melt butter in a small skillet over medium heat. Add cashews, and sauté until lightly browned. Remove cashews from skillet with a slotted spoon; set aside.

Add green onions to butter in skillet, and sauté until tender. Add green onions to rice mixture; stir well. Place rice mixture on a serving platter; sprinkle with cashews. Place hens on top of rice mixture. Brush with reserved ⅓ cup apricot mixture. Yield: 4 servings.   Jeanette C. Phillips

Rebel Recipes
Department of Home Economics, University of Mississippi
Oxford, Mississippi

Peach-Glazed Cornish Hens with Ginger

2 (1½- to 2-pound) Cornish hens, split	2 tablespoons grated fresh ginger
½ teaspoon salt	2 tablespoons brown sugar
1 cup chopped dried peaches	2 tablespoons fresh lime juice
¼ cup fresh orange juice	1 tablespoon soy sauce
1 green onion, thinly sliced	1 tablespoon vegetable oil

Place hens, skin side up, in a 13- x 9- x 2-inch baking dish. Sprinkle with salt; broil 6 inches from heat 3 to 5 minutes or until skin is lightly browned.

Combine peaches and remaining ingredients in a small saucepan. Cook over medium heat 5 minutes, stirring occasionally. Pour sauce over hens. Bake, uncovered, at 375° for 30 minutes or until done. Yield: 4 servings.

One Magnificent Cookbook
The Junior League of Chicago, Illinois

Orange Turkey Scallopini

1 pound turkey breast cutlets	½ cup fresh orange juice
½ cup all-purpose flour	1 tablespoon grated orange rind
¼ teaspoon salt	1 teaspoon dried whole sage
¼ teaspoon freshly ground pepper	¼ teaspoon dried whole thyme
¼ cup plus 2 tablespoons butter, divided	Garnish: chopped fresh parsley
1 tablespoon vegetable oil	
½ cup Chablis or other dry white wine	

Place turkey cutlets between 2 sheets of wax paper; flatten to ⅛-inch thickness, using a meat mallet or rolling pin. Combine flour, salt, and pepper in a medium bowl; stir well. Dredge cutlets in flour mixture.

Combine ¼ cup butter and vegetable oil in a large skillet; cook over medium-high heat until butter melts. Add cutlets, and sauté 30 seconds on each side or until done. Remove cutlets to a serving platter; keep warm. Discard drippings in skillet.

Add wine and orange juice to skillet; cook over high heat, deglazing skillet by scraping particles that cling to bottom. Cook 2 minutes or until mixture is reduced by about one-third. Add orange rind, sage, and thyme; cook until sauce thickens slightly. Remove from heat. Add remaining 2 tablespoons butter, stirring until butter melts. Spoon sauce over turkey cutlets. Garnish, if desired. Yield: 4 servings.

More Than a Tea Party
The Junior League of Boston, Massachusetts

Turkey Tetrazzini

1 (16-ounce) package
  spaghetti
¼ cup butter or margarine,
  melted
3 cups cubed cooked turkey
2 (4¼-ounce) cans chopped
  ripe olives, drained
2 (4-ounce) cans sliced
  mushrooms, drained
1 (4-ounce) jar diced
  pimiento, drained
¼ cup chopped celery
¼ cup diced green pepper

½ teaspoon salt
⅛ teaspoon pepper
½ cup all-purpose flour
⅓ cup dry sherry
2 cups canned diluted
  chicken broth
1 cup half-and-half
⅛ teaspoon garlic powder
½ cup grated Parmesan
  cheese
½ teaspoon seasoned salt
1 (2¼-ounce) package sliced
  natural almonds, toasted

Cook spaghetti according to package directions; drain. Place in a large bowl. Add melted butter, tossing gently to combine. Add turkey and next 7 ingredients; toss gently.

Combine flour and sherry in a medium bowl, beating well with a wire whisk. Add chicken broth, half-and-half, and garlic powder; stir well. Pour broth mixture over spaghetti mixture; stir gently. Spoon into a 13- x 9- x 2-inch baking dish. Sprinkle evenly with cheese, seasoned salt, and almonds. Cover and bake at 350° for 45 minutes. Remove cover, and bake an additional 10 to 12 minutes or until hot and bubbly. Yield: 8 servings.   Betty West Pinkston

Centennial Cookbook
The Orange County Pioneer Council
Newport Beach, California

Turkey Amandine

¼ cup butter or margarine
¼ cup all-purpose flour
2 cups milk
2 tablespoons Chablis or
  other dry white wine
¼ teaspoon salt
Pinch of pepper
2 egg yolks, beaten
2 cups diced cooked turkey
1 cup frozen English peas,
  thawed

⅓ cup slivered almonds,
  toasted and divided
3 tablespoons fine, dry
  breadcrumbs
1 tablespoon butter or
  margarine
2 tablespoons grated
  Parmesan cheese

Melt ¼ cup butter in a heavy saucepan over low heat; add flour, stirring until smooth. Cook 1 minute, stirring constantly. Gradually add milk; cook over medium heat, stirring constantly, until mixture is thickened and bubbly.

Add wine, salt, and pepper to white sauce; stir well. Gradually stir about one-fourth of hot mixture into egg yolks; add to remaining hot mixture, stirring constantly. Cook over medium heat 2 minutes, stirring constantly.

Add diced turkey, peas, and 2 tablespoons almonds to white sauce in saucepan; cook over medium heat 3 to 4 minutes or until thoroughly heated.

Pour turkey mixture into an ungreased 1½-quart baking dish. Sprinkle top with remaining 3 tablespoons plus 1 teaspoon almonds and breadcrumbs. Dot with 1 tablespoon butter, and sprinkle with Parmesan cheese.

Broil 6 inches from heat 1 to 2 minutes or until lightly browned. Yield: 4 servings.   Cheryl Watts

Land of Cotton
John T. Morgan Academy
Selma, Alabama

Duckling with Green Peppercorn Sauce

1 (5- to 6-pound) dressed
  duckling
½ teaspoon salt
⅛ teaspoon pepper

1 onion, peeled
6 fresh parsley sprigs
Green Peppercorn Sauce

Remove giblets from duckling; reserve for other uses. Rinse duckling with cold water, and pat dry. Prick skin with a fork at 2-inch intervals. Sprinkle cavity with salt and pepper. Stuff with onion and parsley.

Place duckling, breast side up, on a lightly greased rack in a roasting pan. Insert meat thermometer in thigh, making sure it does not touch bone. Bake at 450° for 20 minutes. Shield wings and drumsticks with aluminum foil to prevent excessive browning. Reduce heat to 325°, and bake 2 hours and 15 minutes or until thermometer registers 185°. (If duckling starts to brown too much, cover loosely with aluminum foil.) Remove duckling to a serving platter. Serve with Green Peppercorn Sauce. Yield: 4 servings.

Green Peppercorn Sauce

1 tablespoon minced shallots
  or onion
2 tablespoons butter, melted
⅓ cup cognac

½ cup whipping cream
1 tablespoon whole green
  peppercorns
1 tablespoon Dijon mustard

Sauté shallots in butter in a small saucepan over medium heat until tender.

Place cognac in a small long-handled saucepan; heat until warm (do not boil). Remove from heat. Ignite with a long match. When flames subside, add whipping cream; stir well. Cook over medium heat 3 minutes or until slightly thickened. Stir in sautéed shallots, peppercorns, and mustard; reduce heat, and simmer 1 minute. Yield: 1 cup.   Liz and George Vary

Out of This World
Wood Acres Elementary School
Bethesda, Maryland

Roast Breast of Goose

½ pound bulk pork sausage
1 wild goose breast, skinned, boned, and halved
¼ teaspoon dried whole oregano
¼ teaspoon dried whole sage
⅛ teaspoon dried whole tarragon
2 or 3 slices bacon
½ cup water
½ cup bourbon or orange juice

Spread sausage evenly over 1 breast half. Sprinkle sausage with oregano, sage, and tarragon. Top with remaining breast half. Tie securely with heavy string at 2-inch intervals.

Place goose in a shallow roasting pan. Place bacon lengthwise over goose. Pour water and bourbon over goose. Bake at 350° for 45 to 60 minutes or until done, basting frequently with pan drippings. Let stand 5 to 10 minutes before slicing. Yield: 2 servings.

From a Lighthouse Window
The Chesapeake Bay Maritime Museum
St. Michaels, Maryland

Sherried Quail

8 quail, dressed and split
3 tablespoons all-purpose flour
½ teaspoon salt
¼ teaspoon pepper
¼ cup butter, melted
2 tablespoons vegetable oil
1 (10¾-ounce) can chicken broth, undiluted
1 cup dry sherry
1 small bay leaf
Pinch of dried whole thyme

Spread quail open, and pat dry. Combine flour, salt, and pepper; sprinkle over quail.

Brown quail in butter and oil in a large skillet. Add broth and remaining ingredients; cover and cook over medium heat 20 minutes or until quail is done. Remove and discard bay leaf. Remove quail to a serving platter. Serve quail with sherry mixture. Yield: 4 servings.

Cardinal Cuisine
The Mount Vernon Hospital Auxiliary
Alexandria, Virginia

Salads & Salad Dressings

The elaborately carved, 20-foot tall wooden replicas of gods gaze toward the sea at the Pu'uhonua o Honaunau National Historical Park in Hawaii. The 180-acre park includes a walking tour that winds through a grove of coconut palms where royal Hawaiian chiefs once lived.

Plymouth Cranberry Salad

2 cups water, divided
2 cups fresh cranberries
1 cup sugar
2 envelopes unflavored
  gelatin
1 (12-ounce) bottle ginger ale
1 cup peeled, cored, and
  diced pear

1 cup seedless green grapes,
  halved
½ cup diced celery
½ cup chopped walnuts
Boston lettuce leaves
Sugared Cranberries

Combine 1½ cups water, 2 cups cranberries, and sugar in a medium saucepan. Bring to a boil; reduce heat, and simmer, uncovered, 2 minutes or until cranberries pop.

Sprinkle gelatin over remaining ½ cup water in a small bowl; let stand 1 minute.

Add gelatin mixture to cranberry mixture; cook over medium heat, stirring constantly, until gelatin dissolves. Add ginger ale, stirring well. Cover and chill 2 hours or until the consistency of unbeaten egg white.

Fold pear, grapes, celery, and walnuts into gelatin mixture. Spoon gelatin mixture into a lightly oiled 8-cup ring mold. Cover and chill until firm. Unmold onto a lettuce-lined serving plate. Arrange Sugared Cranberries around mold. Yield: 12 servings.

Sugared Cranberries

1 cup fresh cranberries
1 egg white, lightly beaten

1 cup sugar

Place cranberries on a wire rack. Brush cranberries with beaten egg white, using a soft pastry brush. While cranberries are still wet, sprinkle evenly with sugar to create a frosted look; let dry completely. Yield: 1 cup.   Bea Wishnic

What's Cooking?
The Sisterhood of Temple Shalom
Succasunna, New Jersey

Perfection Salad

2 envelopes unflavored
  gelatin
½ cup cold water
2 cups boiling water
¼ cup plus 2 tablespoons
  sugar
¼ cup lemon juice
¼ cup vinegar
½ teaspoon salt

1 cup scraped, grated carrots
1 (15¼-ounce) can crushed
  pineapple, drained
1 cup finely shredded
  cabbage
¼ cup chopped green pepper
1 (2-ounce) jar diced
  pimiento, drained
Lettuce leaves

Combine gelatin and ½ cup cold water in a medium bowl; add 2 cups boiling water, stirring until gelatin dissolves. Add sugar, lemon juice, vinegar, and salt; stir well. Chill until the consistency of unbeaten egg white.

Gently fold carrot and next 4 ingredients into gelatin mixture. Pour gelatin mixture into a lightly oiled 5-cup mold. Cover and chill until firm. Unmold onto a lettuce-lined serving plate. Yield: 6 to 8 servings.   Ann S. Tatum

Shamrock Specialties
The Trinity High School Foundation
Louisville, Kentucky

Antipasto Mold

2 envelopes unflavored
  gelatin
¾ cup cold water
1 cup boiling water
1 chicken-flavored bouillon
  cube
½ cup mayonnaise
1 tablespoon prepared
  horseradish
1 clove garlic, minced
1 teaspoon dry mustard
¼ teaspoon ground white
  pepper

1 (5-ounce) can evaporated
  milk
1 (3¼-ounce) can tuna,
  drained and flaked
½ cup diced salami
½ cup diced provolone
  cheese
½ cup sliced radishes
⅓ cup chopped green onions
¼ cup sliced pimiento-stuffed
  olives
Lettuce leaves

Combine gelatin and ¾ cup cold water in a medium bowl; add 1 cup boiling water and bouillon cube, stirring until gelatin and bouillon cube dissolve. Add mayonnaise, horseradish, garlic, dry mustard, and pepper; stir until smooth. Gradually stir in evaporated milk. Add tuna and next 5 ingredients; stir well. Cover and chill 1 hour or until mixture is the consistency of unbeaten egg white, stirring occasionally.

Spoon gelatin mixture into a lightly oiled 5-cup mold. Cover and chill until firm. Unmold onto a lettuce-lined serving plate. Yield: 6 to 8 servings.

Good Cookin' from Giffin
The Giffin Elementary School PTA
Knoxville, Tennessee

Olive Salad

1 small cauliflower
½ pound fresh mushrooms, sliced
2 medium zucchini, cubed
1 ripe avocado, peeled and chopped
1 medium-size sweet red pepper, chopped
1 medium-size green pepper, chopped
1 (7¾-ounce) jar pimiento-stuffed olives, drained and halved
1 (6-ounce) can small pitted ripe olives, drained and halved
½ cup sliced green onions
½ cup vegetable oil
3 tablespoons lemon juice
3 tablespoons vinegar
1 tablespoon sugar
2 teaspoons salt
Dash of pepper

Remove large outer leaves of cauliflower. Break cauliflower into flowerets. Combine flowerets, mushrooms, and next 7 ingredients in a large bowl; toss well.

Combine oil, lemon juice, vinegar, sugar, salt, and pepper in a jar; cover tightly, and shake vigorously. Pour dressing over vegetable mixture; toss well. Cover and chill at least 4 hours. Yield: 12 to 14 servings.   Virginia Arey

Palate Pleasers II
Redeemer Women's Guild
Elmhurst, Illinois

Cajun Potato Salad

4½ cups water
1½ pounds unpeeled small
  fresh shrimp
2 to 3 tablespoons lemon
  juice
4 medium potatoes
1 clove garlic, halved
½ cup diced celery
½ cup chopped green onions

½ cup sour cream
½ cup mayonnaise
1 teaspoon salt
1 teaspoon dry mustard
½ teaspoon ground red
  pepper
¼ teaspoon dried whole
  tarragon, crushed

Bring water to a boil; add shrimp, and cook 3 to 5 minutes. Drain well; rinse with cold water. Chill. Peel and devein shrimp. Place shrimp in a bowl; add lemon juice, and toss gently. Cover and chill.

Cook potatoes in boiling water to cover 20 to 30 minutes or until tender; drain. Peel and cube potatoes. Set aside.

Rub cut side of garlic on inside of a large salad bowl; discard garlic. Combine chilled shrimp, potato, celery, and green onions in prepared salad bowl; toss gently to combine.

Combine sour cream and remaining ingredients in a small bowl; stir well. Add sour cream mixture to potato mixture, tossing gently to coat evenly. Cover and chill at least 8 hours. Yield: 8 to 10 servings.

Celebrations on the Bayou
The Junior League of Monroe, Louisiana

Charlengne Salad
with Hot Brie Dressing

1 head curly endive, torn
1 head iceberg lettuce, torn
1 head romaine lettuce, torn
10 ounces fully ripened Brie
1 cup olive oil
½ cup white wine vinegar
2 tablespoons lemon juice
1 tablespoon plus 1 teaspoon
  Dijon mustard

2 large cloves garlic, minced
1 teaspoon minced green
  onions
¼ teaspoon pepper
Commercial garlic-flavored
  croutons

Combine endive and lettuces in a large salad bowl; toss well, and set aside.

Remove and discard rind from Brie; cut cheese into small pieces. Combine cheese, olive oil, vinegar, lemon juice, mustard, garlic, green onions, and pepper in a large skillet. Cook over medium heat, stirring constantly, until cheese melts.

Pour warm dressing over greens, tossing gently to coat evenly. Sprinkle salad with croutons, and serve immediately. Yield: 18 to 20 servings.   Barbara Redmont

Critics' Choice
The Corinth Theatre Arts Guild
Corinth, Mississippi

Strawberry-Spinach Salad

8 cups torn spinach
3 kiwifruit, peeled, sliced, and divided
1 cup fresh strawberries, halved and divided
¾ cup coarsely chopped macadamia nuts or pecans, divided

2 tablespoons strawberry jam
2 tablespoons strawberry or cider vinegar
⅓ cup vegetable oil

Combine spinach, half of kiwifruit slices, half of strawberries, and half of chopped nuts in a large bowl; set aside.

Place jam and vinegar in container of an electric blender, and process until combined. With blender running, gradually add oil in a slow, steady stream, and process until blended. Pour dressing over spinach mixture, and toss gently.

Divide spinach mixture evenly among individual salad plates. Top salads evenly with remaining half of kiwifruit, strawberries, and nuts. Yield: 8 servings.

Recipes & Recollections from Terrace Hill
The Terrace Hill Society
Des Moines, Iowa

Spinach Make-Ahead Salad

8 cups torn spinach
½ cup (2 ounces) shredded
   Cheddar cheese
½ cup (2 ounces) shredded
   Swiss cheese
2 cups sliced fresh
   mushrooms
4 hard-cooked eggs, sliced
1 cup mayonnaise

½ cup sour cream
3 tablespoons milk
2 teaspoons lemon juice
2 teaspoons sugar
¼ cup finely chopped green
   onions
4 slices bacon, cooked and
   crumbled

Layer first 5 ingredients in order in a large glass salad bowl. Combine mayonnaise, sour cream, milk, juice, and sugar. Add onions, stirring well. Spread mixture over salad, sealing to edge of bowl. Cover and chill 8 hours. Sprinkle with bacon just before serving. Yield: 6 to 8 servings.   Delma H. George

Aggies, Moms, and Apple Pie
The Federation of Texas A&M University Mothers' Clubs
College Station, Texas

Fried Rice Salad

1 tablespoon plus 1 teaspoon
   vegetable oil
1 cup thinly sliced celery
1 cup minced onion
1 small green pepper, cut
   into julienne strips
½ teaspoon sugar
½ teaspoon salt

¼ to ½ teaspoon pepper
4 cups cooked long-grain rice
1 tablespoon soy sauce
1 medium tomato, diced
1 tablespoon minced fresh
   parsley
3 tablespoons chopped green
   onion tops

Heat oil in a large skillet or wok over medium-high heat; add celery and next 5 ingredients, and stir-fry 3 minutes. Add rice, and stir-fry 2 minutes. Remove from heat; stir in soy sauce.

Spoon rice mixture into a serving bowl; cover and chill at least 3 hours. Top with tomato, parsley, and green onions just before serving. Yield: 12 servings.

The Golden Apple Collection
White Plains Auxiliary of the White Plains Hospital Center
White Plains, New York

The "Anything Goes" Pasta Salad

1 (16-ounce) package wagon
  wheel macaroni
¼ cup olive oil
Salt and pepper to taste
2 (14-ounce) cans artichoke
  hearts, drained and halved
½ cup roasted red pepper
  strips
1 (3-ounce) jar capers, drained
6 to 8 sun-dried tomatoes, cut
  into strips
½ cup grated Parmesan
  cheese

⅓ cup chopped fresh Italian
  parsley
3 cloves garlic, minced
¾ cup olive oil
¼ cup white wine vinegar
¼ cup fresh lemon juice
1 egg yolk
1 teaspoon dry mustard
1 teaspoon dried whole basil
¼ teaspoon salt
⅛ teaspoon pepper
¼ teaspoon hot sauce (optional)
½ cup pine nuts, toasted

Cook macaroni according to package directions; drain. Place macaroni in a large bowl. Add ¼ cup oil and salt and pepper to taste. Add artichoke hearts, roasted pepper, capers, tomato, cheese, and parsley; stir gently to combine. Set aside.

Position knife blade in food processor bowl. Add garlic, next 8 ingredients, and, if desired, hot sauce, and process until smooth. Pour dressing over pasta mixture; toss well. Cover and marinate in refrigerator 1 hour. Sprinkle with pine nuts just before serving. Yield: 12 servings.   Tammy Ostendors

Deal Delights II
Sephardic Women's Organization
Deal, New Jersey

The Golden Apple Collection, *by the White Plains Auxiliary, reflects life in Westchester County, New York. The auxiliary boasts a membership of nearly 500 volunteers who promote the welfare of the White Plains Hospital, its patients, and the community.*

Paella Salad

1½ cups water
½ pound unpeeled
  medium-size fresh shrimp
1 (5-ounce) package yellow
  rice mix
¼ cup tarragon vinegar
2 tablespoons vegetable oil
¼ teaspoon curry powder
⅛ teaspoon ground white
  pepper
⅛ teaspoon dry mustard
2 cups diced cooked chicken
  breast
1 medium tomato, peeled,
  seeded, and chopped
½ cup frozen English peas,
  thawed
⅓ cup thinly sliced celery
¼ cup minced onion
1 (2-ounce) jar diced
  pimiento, drained
Lettuce leaves
Garnish: lemon slices

Bring water to a boil; add shrimp, and cook 3 to 5 minutes. Drain well; rinse with cold water. Chill. Peel and devein shrimp; set aside.

Prepare rice mix according to package directions, omitting butter. Combine rice, vinegar, and next 4 ingredients; stir well. Add reserved shrimp, chicken, tomato, peas, celery, onion, and pimiento; toss well. Cover and chill thoroughly.

Serve salad on lettuce leaves on individual salad plates. Garnish, if desired. Yield: 6 servings.

Gourmet by the Bay
The Dolphin Circle of the King's Daughters and Sons
Virginia Beach, Virginia

Chinese Crab and Noodle Salad

1 medium-size sweet red
  pepper, cut into julienne
  strips
1 tablespoon sesame oil
3 green onions, sliced
1 teaspoon minced fresh
  ginger
1 clove garlic, minced
¼ teaspoon crushed red
  pepper
4 cups cooked fine egg
  noodles, chilled
4 cups torn romaine lettuce
1 pound fresh crabmeat,
  drained and flaked
¼ cup soy sauce
¼ cup red wine vinegar
2 tablespoons sugar
½ teaspoon freshly ground
  pepper

Sauté sweet red pepper in sesame oil in a large skillet 2 minutes. Add green onions, ginger, garlic, and crushed red pepper, and sauté 1 minute.

Combine chilled noodles, red pepper mixture, lettuce, and crab-meat in a large salad bowl; toss gently. Combine soy sauce and remaining ingredients in a small bowl, stirring with a wire whisk. Pour dressing over noodle mixture; toss gently to combine. Cover and chill 30 minutes. Toss again just before serving. Yield: 8 to 10 servings.   Judy Delugach

Memphis in May International Festival Cookbook
Memphis in May International Festival, Inc.
Memphis, Tennessee

Summertime Salmon Salad

2 **pounds skinned salmon fillets**
1 **(16-ounce) package frozen English peas, thawed**
2 **cups mayonnaise**
2 **cups diced celery**
¾ **cup chopped onion**
½ **cup diced green pepper**
½ **cup sweet pickle relish**
1½ **tablespoons fresh lemon juice**
¼ **teaspoon Beau Monde seasoning**
⅛ **teaspoon ground white pepper**
4 **cups cooked corkscrew or seashell macaroni**

Arrange salmon fillets on a steaming rack. Place rack over boiling water; cover and steam salmon 10 to 12 minutes or until fish flakes easily when tested with a fork. Remove salmon from steaming rack, and let cool.

Flake salmon, and place in a large salad bowl. Add peas and next 8 ingredients; stir well. Add macaroni; toss gently to combine. Cover and chill thoroughly. Yield: 12 servings.   Kathy Janssen

Alaska's Cooking, Volume II
The Woman's Club of Anchorage, Alaska

Chicken-Pasta Salad with Basil Dressing

6 skinned, boned, and cooked
  chicken breast halves
2 cups cooked corkscrew
  macaroni, chilled
1 (14-ounce) jar roasted red
  peppers, drained and cut
  into strips
½ cup pitted ripe olives

½ cup olive oil
¼ cup red wine vinegar
1 tablespoon minced fresh
  basil
1 large clove garlic, minced
1 teaspoon salt
¼ teaspoon pepper

Cut chicken into strips. Combine chicken, macaroni, roasted pepper, and olives in a large salad bowl; toss gently. Combine olive oil and remaining ingredients in a small bowl; stir with a wire whisk. Pour dressing over chicken mixture; toss gently. Cover and chill at least 2 hours. Yield: 4 servings.   Suzanne Jennings

Southern California Style
The Assistance League® of Anaheim, California

Macaroni Antipasto

1 (12-ounce) package
  corkscrew macaroni
3 tablespoons walnut oil
2 (6½-ounce) jars marinated
  artichoke hearts, drained
1 (9½-ounce) jar pepper
  salad, drained
1 (5¾-ounce) jar sliced
  pimiento-stuffed olives,
  drained

2 (2¼-ounce) cans sliced ripe
  olives, drained
¼ to ½ pound pepperoni,
  cubed
1 cup cubed salami
½ cup freshly grated
  Parmesan cheese
¼ cup freshly grated Romano
  cheese

Cook macaroni according to package directions; drain. Rinse with cold water; drain well. Combine macaroni and oil in a large salad bowl; toss gently. Add artichoke hearts and remaining ingredients; toss gently. Cover and chill thoroughly. Yield: 12 servings.

Wild about Texas
The Cypress-Woodlands Junior Forum
Houston, Texas

Siam Salad

1 pound flank steak, cooked and thinly sliced
1 medium-size sweet red pepper, cut into julienne strips
1 pound green beans, diagonally sliced and cooked
2½ cups shredded purple or napa cabbage
3 green onions, diagonally sliced
½ cup chopped roasted peanuts
½ cup rice wine vinegar
¼ cup peanut oil
1 tablespoon minced fresh ginger
1 tablespoon soy sauce
1 tablespoon dark sesame oil
1 clove garlic, minced
½ teaspoon sugar
½ teaspoon ground white pepper
¼ teaspoon hot sauce

Combine steak, sweet red pepper, green beans, cabbage, onions, and peanuts in a large salad bowl; toss gently.

Combine vinegar and remaining ingredients in a jar. Cover tightly, and shake vigorously. Pour dressing over steak mixture; toss well. Yield: 8 servings.

From Scratch Cookbook
The Assistance League® of Glendale, California

Buckhorn Dressing

1 cup mayonnaise
1 medium onion, chopped
½ cup vegetable oil
½ cup chili catsup
½ cup catsup
3 tablespoons lemon juice
1 tablespoon prepared horseradish
1 tablespoon Worcestershire sauce
1 clove garlic, crushed
1 teaspoon paprika
1 teaspoon pepper
¼ teaspoon salt
Dash of hot sauce

Combine all ingredients in container of an electric blender or food processor, and process until smooth. Serve dressing over salad greens. Yield: 4 cups.

Seasoned with Sun
The Junior League of El Paso, Texas

Peppercorn Dressing

1 beef-flavored bouillon cube
1 tablespoon plus 1 teaspoon
  boiling water
¾ cup plus 2 tablespoons
  sour cream
¼ cup mayonnaise

2 tablespoons lemon juice
1 tablespoon plus ½ teaspoon
  cracked pepper
1 teaspoon Worcestershire
  sauce
Pinch of salt

Dissolve bouillon cube in boiling water. Add remaining ingredients; stir until blended. Cover and chill 3 hours. Serve over salad greens. Yield: 2 cups.   Linda D. Orsini

Three Rivers Cookbook, Volume III
Child Health Association of Sewickley, Pennsylvania

Honey-Mustard Dressing

1 cup mayonnaise
¾ cup vegetable oil
½ cup honey
⅓ cup vinegar
¼ cup finely chopped onion

¼ cup chopped fresh parsley
¼ cup prepared mustard
1 tablespoon sugar
¾ teaspoon salt

Position knife blade in food processor bowl; add all ingredients, and process until smooth. Cover and chill 4 hours. Serve dressing over salad greens. Yield: 3 cups.   Casa Blanca

Spokane Cooks!© Northwest
The Community Centers Foundation of Spokane, Washington

Regency Dressing

1 cup mayonnaise
¼ cup chopped fresh parsley
2 tablespoons chopped fresh
  chives

2 teaspoons prepared
  horseradish
Dash of salt

Combine all ingredients in a small bowl, stirring well. Chill. Serve dressing over salad greens. Yield: 1 cup.   Mardella Preble

Mothers of Twins Cookbook
Twice as Nice, Mothers of Twins Club
Gillette, Wyoming

Sauces & Condiments

A simple hand-drawn ferry relies on manpower to transport vehicles across a short span of water in Los Banos, Texas. Los banos means the watering-place in Spanish.

Hrvatska Krema (Custard Sauce)

1 envelope unflavored gelatin
½ cup water
¾ cup sugar
1 cup whipping cream

1½ cups sour cream
1 teaspoon vanilla extract
Garnish: fresh fruit

Sprinkle gelatin over water in a small saucepan; let stand 1 minute. Add sugar, and bring mixture to a boil. Cook over medium heat, stirring constantly, until sugar and gelatin dissolve. Remove from heat, and stir in whipping cream. Add sour cream and vanilla; stir well.

Pour mixture into individual dessert dishes; chill at least 4 hours. If desired, stir sauce before serving. Garnish, if desired. Yield: 6 servings.   Ruzarija Zampera

Dobar Tek
The Yugoslav Women's Club
Seattle, Washington

Macadamia Nut-Orange Dessert Sauce

3 large navel oranges
½ cup water
¾ cup sugar
½ cup light corn syrup
1 tablespoon lemon juice

⅔ cup coarsely chopped
   macadamia nuts
3 to 4 tablespoons Grand
   Marnier or other
   orange-flavored liqueur

Remove rind from oranges; cut rind into 1½- x 1/16-inch strips. Squeeze oranges, and reserve juice.

Combine orange rind, juice, and water in a small saucepan. Bring to a boil; reduce heat, and simmer, uncovered, 5 minutes. Add sugar, corn syrup, and lemon juice. Bring to a boil; reduce heat, and simmer 5 minutes, stirring constantly. Simmer, without stirring, an additional 15 minutes. Remove from heat, and let cool completely.

Add nuts and liqueur, stirring well. Serve warm over pound cake or vanilla ice cream. Yield: 2 cups.   Harley W. Lake

Capital Connoisseur
The Lawrence Center Independence House
Schenectady, New York

Peach Sauce

1 (16-ounce) can sliced
  peaches, undrained
¼ cup cream sherry

Dash of ground cinnamon
Dash of ground nutmeg

Combine all ingredients in a large glass jar. Cover tightly, and shake vigorously. Chill at least 8 hours. Serve sauce over vanilla ice cream. Yield: 2 cups.
                Ann Esselman

Gingerbread . . . and all the trimmings
The Junior Service League of Waxahachie, Texas

Raspberry Fudge Sauce

½ cup fresh raspberries
3 (4-ounce) bars semisweet
  chocolate, broken into small
  pieces
½ cup unsalted butter, cut
  into small pieces

2 egg yolks
1 cup whipping cream
2 tablespoons Chambord or
  other raspberry-flavored
  liqueur

Place raspberries in container of an electric blender, and process until smooth. Strain raspberry puree; discard seeds. Set puree aside.

Combine chocolate and butter in top of a double boiler; bring water to a boil. Reduce heat to low; cook until chocolate and butter melt, stirring occasionally. Add egg yolks to chocolate mixture, stirring with a wire whisk. Add raspberry puree and whipping cream; stir well. Remove from heat, and stir in liqueur. Serve warm over ice cream or crêpes. Yield: 3 cups.

A Matter of Taste
The Junior League of Morristown, New Jersey

Jezebel Sauce

1 (12-ounce) jar pineapple
  preserves
1 (12-ounce) jar apple jelly
⅓ cup prepared horseradish

¾ cup dry mustard
¼ teaspoon salt
⅛ teaspoon freshly ground
  pepper

Combine all ingredients in container of an electric blender, and process until mixture is smooth. Store sauce in an airtight container in refrigerator. Serve with ham or over cream cheese with crackers. Yield: 3 cups.   Judy Campbell

Pegasus Presents
Pegasus of Germantown, Tennessee

Marmalade Sauce for Chicken

1 cup orange marmalade	2 tablespoons chopped onion
1 (8-ounce) can tomato sauce	1½ teaspoons soy sauce
½ cup sliced almonds	1 teaspoon ground ginger

Combine all ingredients in a medium saucepan; stir well. Cook over low heat until thoroughly heated, stirring frequently. Serve sauce warm with chicken. Yield: 2 cups.

It's Our Serve!
The Junior League of Long Island
Roslyn, New York

The Junior League of Long Island celebrated 39 years of community service with **It's Our Serve!** *Proceeds from the sale of their cookbook will support league projects such as Lifeline, a resource guide for those who need assistance dealing with life-threatening illness, and Involvement Theater, a league project which, for 30 years, has brought live performances to between 3,000 and 5,000 emotionally and physically handicapped children.*

Miriam's Creole Sauce

2 onions, chopped
2 medium-size green peppers, chopped
1 cup sliced fresh mushrooms
2 cloves garlic, minced
2 tablespoons butter or margarine, melted
1 tablespoon vegetable oil

2 (8-ounce) cans tomato sauce
1 tablespoon dried whole basil
1 tablespoon sugar
1 large bay leaf
¼ teaspoon ground thyme
¼ to ½ teaspoon salt
Dash of hot sauce

Sauté chopped onion, green pepper, sliced mushrooms, and garlic in butter and oil in a large skillet 3 to 5 minutes or until vegetables are tender. Add tomato sauce and remaining ingredients. Bring mixture to a boil; cover, reduce heat, and simmer 20 minutes. Remove and discard bay leaf. Serve sauce with omelets or scrambled eggs. Yield: 2¼ cups.   Paula A. Doebler

Three Rivers Cookbook, Volume III
Child Health Association of Sewickley, Pennsylvania

Mushroom-Onion Sauce

½ pound fresh mushrooms, sliced
¼ cup butter or margarine, melted
¾ cup canned diluted beef broth

¼ cup chopped green onions
1 teaspoon salt
¼ cup Sauterne or other sweet white wine
1 tablespoon cornstarch

Sauté mushrooms in melted butter in a large skillet until tender. Add broth, onions, and salt; stir well. Bring to a boil. Combine Sauterne and cornstarch; stir well. Gradually add wine mixture to mushroom mixture, stirring constantly. Cook over medium heat, stirring constantly, 1 minute or until thickened and bubbly. Serve warm over grilled steaks or hamburgers. Yield: 2 cups.

Bound to Please
The Junior League of Boise, Idaho

Country Barbecue Sauce

1 onion, chopped
1 medium-size green pepper, chopped
1 stalk celery with leaves, chopped
3 cloves garlic, chopped
1 tablespoon chopped fresh sage
1 cup butter or margarine, melted

3 cups tomato juice
2¼ cups catsup
1½ cups vinegar
¾ cup firmly packed brown sugar
1 (6-ounce) can tomato paste
½ teaspoon salt
1 cup bourbon
Rind of 3 lemons
Juice of 3 lemons

Sauté onion, green pepper, celery, garlic, and sage in butter in a Dutch oven until vegetables are tender. Add tomato juice and next 5 ingredients; stir well. Bring to a boil; reduce heat, and simmer, uncovered, 2 hours. Stir in bourbon, lemon rind, and juice. Cover and simmer 30 minutes. Use as a basting sauce for chicken or pork during cooking. Yield: 9 cups.   Mrs. Oneitha Roane

Gracious Goodness: The Taste of Memphis
The Symphony League of Memphis, Tennessee

Pacific Barbecue Sauce

1 cup soy sauce
1 small onion, grated
1 tablespoon sugar
2 tablespoons minced fresh ginger

2 tablespoons bourbon
2 cloves garlic, minced
1 teaspoon dry mustard
1 teaspoon hot sauce

Combine all ingredients in a medium bowl; stir well. Use as a marinade for beef, pork, or chicken and as a basting sauce during cooking. Yield: 1½ cups.

Gourmet LA
The Junior League of Los Angeles, California

Memphis in May Magnificent Marinade

1½ cups vegetable oil
¾ cup lemon juice
¾ cup soy sauce
½ cup rosé or other dry pink wine
¼ cup Worcestershire sauce

2 tablespoons dry mustard
1 tablespoon herb pepper
2½ teaspoons seasoned salt
2 teaspoons chopped fresh parsley
½ teaspoon garlic powder

Combine first 5 ingredients in a large jar; cover tightly, and shake vigorously. Combine dry mustard, herb pepper, seasoned salt, parsley, and garlic powder; add to oil mixture. Cover tightly, and shake vigorously. Use as a basting sauce for chicken or pork during cooking. Yield: 3¾ cups.   Tom Conlee

Memphis in May International Festival Cookbook
Memphis in May International Festival, Inc.
Memphis, Tennessee

Waterford Hot Applesauce

12 large Granny Smith apples
1¾ cups apple cider
¼ cup unsalted butter or margarine
½ cup maple syrup
2 teaspoons grated lemon rind
1½ teaspoons ground cinnamon

½ teaspoon ground allspice
½ teaspoon ground nutmeg
⅛ teaspoon ground ginger
1 tablespoon plus 1 teaspoon unsalted butter or margarine

Peel and core apples; cut into wedges. Combine apple wedges, cider, and ¼ cup butter in a Dutch oven; bring to a boil. Cover, reduce heat, and simmer 25 minutes or until apples are tender.

Remove cover, and lightly mash apples. Add maple syrup and next 5 ingredients; stir well. Cook, uncovered, 10 minutes or until mixture thickens. Remove from heat; add 1 tablespoon plus 1 teaspoon butter, stirring until butter melts. Serve warm or cold with turkey, ham, or pork. Yield: 9½ cups.

Cardinal Cuisine
The Mount Vernon Hospital Auxiliary
Alexandria, Virginia

Cranberry-Currant Walnut Sauce

1 pound fresh cranberries
1¼ cups sugar
1 cup red currant preserves
  or jelly
1 cup water

1 cup coarsely chopped
  walnuts
2 tablespoons grated orange
  rind

Combine first 4 ingredients in a large saucepan. Bring to a boil; reduce heat, and simmer, uncovered, 20 minutes, stirring occasionally. Remove from heat, and skim off foam with a metal spoon. Add walnuts and orange rind; stir well. Cover and chill at least 8 hours. Serve with game, turkey, or ham. Yield: 4 cups.   Marilyn Putz

Aggies, Moms, and Apple Pie
The Federation of Texas A&M University Mothers' Clubs
College Station, Texas

Delaware City Brandied Peaches

3 cups water
2 cups sugar
6 small, firm, ripe peaches,
  peeled

¼ cup brandy

Combine water and sugar in a medium saucepan; bring to a boil. Boil 10 minutes, stirring occasionally. Add peaches, and cook 5 minutes or until peaches are tender.

Pack peaches into hot sterilized jars; pour syrup over peaches, leaving ½-inch headspace. Pour 2 tablespoons brandy into each jar. Remove air bubbles, and wipe jar rims. Cover at once with metal lids, and screw on bands. Process in boiling-water bath 15 minutes. Serve brandied peaches over vanilla ice cream or with lamb or chicken. Yield: 2 pints.   Elmer L. Snow, III

The Delaware Heritage Cookbook
The Delaware Heritage Commission
Wilmington, Delaware

Pesto alla Genovese

2 cups packed fresh basil
  leaves
¾ cup olive oil
1 cup chopped fresh parsley
½ cup pine nuts (optional)

10 to 12 cloves garlic
1½ teaspoons salt
½ cup freshly grated
  Parmesan cheese

Position knife blade in food processor bowl; add basil leaves, and process until finely chopped. Add oil, parsley, pine nuts, if desired, garlic, and salt; process until smooth. Stir in cheese. Serve over pasta. Yield: 1¼ cups.

Stanford University Medical Center Auxiliary Cookbook
Stanford University Medial Center Auxiliary
Palo Alto, California

Herb-Cheese Butter

½ cup butter or margarine,
  softened
¼ cup grated Parmesan cheese
3 tablespoons finely chopped
  fresh parsley

½ teaspoon dried Italian
  seasoning
¼ teaspoon garlic salt
¼ teaspoon pepper

Combine all ingredients in a small bowl; stir well. Serve as a topping for baked potatoes or cooked vegetables. Yield: ½ cup.

Con Mucho Gusto
The Desert Club of Mesa, Arizona

Mustard Butter

1 cup unsalted butter, softened
⅓ cup minced green onions
⅓ cup minced celery
¼ cup Dijon mustard
2 tablespoons chopped fresh
  parsley

2 teaspoons Worcestershire
  sauce
½ teaspoon lemon juice
⅛ teaspoon salt
5 drops of hot sauce

Combine all ingredients in a medium bowl, and stir well with a wire whisk. Shape butter mixture into a ball, and chill until firm. Let butter soften slightly before serving. Serve as a spread for sand-wiches. Yield: 1½ cups.   Marty White Mauldin

Rebel Recipes
Department of Home Economics, University of Mississippi
Oxford, Mississippi

Onion Jam

8 large purple onions, thinly
  sliced
¼ cup butter or margarine,
  melted
2 tablespoons olive oil

1 to 2 teaspoons salt
½ teaspoon freshly ground
  pepper
2 or 3 fresh rosemary sprigs
2 tablespoons brown sugar

Sauté onion in butter and oil in a Dutch oven until tender. Add salt, pepper, and rosemary. Reduce heat to medium; cook 30 minutes, stirring frequently. Stir in sugar. Remove and discard rosemary sprigs. Serve jam with chicken or pork. Yield: 5 cups.

Only in California
The Children's Home Society of California
Los Angeles, California

Grape-Apple Jelly

2 cups grape juice
1 cup unsweetened apple
  juice

1 (1¾-ounce) package
  powdered pectin
3½ cups sugar

Combine juices and pectin in a Dutch oven; stir well. Bring to a boil, stirring occasionally. Add sugar, and bring mixture to a full, rolling boil. Boil 1 minute, stirring constantly. Remove from heat; skim off foam with a metal spoon. Pour jelly into hot sterilized jars, leaving ¼-inch headspace; wipe jar rims. Cover at once with metal lids, and screw on bands. Process in boiling-water bath 5 minutes. Yield: 5 half pints.   Mary Pope

Heritage of Red Cloud
Heritage of Red Cloud
Red Cloud, Nebraska

Lime-Zucchini Marmalade

4 cups shredded zucchini
1 cup water
½ cup fresh lime juice
1 (1¾-ounce) package
  powdered pectin

5 cups sugar
3 tablespoons grated lime
  rind

Combine first 3 ingredients in a Dutch oven. Bring to a boil; reduce heat, and simmer 10 minutes. Add pectin; stir well. Bring to a boil; stir in sugar and rind. Bring to a full, rolling boil; boil 2 minutes, stirring constantly. Remove from heat; stir 5 minutes.

Quickly pour into hot sterilized jars, leaving ¼-inch headspace; wipe jar rims. Cover at once with metal lids, and screw on bands. Process in boiling-water bath 10 minutes. Yield: about 6 half pints.

Merrymeeting Merry Eating
The Regional Memorial Hospital Auxiliary
Brunswick, Maine

Peach-Cantaloupe Conserve

3 cups peeled, chopped fresh
  peaches
3 cups peeled, chopped
  cantaloupe
4¼ cups sugar
3 tablespoons lemon juice

⅓ cup slivered blanched
  almonds
½ teaspoon ground nutmeg
¼ teaspoon salt
¼ teaspoon grated orange
  rind

Combine peaches and cantaloupe in a large Dutch oven. Bring mixture to a boil, stirring constantly. Add sugar and lemon juice; bring to a boil, stirring constantly. Boil, uncovered, 12 minutes, stirring occasionally. Add almonds and remaining ingredients. Bring to a boil; boil 10 to 12 minutes or until mixture registers 221° on a candy thermometer, stirring frequently. Remove from heat; skim off foam with a metal spoon, if necessary.

Quickly pour into hot sterilized jars, leaving ¼-inch headspace; wipe jar rims. Cover at once with metal lids, and screw on bands. Process in boiling-water bath 5 minutes. Yield: 5 half pints.

Recipes to Cherish
Women's Missionary and Service Commission
Harrisonburg, Virginia

Soups & Stews

A hiker enjoys a trail winding through the redwoods of the Cascade Range in Oregon. The Cascade Range is part of the Pacific Coast Ranges, extending northward more than 700 miles from Lassen Peak in northern California, through Oregon and Washington, to the Fraser River in southern British Columbia, Canada.

Apricot-Wine Soup

2 (16-ounce) cans apricots,
  undrained
1 (8-ounce) carton sour cream
1 cup Chablis or other dry
  white wine
¼ cup apricot liqueur

2 tablespoons lemon juice
2 teaspoons vanilla extract
¼ teaspoon ground cinnamon
Garnishes: sour cream and
  ground cinnamon

Combine all ingredients except garnishes in container of an electric blender, and process until smooth. Cover and chill thoroughly. Ladle soup into individual soup bowls. Garnish, if desired. Yield: 6 cups.   Leckie Kern Stack

Georgia on My Menu
The Junior League of Cobb-Marietta, Georgia

Blueberry-Yogurt Soup

4 cups fresh blueberries
1 (3-inch) stick cinnamon
2 cups water
½ cup sugar
⅛ teaspoon salt

2 tablespoons cornstarch
½ cup milk
2 cups plain low-fat yogurt
¼ cup Burgundy or other dry
  red wine

Wash blueberries; reserve ¼ cup blueberries for garnish.

Combine remaining 3¾ cups blueberries and next 4 ingredients in a medium saucepan. Bring to a boil; reduce heat, and simmer 5 minutes or until berries begin to burst. Remove from heat. Remove and discard cinnamon stick.

Spoon half of blueberry mixture into container of an electric blender, and process until smooth. Repeat procedure with remaining half of blueberry mixture. Return pureed mixture to saucepan.

Combine cornstarch and milk; stir well. Add to blueberry mixture; stir well. Cook over medium heat, stirring constantly, until mixture thickens. Remove from heat. Let cool slightly; stir in yogurt and wine. Cover and chill thoroughly.

Ladle soup into individual soup bowls. Top each serving evenly with reserved blueberries. Yield: 8 cups.   Zeva Appel

What's Cooking?
The Sisterhood of Temple Shalom
Succasunna, New Jersey

Mexican Avocado Soup

1 medium-size ripe avocado,
  peeled and coarsely
  chopped
2 cups milk
½ cup minced purple onion
½ cup chopped green chiles
¼ cup sour cream

½ teaspoon ground cumin
¼ teaspoon salt
¼ teaspoon freshly ground
  black pepper
Dash of ground red pepper
Garnish: tortilla chips

Place avocado in container of an electric blender or food processor, and process until smooth.

Combine pureed avocado, milk, and next 7 ingredients; stir well. Cover and chill thoroughly. Ladle into individual soup bowls. Garnish, if desired. Yield: 4 cups.

License to Cook New Mexico Style
New Mexico Federation of Business and Professional Women
Albuquerque, New Mexico

Curried Broccoli Soup

2 pounds fresh broccoli
2 (14½-ounce) cans
  ready-to-serve chicken
  broth, divided
3 tablespoons butter or
  margarine

2 onions, chopped
1½ teaspoons curry powder
Sour cream
Chopped roasted peanuts

Trim off large leaves of broccoli, and remove tough ends of lower stalks. Wash broccoli thoroughly. Cut broccoli into flowerets, and coarsely chop stalks. Set aside.

Place 1 cup broth in a large saucepan; bring to a boil. Add half of broccoli flowerets, and cook 3 to 4 minutes or until crisp-tender. Drain, reserving broth. Chill cooked broccoli flowerets.

Melt butter in a large saucepan. Add onion and curry powder, and sauté until onion is tender. Stir in chopped broccoli stalks, remaining half of flowerets, reserved cooking broth, and remaining chicken broth. Bring to a boil; cover, reduce heat, and simmer 12 minutes or until broccoli is tender.

Transfer half of broccoli mixture to container of an electric blender or food processor, and process until mixture is smooth.

Repeat procedure with remaining broccoli mixture. Transfer pureed mixture to a medium bowl. Cover and chill thoroughly.

To serve, ladle soup into individual soup bowls. Top each serving with chilled flowerets, sour cream, and peanuts. Yield: 6 cups.

Stanford University Medical Center Auxiliary Cookbook
Stanford University Medical Center Auxiliary
Palo Alto, California

Red Pepper Soup

4 cups chopped leeks
6 large sweet red peppers, thinly sliced
1 cup unsalted butter, melted
2 tablespoons vegetable oil

3 cups canned diluted chicken broth
½ teaspoon salt
¼ teaspoon ground white pepper
6 cups buttermilk

Sauté leeks and red pepper in butter and oil in a Dutch oven until tender. Add broth, salt, and pepper; stir well. Bring to a boil; cover, reduce heat, and simmer 30 minutes. Pour one-third of pepper mixture into container of an electric blender or food processor; process until smooth. Repeat procedure twice with remaining pepper mixture. Strain pureed pepper mixture; let cool slightly. Stir in buttermilk. Cover and chill. Yield: 14 cups.

From Scratch Cookbook
The Assistance League® of Glendale, California

License to Cook New Mexico Style *by the New Mexico Federation of Business and Professional Women offers the cuisine of the Southwest along with interesting facts about "the land of enchantment." Proceeds will benefit their scholarship fund.*

San Fernando Salad Soup

1 (46-ounce) can tomato juice
3 medium tomatoes, diced
1 medium-size green pepper, diced
1 medium cucumber, seeded and diced
1 cup scraped, shredded carrots
1 cup thinly sliced celery
¼ cup thinly sliced green onions

¼ cup olive oil
2 tablespoons lemon juice
1 tablespoon sugar
1½ teaspoons salt
1 clove garlic, crushed
1 teaspoon Worcestershire sauce
Garnish: commercial croutons

Combine all ingredients except garnish in a large bowl; stir well. Cover and chill thoroughly. Ladle into individual soup bowls. Garnish, if desired. Yield: 10½ cups.   Naomi F. Eber

Bach to the Kitchen
Cappella Cantorum
Essex, Connecticut

White Spanish Gazpacho

3 medium cucumbers, peeled and cut into 2-inch pieces
1 tablespoon salt
1 clove garlic
3 cups canned diluted chicken broth, divided
3 cups sour cream
3 tablespoons vinegar

3 cups peeled, chopped tomato
¾ cup sliced natural almonds, toasted
½ cup finely chopped fresh parsley
½ cup chopped green onions
Garnishes: radish slices and scraped shredded carrot

Combine cucumber and salt in a medium bowl; let stand 30 minutes. Drain and rinse well.

Position knife blade in food processor bowl; add cucumber, and garlic, and process until smooth. With processor running, pour 1 cup chicken broth through food chute in a slow, steady stream; process 30 seconds. Combine pureed cucumber mixture, remaining 2 cups chicken broth, sour cream, and vinegar, stirring with a wire whisk until blended. Cover and chill thoroughly.

Ladle gazpacho into individual wide, shallow soup bowls; nestle bowls in crushed ice. Top each serving evenly with chopped tomato, toasted almonds, chopped parsley, and green onions. Garnish, if desired. Yield: 9 cups.   Roy Jefferson

Cooking with the Skins
The National Multiple Sclerosis Society/National Capital Chapter
Washington, DC

French Onion Soup and Croutons

4 cups thinly sliced onions
¼ cup butter or margarine, melted
2 tablespoons all-purpose flour
2 (10½-ounce) cans chicken broth, undiluted

2 (10½-ounce) cans beef broth, undiluted
1⅓ cups water
Puffy Cheese Croutons

Sauté onion in butter in a large Dutch oven until tender. Add flour; stir well. Add chicken broth, beef broth, and water, stirring well. Bring to a boil; cover, reduce heat, and simmer 30 minutes. Ladle into individual soup bowls. Top each serving with Puffy Cheese Croutons. Yield: 8 cups.

Puffy Cheese Croutons

¼ teaspoon butter or margarine
1 cup (4 ounces) shredded Cheddar cheese

1 tablespoon milk
2 egg whites
5 (1-ounce) slices French bread, cut into 1-inch cubes

Place butter in top of a double boiler; bring water to a boil. Reduce heat to low; cook until butter melts. Add cheese and milk; cook, stirring constantly, until cheese melts.

Beat egg whites (at room temperature) at high speed of an electric mixer until stiff peaks form. Fold egg whites into cheese mixture. Dip bread cubes into cheese mixture, and place on a baking sheet. Bake at 400° for 8 minutes or until puffed and lightly browned. Yield: 40 croutons.   Eunice G. Johnson

Woman to Woman Cookbook
The Zonta Club of the Black Hills
Rapid City, South Dakota

Cheesecake Soup

¾ cup chopped onion
½ cup chopped celery
½ cup butter or margarine, melted
½ cup all-purpose flour
1 (10¾-ounce) can chicken broth, undiluted
2¾ cups water
1 (8-ounce) package cream cheese, softened
1 cup plain low-fat yogurt
2 egg yolks, beaten
½ teaspoon salt
¼ teaspoon ground white pepper
Garnish: chopped fresh parsley

Sauté onion and celery in butter in a Dutch oven. Add flour, stirring until smooth. Cook 1 minute, stirring constantly. Gradually add broth and water. Bring to a boil; cover, reduce heat, and simmer 7 minutes, stirring occasionally. Remove cover, and simmer 8 minutes, stirring occasionally.

Combine cream cheese, yogurt, and egg yolks in a medium bowl; beat at low speed of an electric mixer until smooth. Gradually stir about 2 cups hot mixture into yolks; add to remaining hot mixture, stirring constantly. Cook over low heat, stirring constantly, until mixture is thoroughly heated. Add salt and pepper; stir well. Ladle into individual soup bowls. Garnish, if desired. Yield: 6½ cups.

"One Lump or Two?"
All Children's Hospital Guild
St. Petersburg, Florida

"One Lump or Two?" *was created by the All Children's Hospital Guild to raise funds for the All Children's Hospital. Its purpose is to care for any child in need, regardless of race, religion, or ability to pay. Monies earned from the sale of this cookbook will go toward the building of a barrier-free playground.*

Creamy Cheddar Soup

⅔ cup scraped, shredded
  carrots
⅔ cup thinly sliced celery
¼ cup finely chopped onion
¼ cup butter or margarine,
  melted
¼ cup all-purpose flour

4 cups milk
1 teaspoon salt
Dash of pepper
2 cups (8 ounces) shredded
  sharp Cheddar cheese
1 cup cubed cooked ham

Sauté carrot, celery, and onion in butter in a small Dutch oven until tender. Add flour, stirring until smooth. Cook 1 minute, stirring constantly. Gradually add milk; cook over medium heat, stirring constantly, until mixture is thickened and bubbly. Add salt and pepper; stir well. Add cheese and ham, stirring until cheese melts. Serve immediately. Yield: 6 cups.   Pauline Nelson

Port's Galley
The Port Council of Port of Portland, Oregon

Golden Gate Cheese Soup

⅔ cup scraped, finely
  chopped carrots
½ cup finely chopped celery
⅓ cup finely chopped onion
¼ cup butter or margarine,
  melted
⅓ cup all-purpose flour

2 cups canned diluted
  chicken broth
2 cups milk
1 cup (4 ounces) shredded
  Cheddar cheese
1 tablespoon brandy
¼ teaspoon salt

Sauté carrot, celery, and onion in butter in a large saucepan 5 minutes or until vegetables are tender. Add flour, stirring until smooth. Cook 1 minute, stirring constantly. Gradually add chicken broth and milk; cook over medium heat, stirring constantly, until mixture is thickened and bubbly.

Stir in shredded cheese, brandy, and salt. Reduce heat to low, and cook, stirring constantly, until cheese melts. Serve soup immediately. Yield: 5 cups.   Marlene Taylor

Southern California Style
The Assistance League® of Anaheim, California

Monterey Jack Cheese Soup

2 cups canned diluted
   chicken broth
1 cup finely chopped onion
1 cup peeled, diced tomato
1 (4-ounce) can chopped
   green chiles, undrained
1 teaspoon minced garlic
¼ cup plus 2 tablespoons
   butter or margarine

¼ cup plus 2 tablespoons
   all-purpose flour
5 cups milk, divided
3 cups (12 ounces) shredded
   Monterey Jack cheese
½ teaspoon salt
⅛ teaspoon pepper

Combine first 5 ingredients in a large saucepan. Bring to a boil; cover, reduce heat, and simmer 10 to 12 minutes or until vegetables are tender. Remove from heat, and set aside.

Melt butter in a heavy saucepan over low heat; add flour, stirring until smooth. Cook 1 minute, stirring constantly. Gradually add 3½ cups milk; cook over medium heat, stirring constantly, until mixture is thickened and bubbly. Add reserved vegetable mixture, remaining 1½ cups milk, shredded cheese, salt, and pepper; cook, stirring constantly, until cheese melts and soup is thoroughly heated. Serve immediately. Yield: 9½ cups.   Alison McAuliffe

Black-Eyed Susan Country
The Saint Agnes Hospital Auxiliary
Baltimore, Maryland

French Potato Soup

2 large leeks
1 cup scraped, chopped
   carrots
1 cup peeled, chopped turnip
½ cup chopped celery
½ cup chopped onion
2 tablespoons olive oil or
   butter, melted
4 cups canned diluted
   chicken broth

3 cups peeled, chopped
   baking potatoes
2 bay leaves
½ teaspoon salt
¼ teaspoon pepper
½ cup whipping cream
   (optional)

Chop white portion of leeks; discard tops. Sauté leeks, carrot, turnip, celery, and onion in oil in a Dutch oven until tender. Add chicken broth, potato, bay leaves, salt, and pepper. Bring to a boil;

cover, reduce heat, and simmer 20 minutes or until potato is tender. Remove and discard bay leaves.

Position knife blade in food processor bowl; add half of potato mixture, and process until smooth. Repeat procedure with remaining potato mixture. Return pureed potato mixture to Dutch oven; cook over low heat until thoroughly heated. Stir in whipping cream, if desired. Yield: 7 cups.   Au Croissant

Spokane Cooks!© Northwest
The Community Centers Foundation of Spokane, Washington

Swiss Potato Soup

4 large baking potatoes, peeled and sliced
3 cups water
2 tablespoons chopped celery leaves
1½ teaspoons salt
¼ teaspoon dried whole marjoram
3 green onions
2 tablespoons butter or margarine

2 tablespoons all-purpose flour
3 cups milk
2 green onions, finely chopped
½ cup minced fresh parsley
¼ teaspoon pepper
1½ cups (6 ounces) shredded Swiss cheese

Combine first 5 ingredients in a large Dutch oven. Finely chop white portion of 3 green onions; reserve tops for other uses. Add to potato mixture. Bring to a boil over medium heat; reduce heat, and simmer 25 minutes or until potato is tender. Remove from heat; mash potato mixture.

Melt butter in a large saucepan over low heat; add flour, stirring until smooth. Cook 1 minute, stirring constantly. Gradually add milk; cook over medium heat, stirring constantly, until mixture is thickened and bubbly. Add white sauce to potato mixture; cook over low heat until thoroughly heated. Stir in 2 chopped green onions, parsley, and pepper; cover and let stand 5 minutes. Ladle into individual soup bowls. Sprinkle each serving evenly with shredded cheese. Yield: 9½ cups.   Vicki Scheck

A Taste of Hope
The Camarillo Chapter of City of Hope
Camarillo, California

Vichysquash

1 medium onion, sliced
2 tablespoons butter or
  margarine, melted
6 medium-size yellow squash,
  sliced
½ cup canned diluted
  chicken broth

1 cup half-and-half or milk
Salt and freshly ground
  pepper to taste
Garnish: chopped fresh
  chives

Sauté onion in butter in a large saucepan over medium heat until tender. Add squash and broth. Bring to a boil; cover, reduce heat, and simmer 15 minutes or until squash is tender.

Transfer squash mixture to container of an electric blender or food processor, and process until smooth. Let cool slightly. Add half-and-half and salt and pepper to taste; stir well. Garnish, if desired. Yield: 4¾ cups.   Dick Wylly

The Mark Twain Library Cookbook, Volume III
The Mark Twain Library Association
Redding, Connecticut

Cream of Pumpkin Soup
with Cinnamon Croutons

1 cup chopped onion
2 tablespoons butter or
  margarine, melted
2 (10¾-ounce) cans chicken
  broth, undiluted
1 (16-ounce) can cooked,
  mashed pumpkin

1 teaspoon salt
¼ teaspoon ground cinnamon
⅛ teaspoon ground ginger
⅛ teaspoon pepper
1 cup whipping cream
Cinnamon Croutons

Sauté onion in butter in a medium saucepan until tender. Add 1 can chicken broth; stir well. Bring to a boil; cover, reduce heat, and simmer 15 minutes.

Pour broth mixture into container of an electric blender, and process until smooth. Return mixture to saucepan. Add remaining 1 can chicken broth, pumpkin, and next 4 ingredients; stir well. Bring to a boil; cover, reduce heat, and simmer 10 minutes, stirring occasionally. Stir in cream, and cook until thoroughly heated (do not boil). Ladle into individual soup bowls. Top each serving with Cinnamon Croutons. Yield: 6 cups.

Cinnamon Croutons

3 tablespoons butter or margarine, softened
1 tablespoon brown sugar

¼ teaspoon ground cinnamon
4 slices whole wheat bread

Combine butter, brown sugar, and cinnamon; stir well. Spread butter mixture evenly over one side of bread slices. Place bread, buttered side up, on a baking sheet. Bake at 400° for 8 to 10 minutes or until bread is crisp and topping is bubbly. Cut each slice of bread into 8 small triangles or squares. Yield: 32 croutons.

Hearts & Flour
The Womens' Club of Pittsford, New York

Bayliner Peanut Soup

1 onion, chopped
1¼ cups chopped celery
¼ cup butter, melted
3 tablespoons all-purpose flour
3 (10½-ounce) cans chicken broth, diluted

⅓ cup water
2 cups creamy peanut butter
1¾ cups half-and-half
Chopped roasted peanuts

Sauté onion and celery in butter in a large Dutch oven over medium heat until tender. Transfer sautéed vegetable mixture to container of an electric blender, and process until smooth. Return pureed mixture to Dutch oven; add flour, stirring until smooth. Cook 1 minute, stirring constantly. Gradually add chicken broth and water; cook over medium heat until thoroughly heated. Add peanut butter, stirring until smooth. Gradually add half-and-half; cook until thoroughly heated (do not boil). Ladle into individual soup bowls. Sprinkle each serving with chopped peanuts. Yield: 13 cups.

From a Lighthouse Window
The Chesapeake Bay Maritime Museum
St. Michaels, Maryland

Crab Bisque

½ cup scraped, finely
  shredded carrot
¼ cup finely chopped onion
¼ cup butter or margarine,
  melted
3 tablespoons all-purpose
  flour
2 cups canned diluted
  chicken broth
4 cups half-and-half

2 cups fresh crabmeat,
  drained and flaked
¼ cup dry sherry
1 teaspoon salt
⅓ cup finely chopped
  watercress
Dash of ground red pepper
Freshly ground black pepper
  to taste

Sauté carrot and onion in butter in a skillet until tender. Reduce
heat to low; add flour, stirring until smooth. Cook 1 minute, stirring
constantly. Gradually add broth; cook over medium heat, stirring
constantly, until thickened and bubbly. Add half-and-half and next
3 ingredients; stir well. Cook until thoroughly heated (do not boil).
Stir in watercress, red pepper, and black pepper. Yield: 9½ cups.

Quiltie Ladies Scrapbook
Variable Star Quilters
Souderton, Pennsylvania

Maxon's Green Chile Chowder

1 poblano chile
4 cups canned diluted
  chicken broth
4 medium-size baking
  potatoes, peeled and cut
  into ½-inch cubes
1 cup finely chopped onion
½ jalapeño pepper, seeded
  and minced

½ teaspoon seasoned salt
¼ cup butter or margarine
¼ cup all-purpose flour
1½ cups half-and-half
1½ cups milk
Shredded Cheddar cheese

Wash and dry chile; place on an aluminum foil-lined baking sheet.
Bake at 425° for 45 minutes. Place in a plastic bag; close tightly, and
let stand 10 minutes. Peel chile; remove core and seeds. Chop chile.
Combine chile and next 5 ingredients in a Dutch oven. Bring to a
boil; cover, reduce heat, and simmer 20 minutes or until potato is
tender. Drain, reserving 3 cups liquid. Set half of potato mixture
aside. Mash remaining half of potato mixture; set aside.

Melt butter in Dutch oven over low heat; add flour, stirring until smooth. Cook 1 minute, stirring constantly. Gradually add reserved potato liquid, half-and-half, and milk; cook over medium heat, stirring constantly, until mixture is thickened and bubbly. Remove from heat; add reserved potato mixtures, stirring well. Ladle into individual soup bowls. Sprinkle with cheese. Yield: 9 cups.

Seasoned with Sun
The Junior League of El Paso, Texas

Boston Bouillabaisse

4 cups water (optional)
2 (8-ounce) frozen lobster tails, thawed (optional)
¾ cup chopped onion
¾ cup sliced celery
1 large clove garlic, minced
⅓ cup butter or margarine, melted
2 (16-ounce) cans whole tomatoes, undrained and chopped
2 cups clam juice
1 cup water
1 pound cod fillets, cut into 2-inch pieces

1 pound perch fillets, cut into 2-inch pieces
1 pound pollack fillets, cut into 2-inch pieces
1 large bay leaf, crushed
½ teaspoon dried whole thyme
½ teaspoon saffron threads, crushed (optional)
½ teaspoon salt
½ teaspoon pepper
1 pound fresh sea scallops

If desired, bring 4 cups water to a boil in a large saucepan; add lobster tails. Return to a boil; cook 5 minutes. Remove lobster tails with tongs; rinse with cold water. Drain. Split tails lengthwise; remove and coarsely chop meat. Set aside.

Sauté onion, celery, and garlic in melted butter in a large Dutch oven until vegetables are tender. Add tomatoes and next 10 ingredients; stir well. Bring to a boil; reduce heat, and simmer 10 minutes. Add scallops; simmer 10 minutes. If desired, stir in reserved lobster meat, and cook until thoroughly heated. Serve immediately. Yield: 16 cups.

Scoops from the Bay
Cape Cod Academy
Osterville, Massachusetts

White Chili

4 chicken breast halves,
skinned, boned, and cut
into 1-inch pieces
1 (15-ounce) can cannellini
beans, drained
1 (15-ounce) can garbanzo
beans, drained
1½ cups water
1 (11-ounce) can white corn,
drained
2 (4-ounce) cans chopped
green chiles, undrained

2 chicken-flavored bouillon
cubes
1 onion, chopped
1 clove garlic, minced
1 teaspoon ground cumin
1 tablespoon vegetable oil
Hot sauce to taste
1 cup (4 ounces) shredded
Monterey Jack cheese
Garnish: fresh parsley sprigs

Combine first 7 ingredients in a 2½-quart baking dish; stir well, and set aside. Sauté onion, garlic, and cumin in oil in a skillet until onion is tender. Add to chicken mixture, stirring well. Cover and bake at 350° for 50 minutes or until chicken is done. Remove from oven. Add hot sauce to taste; stir well. Sprinkle with cheese. Garnish, if desired. Yield: 8 cups.   Cathleen Patton

Favorite Recipes of Edmonds
Edmonds United Methodist Women
Edmonds, Washington

Two-Alarm Chili

2 pounds boneless chuck
roast, coarsely ground
1 (29-ounce) can tomato
sauce
1 cup water
¼ cup plus 2 tablespoons
chili powder
1½ teaspoons garlic powder
1½ teaspoons onion powder
1½ teaspoons ground cumin

1½ teaspoons dried Italian
seasoning
1 teaspoon salt
1 teaspoon ground red
pepper (optional)
1 teaspoon paprika
1 (30-ounce) can chili beans,
drained
2 tablespoons white cornmeal
2 tablespoons water

Cook ground chuck in a Dutch oven until browned, stirring to crumble; drain. Add tomato sauce and next 9 ingredients. Bring to a boil; cover, reduce heat, and simmer 1 hour and 15 minutes.

Add beans, stirring well. Combine cornmeal and 2 tablespoons water; add to chili mixture, stirring well. Cover; simmer 15 minutes or until thoroughly heated. Yield: 10½ cups.   Ed Voris

Home on the Range
West Marin Health Project and Dance Palace Community Center
Point Reyes, California

Beef Ragout

⅔ cup all-purpose flour
1 teaspoon salt
⅛ teaspoon pepper
1 (3-pound) boneless chuck
 roast, cut into 1½-inch cubes
⅓ cup vegetable oil, divided
1 cup chopped onion
1 cup chopped celery
½ cup chopped green pepper
2 cloves garlic, crushed
2 (10½-ounce) cans beef
 consommé, undiluted

1 (16-ounce) can whole
 tomatoes, undrained
1 (6-ounce) can tomato paste
2 teaspoons Worcestershire
 sauce
2 tablespoons chopped fresh
 parsley
2 teaspoons paprika
12 new potatoes (about 1¼
 pounds)
Garnish: chopped fresh
 parsley

Combine flour, salt, and pepper; stir well. Dredge beef cubes in flour mixture. Reserve any remaining flour mixture.

Brown beef on all sides in 3 tablespoons oil in a large Dutch oven, adding remaining 2 tablespoons plus 1 teaspoon oil as needed. Remove meat, reserving drippings in Dutch oven. Drain meat on paper towels.

Add onion, celery, green pepper, and garlic to drippings, and sauté until vegetables are tender. Add reserved flour mixture; cook 1 minute, stirring constantly. Gradually add beef consommé; cook over medium heat, stirring constantly, until mixture is thickened and bubbly. Add reserved beef cubes, tomatoes, and next 4 ingredients. Bring to a boil, stirring constantly; cover, reduce heat, and simmer 1½ hours. Add potatoes; cover and simmer 1 hour or until potatoes are tender. Garnish, if desired. Yield: 10 servings.

Terry Home Presents Food & Fun from Celebrities & Us
Terry Home, Inc.
Sumner, Washington

Creole Black-Eyes and Rice

1 (16-ounce) package dried
    black-eyed peas
½ pound salt pork, quartered
4 cups water
3 cups chopped onion
1 cup chopped green onions
1 cup chopped fresh parsley
1 cup chopped green pepper
1 (8-ounce) can tomato sauce
1 tablespoon Worcestershire
    sauce
2 cloves garlic, crushed
1 to 1½ teaspoons salt

1 teaspoon ground red
    pepper
1 teaspoon black pepper
¼ teaspoon dried whole
    thyme
¼ teaspoon dried whole
    oregano
3 dashes of hot sauce
2 pounds smoked sausage,
    cut into 1-inch pieces
Hot cooked rice
Garnish: green onion fans

Sort and wash peas; place in a large Dutch oven. Cover with water 2 inches above peas; let soak 8 hours. Drain. Return peas to Dutch oven; add salt pork and 4 cups water. Bring to a boil; cover, reduce heat, and simmer 45 minutes.

Add onion and next 12 ingredients, stirring well. Cover and simmer 45 minutes to 1 hour or until peas are tender. Add sausage; simmer, uncovered, 45 minutes. Serve over rice in individual soup bowls. Garnish, if desired. Yield: 16 cups.   Mary E. Wigelius

The Florida Cooking Adventure
The Florida Federation of Women's Clubs
Lakeland, Florida

Vegetables

*The oldest dated bell in Christendom, A.D. 1247, was acquired
by the owner of the Glenwood Mission Inn in Riverside,
California. The bell, found in England, bears an inscription
in Latin regarding the patron saint of Spain.*

Stir-Fry Asparagus with Cashews

1½ pounds fresh asparagus spears
2 tablespoons olive oil
2 teaspoons light sesame oil
2 teaspoons minced fresh ginger

½ cup fresh shiitake mushrooms
½ cup roasted cashews
1 tablespoon soy sauce

Snap off tough ends of asparagus. Remove scales from stalks with a knife or vegetable peeler, if desired. Cut asparagus diagonally into 2-inch pieces; set aside.

Pour oils around top of a preheated wok, coating sides; heat at medium high (325°) for 2 minutes. Add ginger; stir-fry 30 seconds. Add asparagus, and stir-fry 2 minutes. Add mushrooms, and stir-fry 5 minutes or until asparagus is crisp-tender. Add cashews and soy sauce; toss gently. Serve immediately. Yield: 6 servings.

Gourmet LA
The Junior League of Los Angeles, California

Green Beans Provençal

1 pound fresh green beans
4 slices bacon
½ cup chopped onion
½ cup chopped celery
2 tomatoes, peeled and cut into wedges

1 teaspoon salt
½ teaspoon dried whole oregano
⅛ teaspoon pepper

Wash beans and remove strings. Cut beans into 1½-inch pieces; set aside.

Cook bacon in a large skillet until crisp; remove bacon, reserving 2 tablespoons drippings in skillet. Crumble bacon, and set aside.

Sauté onion and celery in drippings until tender. Add green beans, tomato, salt, oregano, and pepper. Cover and cook over medium heat 8 to 10 minutes or until beans are tender. Sprinkle with crumbled bacon. Yield: 4 servings.   Velma Booth

Heavenly Delights
United Methodist Women, First United Methodist Church
Noblesville, Indiana

Broccoli with Mustard Seeds and Horseradish

¾ pound fresh broccoli
2 tablespoons butter or margarine
1 tablespoon mustard seeds

2 teaspoons prepared horseradish
1 teaspoon fresh lemon juice
Salt and pepper to taste

Trim off large leaves of broccoli, and remove tough ends of lower stalks. Wash broccoli thoroughly, and cut into spears. Arrange broccoli in a vegetable steamer over boiling water. Cover and steam 5 minutes or until crisp-tender. Set aside, and keep warm.

Melt butter in a medium saucepan over medium heat; add mustard seeds. Cover and cook 10 to 15 minutes or until mustard seeds begin to pop; remove from heat. Stir in horseradish, lemon juice, and salt and pepper to taste. Pour mustard seed mixture over broccoli, and toss gently to combine. Serve immediately. Yield: 2 to 4 servings.

Nancy Tighe

Bach to the Kitchen
Cappella Cantorum
Essex, Connecticut

Marinated Brussels Sprouts

1¼ pounds fresh brussels sprouts or 2 (10-ounce) packages frozen brussels sprouts, thawed
1 teaspoon salt
⅓ cup vegetable oil
3 tablespoons white wine vinegar
½ cup sliced water chestnuts

¼ cup finely chopped cooked ham or 6 slices bacon, cooked and crumbled
2 tablespoons thinly sliced green onions
1 (2-ounce) jar sliced pimiento, drained
Salt and pepper to taste

Wash brussels sprouts thoroughly, and remove discolored leaves. Cut off stem ends, and cut in half lengthwise. Combine brussels sprouts and 1 teaspoon salt in a large saucepan; add water to cover. Bring to a boil; cover, reduce heat, and simmer 6 to 8 minutes or until brussels sprouts are tender. Drain well. Transfer brussels sprouts to a serving bowl; set aside, and keep warm.

Combine oil and vinegar; stir with a wire whisk until blended. Add water chestnuts and remaining ingredients; toss well.

Pour dressing mixture over brussels sprouts; toss gently to coat well. Serve warm, or cover and chill 4 to 6 hours. Yield: 8 to 10 servings.   Laura Quinn

Southern California Style
The Assistance League® of Anaheim, California

Brussels Sprouts with Walnuts

1 pound fresh brussels
  sprouts
1 cup water
¼ cup butter or margarine,
  divided
1½ tablespoons all-purpose
  flour

¾ cup canned diluted
  chicken broth
½ to 1 teaspoon salt
¼ teaspoon pepper
1 cup coarsely chopped
  walnuts
½ cup soft breadcrumbs

Wash brussels sprouts thoroughly, and remove discolored leaves. Cut off stem ends, and slash bottom of each sprout with a shallow X.

Combine brussels sprouts and water in a medium saucepan; bring water to a boil over medium-high heat. Cover, reduce heat, and simmer 8 minutes or until brussels sprouts are tender. Drain well, and set aside.

Melt 2 tablespoons butter in a medium saucepan over low heat; add flour, stirring until smooth. Cook 1 minute, stirring constantly. Gradually add chicken broth; cook over medium heat, stirring constantly, until mixture is thickened and bubbly. Add salt and pepper; stir well. Add reserved brussels sprouts and walnuts; toss gently to coat evenly. Cook just until brussels sprouts are thoroughly heated. Transfer to a serving bowl, and keep warm.

Melt remaining 2 tablespoons butter in a small saucepan over medium heat. Add breadcrumbs, and cook, stirring occasionally, 4 minutes or until golden brown. Sprinkle breadcrumb mixture over brussels sprouts. Yield: 8 servings.

Celebrations on the Bayou
The Junior League of Monroe, Louisiana

Skillet Cabbage

1 tablespoon vegetable oil
3 cups shredded cabbage
1 cup chopped celery
1 small green pepper,
   chopped

1 small onion, chopped
½ cup sliced water chestnuts
½ teaspoon salt
¼ teaspoon pepper

Heat oil in a large skillet over medium heat. Add cabbage and remaining ingredients; cover and cook 5 minutes or until vegetables are crisp-tender, stirring occasionally. Serve immediately. Yield: 4 servings.   Marie Paxson

Pioneers of Alaska Cookbook
The Pioneers of Alaska Auxiliary #4
Anchorage, Alaska

Carrots and Water Chestnuts

1 pound carrots, scraped and
   diagonally sliced
2 tablespoons butter or
   margarine
1 (6-ounce) can sliced water
   chestnuts, drained
¾ teaspoon dried whole
   thyme, crushed

¼ teaspoon ground ginger
3 tablespoons Chablis or
   other dry white wine
1 tablespoon chopped fresh
   parsley

Cook carrot in a small amount of boiling water 6 to 8 minutes or until tender; drain. Set aside.

Melt butter in a large skillet over medium-low heat. Add water chestnuts, thyme, and ginger, and cook 2 minutes. Add reserved carrot and wine; cook just until thoroughly heated. Transfer vegetable mixture to a serving bowl; sprinkle with chopped fresh parsley. Yield: 4 to 6 servings.   Pat Perkins

Out of This World
Wood Acres Elementary School
Bethesda, Maryland

Carrots Raspberry

2 large carrots, scraped and
  thinly sliced
2 tablespoons water
1½ teaspoons unsalted butter
  or margarine

1 tablespoon lemon juice
1 teaspoon raspberry vinegar
1½ teaspoons honey

Combine carrot, water, and butter in a small saucepan. Bring to a
boil; cover, reduce heat, and simmer 10 minutes or until carrot is
crisp-tender, stirring occasionally.

Add lemon juice, vinegar, and honey; stir gently. Remove from
heat; let stand 2 minutes. Yield: 2 servings.   Lillian Johnson

The Less Fat Cookbook
The Cancer Education and Prevention Center
Oakland, California

Cauliflower with Raisins
and Pine Nuts

2 tablespoons raisins
1 small cauliflower
4 quarts water
2 teaspoons minced garlic
¼ cup extra-virgin olive oil
2 tablespoons pine nuts

¼ teaspoon salt
⅛ teaspoon freshly ground
  pepper
2 tablespoons chopped fresh
  parsley

Place raisins in a small bowl; add water to cover, and let stand 15
minutes. Drain well, and set aside.

Remove outer leaves and stalk of cauliflower. Wash cauliflower;
leave head whole.

Bring 4 quarts water to a boil in a large Dutch oven; add cauliflower. Return to a boil, and cook 6 to 7 minutes or until crisp-
tender. Drain; break cauliflower into flowerets.

Sauté garlic in olive oil in a large skillet until tender. Add reserved
raisins, cauliflower, pine nuts, salt, and pepper. Cover and cook over
low heat 8 to 10 minutes or until cauliflower is tender, stirring
occasionally. Sprinkle with chopped parsley; serve immediately.
Yield: 4 to 6 servings.

One Magnificent Cookbook
The Junior League of Chicago, Illinois

Spanish Corn-Zucchini

2 medium zucchini (about 1 pound), thinly sliced
½ cup chopped onion
¼ cup chopped green pepper
1 clove garlic, minced
¼ cup butter or margarine, melted
2 medium tomatoes, peeled and chopped
1½ cups frozen whole kernel corn, thawed
1 teaspoon sugar
½ teaspoon salt
½ teaspoon chili powder
¼ teaspoon dried whole oregano
⅛ teaspoon pepper

Sauté zucchini, onion, green pepper, and garlic in melted butter in a large skillet 5 minutes or until crisp-tender. Add tomato and remaining ingredients. Cook over low heat 10 minutes or until vegetables are tender. Yield: 4 to 6 servings.   Ray Hume

Port's Galley
The Port Council of Port of Portland, Oregon

Connie's Corn Scallop

1 (17-ounce) can cream-style corn
½ cup crushed saltine crackers
¼ cup scraped, finely shredded carrot
¼ cup chopped celery
¼ cup chopped green pepper
1 teaspoon chopped onion
¼ cup butter or margarine, melted
¼ cup evaporated milk
2 eggs, beaten
6 drops of hot sauce
½ teaspoon salt
½ teaspoon sugar
½ cup (2 ounces) shredded Cheddar cheese
½ teaspoon paprika

Combine first 12 ingredients in a large bowl; stir well. Pour corn mixture into a greased 8-inch square baking dish. Bake at 350° for 20 minutes or until set. Sprinkle with shredded cheese and paprika; bake an additional 10 minutes or until cheese melts. Yield: 6 servings.   Connie Marshall

Ancestral Stirrings
The New England Historic Genealogical Society
Boston, Massachusetts

Mexican Eggplant Casserole

1 large eggplant, unpeeled
¼ cup vegetable oil
1 (15-ounce) can tomato sauce
2 (4-ounce) cans chopped
  green chiles, drained
½ cup thinly sliced green
  onions

1 (2¼-ounce) can sliced ripe
  olives, drained
½ teaspoon ground cumin
¼ teaspoon garlic powder
1½ cups (6 ounces) shredded
  Cheddar cheese
½ cup sour cream

Cut eggplant into ½-inch slices; brush both sides of slices with oil. Place on a large baking sheet. Bake at 450° for 15 minutes or until tender; set aside.

Combine tomato sauce and next 5 ingredients in a medium saucepan. Bring to a boil; cover, reduce heat, and simmer 10 minutes.

Arrange half of eggplant slices in bottom of a 2-quart casserole. Spoon half of tomato sauce mixture over eggplant; sprinkle with half of cheese. Repeat layers with remaining half of eggplant, sauce, and cheese. Bake, uncovered, at 350° for 20 to 25 minutes or until cheese melts and mixture is thoroughly heated. Serve with sour cream. Yield: 6 servings.

Stanford University Medical Center Auxiliary Cookbook
Stanford University Medial Center Auxiliary
Palo Alto, California

Monies earned from the Stanford University Medical Center Auxiliary's member-staffed gift shop, sale of the **Stanford University Medical Center Auxiliary Cookbook,** *and baby photo sales will be used to purchase hospital equipment, fund scholarships, and provide financial aid to the social services and chaplaincy departments.*

Mushrooms Florentine

18 large fresh mushrooms
1 (10-ounce) package frozen
   chopped spinach, thawed
¼ cup butter or margarine,
   melted
1 medium onion, minced
1 egg yolk, beaten

¼ cup grated Parmesan
   cheese, divided
½ teaspoon salt
⅛ teaspoon freshly ground
   nutmeg
⅛ teaspoon pepper

Clean mushrooms with a damp paper towel. Remove and finely chop stems. Set mushroom caps and chopped stems aside.

Cook spinach according to package directions; drain well, and press between paper towels to remove excess moisture.

Dip mushroom caps in melted butter; place in a 13- x 9- x 2-inch baking dish, cap side down. Sauté reserved chopped mushroom stems and onion in any remaining melted butter in a skillet. Add spinach; stir well. Set aside.

Combine egg yolk, 2½ tablespoons Parmesan cheese, salt, nutmeg, and pepper in a small bowl; stir well. Add to spinach mixture, stirring well.

Spoon spinach mixture evenly into mushroom caps; sprinkle evenly with remaining 1½ tablespoons Parmesan cheese. Bake at 325° for 20 to 25 minutes or until stuffed mushrooms are thoroughly heated. Yield: 6 servings.   Katharina Casper

St. George Women's Auxiliary Cookbook
St. George Women's Auxiliary
Oakland, California

Scalloped Onions and Almonds

12 small boiling onions
1 cup diced celery
½ cup sliced almonds,
   toasted
2 tablespoons grated
   Parmesan cheese
¼ cup butter or
   margarine

3 tablespoons all-purpose
   flour
1 cup milk
½ cup half-and-half
½ to 1 teaspoon salt
⅛ teaspoon pepper
Paprika

Cook onions and diced celery in boiling water to cover 10 to 15 minutes or until vegetables are tender; drain well. Place vegetables in a lightly greased 2-quart casserole. Sprinkle with sliced almonds and Parmesan cheese. Set aside.

Melt butter in a heavy saucepan over low heat; add flour, stirring until smooth. Cook 1 minute, stirring constantly. Gradually add milk and half-and-half; cook over medium heat, stirring constantly, until mixture is thickened and bubbly. Add salt and pepper; stir well. Pour sauce over onion mixture. Sprinkle with paprika. Bake at 350° for 30 minutes. Yield: 6 servings.   Shelley Hargus Wells

Central Texas Style
The Junior Service League of Killeen, Texas

Herbed Onion Slices

3 tablespoons butter or margarine
1 tablespoon brown sugar
½ teaspoon salt
Dash of pepper
2 large onions, cut into ½-inch slices
¼ cup finely chopped celery
2 tablespoons minced fresh parsley
2 tablespoons grated Parmesan cheese
¼ teaspoon dried whole oregano, crushed

Melt butter in a large skillet over medium-low heat; stir in brown sugar, salt, and pepper. Arrange onion slices in a single layer over butter mixture in skillet. Sprinkle with chopped celery; cover and cook 10 minutes.

Turn onion slices; sprinkle with parsley, Parmesan cheese, and oregano. Cover and cook an additional 10 minutes or until onions are tender. Yield: 4 servings.   Julie Parker

For Crying Out Loud . . . Let's Eat!
The Service League of Hammond, Indiana

Black-Eyed Peas and Smoked Ham Hocks

3 cups dried black-eyed peas
8 cups water
3 pounds smoked ham hocks
1 (16-ounce) can stewed tomatoes, undrained
1¼ cups chopped onion
1 cup chopped green pepper
2 tablespoons brown sugar
1 teaspoon salt

Sort and wash peas; place in a large Dutch oven. Cover with water 2 inches above peas; let soak 8 hours. Drain peas, and return to Dutch oven. Add 8 cups water and remaining ingredients. Bring to a boil; cover, reduce heat, and simmer 1½ hours or until peas are tender, stirring occasionally.

Remove ham hocks. Cut ham from ham hocks, and chop meat. Return meat to peas. Yield: 8 servings.   Carolyn Lowery

Crossroads Cuisine
The Winona Manor Christmas Fund
Kilmichael, Mississippi

Stir-Fried Sugar Snap Peas

¾ pound Sugar Snap peas
2 tablespoons vegetable oil
1 sweet red pepper, cut into julienne strips
1 (8-ounce) can sliced water chestnuts, drained
½ cup chopped green onions
1 clove garlic, crushed
1 tablespoon plus 1 teaspoon soy sauce
1 teaspoon rice wine vinegar
½ teaspoon light sesame oil
⅛ teaspoon ground ginger
Salt and pepper to taste

Wash peas; trim ends, and remove strings. Cook peas in boiling water to cover 2 minutes or until crisp-tender. Drain; set aside.

Pour vegetable oil around top of a preheated wok, coating sides; heat at medium high (325°) for 2 minutes. Add pepper strips, water chestnuts, green onions, and garlic; stir-fry 3 to 4 minutes or until vegetables are crisp-tender. Add Sugar Snap peas, soy sauce, and remaining ingredients; stir-fry 1 minute or until thoroughly heated. Yield: 6 servings.   Debbie Slotnick

The Best Specialties of the House . . . and More
North Suburban Guild of Children's Memorial Medical Center
Chicago, Illinois

Famous Saratoga Creamed Potatoes

8 medium-size baking
  potatoes, peeled and diced
1 cup whipping cream

1 cup butter or margarine,
  melted
1 teaspoon salt

Combine all ingredients in a large Dutch oven. Cook, uncovered, over low heat 2½ to 3 hours or until potato is tender, stirring occasionally. Yield: 12 to 14 servings. Almeda C. Dake

Capital Connoisseur
The Lawrence Center Independence House
Schenectady, New York

German Potato Bake

2 pounds red potatoes,
  unpeeled
1 cup chopped onion
¼ cup butter or margarine,
  melted
2 tablespoons all-purpose
  flour
2 cups canned diluted
  chicken broth

2 tablespoons spicy brown
  mustard
1 teaspoon prepared
  horseradish
¼ teaspoon pepper
¼ cup fine, dry breadcrumbs

Cook potatoes, covered, in boiling water to cover 20 minutes or until tender; drain and let cool slightly. Cut potatoes into ½-inch-thick slices; layer slices in a greased 2-quart baking dish. Set aside.

Sauté onion in butter in a large skillet until tender; add flour, stirring until smooth. Cook 1 minute, stirring constantly. Gradually add broth; cook over medium heat, stirring constantly, until mixture is thickened and bubbly. Remove from heat, and stir in mustard, horseradish, and pepper.

Pour sauce over potato slices; sprinkle with breadcrumbs. Bake, uncovered, at 375° for 20 minutes or until thoroughly heated. Yield: 6 to 8 servings. Janie Gardner

100th Anniversary Cookbook
Auxiliary of Harrisburg Hospital
Harrisburg, Pennsylvania

Potato Pancake Pie

2 tablespoons butter or
  margarine, melted
2 large baking potatoes,
  peeled and shredded
1 egg, lightly beaten
½ to ¾ teaspoon salt
Dash of pepper

2 tablespoons all-purpose
  flour
¼ cup (2 ounces) finely
  shredded Gruyère or
  Cheddar cheese
½ teaspoon paprika

Place melted butter in a 9-inch pieplate; set aside.

Rinse shredded potato; drain well. Press potato between paper towels to remove excess moisture. Combine potato, egg, salt, and pepper; stir well. Add flour, and stir well. Firmly press potato mixture into pieplate. Sprinkle with cheese and paprika. Bake at 400° for 35 to 40 minutes or until golden brown. To serve, cut into wedges. Yield: 6 servings.   Julie Ann Adamski

Na Zdrowie II
The Women's Auxiliary-Polish American Club of Agawam
Feeding Hills, Massachusetts

Pineapple-Filled Sweet Potatoes

3 large sweet potatoes
1 (8-ounce) can crushed
  pineapple, undrained
1 tablespoon whipping
  cream

1 tablespoon butter or
  margarine
½ teaspoon salt
6 large marshmallows, cut
  into pieces

Wash potatoes; bake at 400° for 45 minutes or until done. Allow potatoes to cool to touch. Cut potatoes in half lengthwise; carefully scoop out pulp, leaving shells intact. Set potato pulp aside. Place potato shells in a 13- x 9- x 2-inch baking dish; set aside.

Drain pineapple, reserving 2 tablespoons juice; set juice aside. Mash potato pulp. Add pineapple, cream, butter, and salt; stir well. Stuff shells with potato mixture; top with marshmallows. Brush pineapple juice over potatoes. Bake at 325° for 20 minutes or until thoroughly heated. Yield: 6 servings.   Rena Nichman

Black-Eyed Susan Country
The Saint Agnes Hospital Auxiliary
Baltimore, Maryland

Spinach and Carrot Medley

5 medium carrots, scraped
   and thinly sliced
1 medium onion, sliced and
   separated into rings
1 (10-ounce) package frozen
   chopped spinach
3 tablespoons butter or
   margarine
3 tablespoons all-purpose
   flour

1½ cups milk
1 cup (4 ounces) shredded
   process American cheese
¼ teaspoon salt
Dash of pepper
½ cup soft breadcrumbs
1 tablespoon butter or
   margarine, melted

Place sliced carrot and onion rings in a medium saucepan; add water to cover. Bring to a boil over medium heat; reduce heat, and simmer 8 minutes or until vegetables are crisp-tender. Drain well, and set aside.

Cook spinach according to package directions; drain. Set aside, and let cool.

Melt 3 tablespoons butter in a small saucepan over low heat; add flour, stirring until mixture is smooth. Cook 1 minute, stirring constantly. Gradually add milk, and cook over medium heat, stirring constantly, until mixture is thickened and bubbly. Add American cheese, salt, and pepper, stirring just until cheese melts. Set cheese sauce aside.

Layer half of spinach, half of carrot mixture, and half of cheese sauce in a 1-quart casserole. Repeat layers with remaining spinach, carrot mixture, and cheese sauce.

Combine soft breadcrumbs and 1 tablespoon melted butter in a small bowl; stir to coat well. Sprinkle breadcrumb mixture evenly over cheese sauce. Bake at 350° for 15 to 20 minutes or until top is lightly browned and vegetable mixture is thoroughly heated. Yield: 4 to 6 servings.

Jeanne Powell Orman

Georgia on My Menu
The Junior League of Cobb-Marietta, Georgia

Thanksgiving Squash

3 medium acorn squash
½ pound mild Italian sausage
½ cup chopped onion
¼ cup chopped celery with
  leaves
1½ cups crumbled day-old
  cornbread or cornbread
  stuffing mix
3 tablespoons chopped fresh
  parsley

¼ teaspoon dried whole
  thyme
¼ to ½ cup canned diluted
  chicken broth
½ cup chopped pecans or
  walnuts
¼ teaspoon salt
⅛ teaspoon ground white
  pepper
Dash of ground nutmeg

Cut squash in half lengthwise; remove and discard seeds and membranes. Place squash, cut side down, in a 13- x 9- x 2-inch baking dish. Pour water into dish to a depth of 1 inch. Bake at 350° for 35 minutes. Remove from oven; drain well. Return squash halves to dish, placing squash cut side up. Set aside.

Remove casings from sausage; sauté sausage in a large skillet over medium heat until browned, stirring to crumble meat. Remove sausage with a slotted spoon, reserving drippings. Set sausage aside.

Sauté onion and celery in drippings until tender. Drain, discarding drippings. Place sautéed vegetables in a large bowl. Add reserved sausage, cornbread, parsley, and thyme; stir well. Add chicken broth; stir until dry ingredients are moistened. Add pecans and remaining ingredients; stir well.

Spoon cornbread mixture evenly into squash cavities. Bake at 350° for 15 to 20 minutes or until squash is tender and stuffing is thoroughly heated. Yield: 6 servings.   Mary Pollock

The Educated Palate
The Calhoun School Parents Association
New York, New York

Baked Acorn Squash with Applesauce Filling

3 acorn squash
2 cups applesauce
⅓ cup firmly packed brown
  sugar
⅓ cup raisins

¼ cup chopped walnuts
1 tablespoon lemon juice
2 tablespoons butter or
  margarine

Cut squash in half lengthwise; remove and discard seeds and membranes. Place squash, cut side up, in a 13- x 9- x 2-inch baking dish. Add boiling water to dish to a depth of 1 inch.

Combine applesauce and next 4 ingredients; stir well. Spoon into shells; dot with butter. Cover and bake at 350° for 25 minutes. Remove cover, and bake an additional 25 minutes or until squash is tender. Yield: 6 servings.   Betsy Sersted Maier

Rosemalers' Recipes
The Vesterheim-Norwegian American Museum
Decorah, Iowa

Stuffed Squash Surprise

6 medium-size yellow squash
1 (10-ounce) package frozen chopped spinach
1 (3-ounce) package cream cheese, softened
1 egg, beaten
2 tablespoons butter or margarine, melted
¾ teaspoon sugar
½ teaspoon pepper
¼ teaspoon seasoned salt
¼ teaspoon onion salt
½ cup round buttery cracker crumbs
4 slices bacon, cooked and crumbled
Paprika

Cook squash in boiling water to cover 10 minutes or until tender. Drain; let cool slightly. Trim off stems. Cut squash in half lengthwise; scoop out pulp, leaving a ¼-inch shell. Set squash pulp and shells aside.

Cook spinach according to package directions, omitting salt. Drain well; set aside.

Beat cream cheese at medium speed of an electric mixer until smooth. Add squash pulp and spinach, stirring well. Add egg and next 5 ingredients; stir well. Spoon squash mixture into reserved shells. Sprinkle with cracker crumbs, bacon, and paprika.

Place stuffed shells on a lightly greased baking sheet; cover with aluminum foil. Bake at 325° for 20 minutes. Remove cover, and bake an additional 15 minutes or until lightly browned and thoroughly heated. Yield: 12 servings.   Dr. Annette Shelby

The Cookbook
East Lake United Methodist Church
Birmingham, Alabama

Shamu's Italian Casserole

1 small onion, sliced and
separated into rings
2 tablespoons butter or
margarine, melted
4 small zucchini, sliced
1 (14½-ounce) can whole
tomatoes, undrained and
finely chopped

¼ teaspoon salt
⅛ teaspoon pepper
1 cup commercial croutons
¼ cup (1 ounce) shredded
Cheddar cheese

Sauté onion rings in melted butter in a large skillet 5 minutes or until tender. Add sliced zucchini, chopped tomatoes, salt, and pepper, stirring well.

Spoon vegetable mixture into a greased 2-quart casserole. Sprinkle evenly with croutons and shredded cheese. Cover and bake at 350° for 15 minutes. Remove cover, and bake an additional 15 minutes or until lightly browned and thoroughly heated. Yield: 4 to 6 servings.

An Apple a Day Cookbook
Children's Hospital at Santa Rosa
San Antonio, Texas

Cuisine à la Mode *is a collection of original recipes compiled by Les Dames Richelieu du Rhode Island from Woonsocket, Rhode Island. The service organization is dedicated to the enhancement and promotion of the French language and culture. Proceeds will assist the group in their work with a soup kitchen, rape crisis center, the Leukemia Foundation, and the French Institute, as well as help to provide scholarships for local students.*

Tomatoes Stuffed with Broccoli

4 medium tomatoes
1 (10-ounce) package frozen chopped broccoli
1 (6-ounce) roll process cheese food with garlic
¼ teaspoon salt
¼ teaspoon pepper

Cut a ½-inch slice off top of each tomato; reserve for other uses. Carefully scoop out pulp, leaving shells intact. Reserve pulp for other uses. Invert shells on paper towels to drain.

Cook broccoli according to package directions; drain. Position knife blade in food processor bowl; add broccoli and remaining ingredients to bowl, and process until smooth. Spoon broccoli mixture evenly into tomato shells. Place stuffed tomatoes in a lightly greased 9-inch square baking dish. Bake at 400° for 10 minutes or until thoroughly heated. Yield: 4 servings.   Susan Holey

Gingerbread . . . and all the trimmings
The Junior Service League of Waxahachie, Texas

Vegetables Fromage

3 cups bow tie pasta, uncooked
4 carrots, scraped and cut into julienne strips
2 medium zucchini, cut into julienne strips
1 medium-size green pepper, cut into julienne strips
1 clove garlic, minced
3 tablespoons butter or margarine, melted
1 (8-ounce) loaf process cheese spread, cubed
¼ cup half-and-half
1 teaspoon dried whole basil, crushed

Cook pasta according to package directions; drain and set aside.

Sauté julienned carrot, zucchini, green pepper, and minced garlic in melted butter in a large skillet until vegetables are crisp-tender. Reduce heat to low; add cheese, half-and-half, and basil, stirring until cheese melts. Add reserved cooked pasta, and toss gently. Cook just until mixture is thoroughly heated, stirring occasionally. Yield: 6 to 8 servings.   Laurier Champigny

Cuisine à la Mode
Les Dames Richelieu du Rhode Island
Woonsocket, Rhode Island

Acknowledgments

The editors salute the three national and six regional winners of the 1990 Tabasco® Community Cookbook Awards competition sponsored by McIlhenny Company, Avery Island, Louisiana. **First Place Winner:** *From A Lighthouse Window,* Chesapeake Bay Maritime Museum, St. Michaels, Maryland; **Second Place Winner:** *Gracious Goodness: The Taste of Memphis,* The Memphis Symphony League, Memphis, Tennessee; **Third Place Winner:** *Spice and Spirit: The Complete Kosher Jewish Cookbook,* Lubavitch Women's Organization, Brooklyn, New York; **Northeast:** *Country Kitchen Cookbook,* South County Museum of Narragansett, Rhode Island; **Mideast:** *Historic Lexington Cooks,* Historic Lexington Foundation of Lexington, Virginia; **Southeast:** *Celebrations on the Bayou,* Junior League of Monroe, Louisiana; **Midwest:** *Honest to Goodness,* Junior League of Springfield, Illinois; **Northwest:** *The Two Billion Dollar Cookbook,* Volunteers engaged in the Alaskan oil-spill cleanup, Anchorage, Alaska; and **Southwest:** *Wild About Texas,* Cypress-Woodlands Junior Forum, Houston, Texas.

Special thanks to Dot Gibson and Ellen Rolfes for their continuing efforts to promote the sale of community cookbooks throughout America. While each of the cookbooks listed below is represented by recipes appearing in *America's Best Recipes 1991,* the editors also included descriptions of several of these fund-raising volumes to give a sampling of the diverse nature of the books and organizations represented. Unless otherwise noted, the copyright is held by the sponsoring organization whose mailing address is included below.

100th Anniversary Cookbook, Auxiliary of Harrisburg Hospital, Capital Health System, 17 S. Market Square, P.O. Box 8700, Harrisburg, PA 17105

200th Anniversary Year Cookbook, Christ Evangelical Lutheran Church, 9212 Taylorsville Rd., Jeffersontown, KY 40299

641.5 "Show Me" Recipes, Missouri Association of School Librarians, 24 Glendale, Glen Carbon, IL 62034

Aggies, Moms, and Apple Pie, Federation of Texas A&M University Mothers' Clubs, Drawer C, College Station, TX 77843

Alaska's Cooking, Volume II, Anchorage Woman's Club, P.O. Box 10273, Anchorage, AK 99510

Albertina's II, Albertina Kerr Centers for Children, 424 N.E. 22nd Ave., Portland, OR 97232

Ancestral Stirrings, New England Historic Genealogical Society, 101 Newbury St., Boston, MA 02116

An Apple a Day Cookbook, Children's Hospital at Santa Rosa, 519 W. Houston St., San Antonio, TX 78207

Aspic and Old Lace, Northern Indiana Historical Society, 112 S. Lafayette Blvd., South Bend, IN 46601

Bach to the Kitchen, Cappella Cantorum, Box 714, Essex, CT 06409

The Best Specialties of the House . . . and More, North Suburban Guild of Children's Memorial Medical Center, 243 Aspen Ln., Highland Park, IL 60035

Bethany Christian Community, A Recipe Collection, Bethany Christian Community, 2824 E. 18th St., Anchorage, AK 99508

Black-Eyed Susan Country, Saint Agnes Hospital Auxiliary, 900 Caton Ave., Baltimore, MD 21229

Bound to Please, Junior League of Boise, P.O. Box 6126, Boise, ID 83706

Calling All Cooks Two, Telephone Pioneers of America, 3196 Hwy. 280 S., Rm. 301-NA, Birmingham, AL 35243

Cal Poly Pomona 50th Anniversary, Home Economics Alumni Association, 3801 W. Temple Ave., Pomona, CA 91768

Calvary Collections, Calvary Lutheran Church, 2200 Hwy. 2 East, Kalispell, MT 59901

Capital Classics, Junior League of Washington, 3039 M St. N.W., Washington, DC 20007

Capital Connoisseur, Lawrence Center Independence House, 2660 Albany St., Schenectady, NY 12304

Cardinal Cuisine, Mount Vernon Hospital Auxiliary, 2501 Parker's Ln., Alexandria, VA 22306

Celebrations on the Bayou, Junior League of Monroe, 2811 Cameron, Monroe, LA 71201

Centennial Cookbook, Orange County Pioneer Council, 400 Vista Parada, Newport Beach, CA 92660

Centennial Cookbook: 100 Years of Freemasonry in North Dakota, Masonic Grand Lodge, 201 14th Ave. N., Fargo, ND 58102

Central Texas Style, Junior Service League of Killeen, P.O. Box 1106, Killeen, TX 76540

The Children of Tikvah's Special Cookbook, Volume 3, Tikvah Institute for Childhood Learning Disabilities, 1255 N. Sandburg Terr., #1011, Chicago, IL 60610

A Collection of Recipes, Worcester Country School Development Office, 508 S. Main St., Berlin, MD 21811

Concertos for Cooks, North Group Symphony Women's Committee, Indiana State Symphony Society, Inc., 45 Monument Cir., Indianapolis, IN 46204

Con Mucho Gusto, Desert Club of Mesa, 331 E. Hackamore, Mesa, AZ 85201

Connecticut Cooks III, American Cancer Society, Connecticut Division, Inc., 14 Village Ln., P.O. Box 410, Wallingford, CT 06492

The Cookbook, East Lake United Methodist Church, 7753 1st Ave. S., Birmingham, AL 35206

Cooking Elementary Style, Ridgedale Elementary School PTA, 2900 Ridgedale Rd., Knoxville, TN 37921

Cooking with the Skins, National Multiple Sclerosis Society/National Capital Chapter, 2021 K St. N.W. #100, Washington, DC 20006

Cookin' with the Crusaders, Most Holy Redeemer Inter-Parochial School, 302 E. Linebaugh Ave., Tampa, FL 33612

Cookin' with the Lion, Penn State Alumni Association, 105 Old Main, University Park, PA 16802

Copper Country Recipes, Copper Harbor Improvement Association, U.S. 41, Copper Harbor, MI 49918

Crème de la Congregation, Our Saviors Lutheran Church, 1035 Carol Ln., Lafayette, CA 94549

Critics' Choice, Corinth Theatre Arts Guild, P.O. Box 435, Corinth, MS 38834

Crossroads Cuisine, Winona Manor Christmas Fund, P.O. Box 158, Kilmichael, MS 39747

Cuisine à la Mode, Les Dames Richelieu du Rhode Island, 1 Social St., Box F, Woonsocket, RI 02895

Deal Delights II, Sephardic Women's Organization, P.O. Box 133, Deal, NJ 07723

The Delaware Heritage Cookbook, Delaware Heritage Commission, 820 N. French St., Wilmington, DE 19801

Delectable Edibles from the Livable Forest, Kingwood Women's Club, P.O. Box 5411, Kingwood, TX 77325

Dining with the Daughters, Daughters of Hawaii, 2913 Pali Hwy., Honolulu, HI 96817

Dobar Tek, Yugoslav Women's Club, 4214 S. Holly St., Seattle, WA 98118

Down East Jewish Cooking, Rockland Chapter of Hadassah, 13 Katahdin Ave., Rockland, ME 04841

East Cooper Cuisine, Christ Our King Ladies Club, 1122 Russell Dr., Mt. Pleasant, SC 29464

eating, First Lutheran Church, 6400 State Line Rd., Mission Hills, KS 66208

The Educated Palate, Calhoun School Parents Association, 433 West End Ave., New York, NY 10024

Ex Libris, A Treasury of Recipes, Friends of the Wellesley Free Libraries, 530 Washington St., Wellesley, MA 02181

The Farmer's Daughters, National Multiple Sclerosis Society, #1 Jefferson St., P.O. Box 365, St. Charles, AR 72140

Favorite Recipes from Fishers Island, Island Bowling Center, Whistler Ave., Fishers Island, NY 06390

Favorite Recipes from Our Best Cooks, Volume II, Frederick Chopin Choir, St. Valentine's Polish National Catholic Church, 127 King St., Northampton, MA 01060

Favorite Recipes from St. Demetrios Church, St. Demetrios Greek Orthodox Church, P.O. Box 28218, Baltimore, MD 21234

Favorite Recipes from St. Paul's, St. Paul's Episcopal Church, Main St., Millis¡ MA 02054

Favorite Recipes of Edmonds, Edmonds United Methodist Women, 828 Caspers St., Edmonds, WA 98020

Feed My People, Carter-Westminster United Presbyterian Church, 4950 Pratt, Skokie, IL 60077

Fiesta, Pensacola Junior Woman's Club, P.O. Box 9215, Pensacola, FL 32513

The Florida Cooking Adventure, Florida Federation of Women's Clubs, 215 E. Lime St., Lakeland, FL 33801

For Crying Out Loud . . . Let's Eat!, Service League of Hammond, P.O. Box 4442, Hammond, IN 46324

Friends Come in All Flavors, Buckingham Friends School, P.O. Box 158, Lahaska, PA 18931

From a Lighthouse Window, Chesapeake Bay Maritime Museum, P.O. Box 636, St. Michaels, MD 21663

From Our House to Your House, Thomson Consumer Electronics Employees, Scranton Plant, 200 Keystone Industrial Park, Scranton, PA 18512

From Scratch Cookbook, Assistance League® of Glendale, 1305 California, Glendale, CA 91206

The Galloping Chef, Combined Training Equestrian Team Alliance, 750 Whiskey Hill Rd., Woodside, CA 94062

Georgia on My Menu, Junior League of Cobb-Marietta, Inc., P.O. Box 727, Marietta, GA 30060

Gingerbread . . . and all the trimmings, Junior Service League of Waxahachie, P.O. Box 294, Waxahachie, TX 75165

The Golden Apple Collection, White Plains Auxiliary of the White Plains Hospital Center, P.O. Box 8, Gedney Station, White Plains, NY 10605

Good Cookin' from Giffin, Giffin Elementary School PTA, Beech St., Knoxville, TN 37920

Gourmet by the Bay, Dolphin Circle, International Order of the King's Daughters and Sons, P.O. Box 8335, Virginia Beach, VA 23450

Gourmet LA, Junior League of Los Angeles, Farmers' Market, 3rd and Fairfax, Los Angeles, CA 90036

Gracious Goodness: The Taste of Memphis, Memphis Symphony League, 3100 Walnut Grove Rd., Ste. 402, Memphis, TN 38111

A Grand Heritage, Heritage Academy, P.O. Box 9251, Columbus, MS 39701

Greetings from Atlantic City, Ruth Newman Shapiro Cancer and Heart Fund, 2024 Pacific Ave., Atlantic City, NJ 08401

Holladay 7th Ward Cookbook, Holladay 7th Ward Relief Society, 4407 Fortuna Way, Salt Lake City, UT 84124

Hearts & Flour, Women's Club of Pittsford, P.O. Box 208, Pittsford, NY 14534

Hearts and Flours, Junior League of Waco, 6801 Sanger, Ste. 160B, Waco, TX 76710

Heavenly Delights, United Methodist Women, First United Methodist Church, 2051 E. Monument St., Noblesville, IN 46060

Hemi-demi-semi Flavors, Chamber Music Society of the North Shore, 670 Longwood, Glencoe, IL 60022

Heritage of Red Cloud, Heritage of Red Cloud, 636 N. Locust, Red Cloud, NE 68970

Historic Lexington Cooks: Rockbridge Regional Recipes, Historic Lexington Foundation, 8 E. Washington St., Lexington, VA 24450

Home on the Range, West Marin Health Project and Dance Palace Community Center, P.O. Box 867, Point Reyes, CA 94956

Honest to Goodness, Junior League of Springfield, 426 S. 8th St., P.O. Box 1736, Springfield, IL 62701

Hudson Cooks, Hudson Community Playground, P.O. Box 2201, Hudson, OH 44236

Indiana University Northwest Staff Cookbook, Indiana University Northwest Staff Council, 3400 Broadway, Gary, IN 46408

In the Pink of Things, Muskogee Regional Medical Center Auxiliary, 30 Rockefeller Dr., Muskogee, OK 74401

Island Born and Bred, Harkers Island United Methodist Women, P.O. Box 25, Harkers Island, NC 28531

It's Our Serve!, Junior League of Long Island, 1395 Old Northern Blvd., Roslyn, NY 11576

Joy of Greek Cooking (With an American Accent), Philoptochos Society of the Annunciation Greek Orthodox Cathedral, 707 Lafayette E., Detroit, MI 48226

La Cucina Sammarinese, San Marino Ladies Auxiliary, 1685 E. Big Beaver Rd., Troy, MI 48083

Land of Cotton, John T. Morgan Academy, P.O. Drawer P, Selma, AL 36702

Lasting Impressions, St. Joseph's Hospital of Atlanta Auxiliary, 5665 Peachtree Dunwoody Rd. N.E., Atlanta, GA 30342

The Less Fat Cookbook, Cancer Education and Prevention Center, 380 34th St., Oakland, CA 94610

License to Cook New Mexico Style, New Mexico Federation of Business and Professional Women, Penfield Press, 215 Brown St., Iowa City, IA 52245

Marblehead Cooks, Tower School Associates, 61 W. Shore Dr., Marblehead, MA 01945

The Mark Twain Library Cookbook, Volume III, Mark Twain Library Association, P.O. Box 9, Redding, CT 06875

A Matter of Taste, Junior League of Morristown, Inc., 7 King Pl., Morristown, NJ 07960

Memphis in May International Festival Cookbook, Memphis in May International Festival, Inc., 245 Wagner Pl., #220, Memphis, TN 38103

Merrymeeting Merry Eating, Regional Memorial Hospital Auxiliary, 58 Baribeau Dr., Brunswick, ME 04011

More Memoirs of a Galley Slave, Kodiak Fishermen's Wives Association, P.O. Box 467, Kodiak, AK 99615

More Than a Tea Party, Junior League of Boston, 117 Newbury St., Boston, MA 02116

Mothers of Twins Cookbook, Twice as Nice, Mothers of Twins Club, 4508 Hi-Line Rd., Gillette, WY 82716

Mountain Memories, American Cancer Society, West Virginia Division, Inc., 2428 Kanawha Blvd. E., Charleston, WV 25311

Musical Tastes, Chancel and Bell Choirs, First United Methodist Church, 101 E. Jefferson St., Charlottesville, VA 22901

Na Zdrowie II, Women's Auxiliary-Polish American Club of Agawam, 139 Southwick St., P.O. Box 173, Feeding Hills, MA 01030

Norand 20th Anniversary Cookbook, Norand Corporation, 550 Second St., Cedar Rapids, IA 52401 ,

"One Lump or Two?", All Children's Hospital Guild, 801 5th St. S., P.O. Box 3142, St. Petersburg, FL 33701

One Magnificent Cookbook, Junior League of Chicago, Inc., 1447 N. Astor St., Chicago, IL 60610

Only in California, Children's Home Society of California, 2727 W. Sixth St., Los Angeles, CA 90057

Our Favorite Recipes, St. Edmond's Church, 2130 S. 21st St., Philadelphia, PA 19145

Our Town Cookbook, Peterborough Historical Society, 19 Grove St., Peterborough, NH 03458

Out of This World, Wood Acres Elementary School, 5800 Cromwell Dr., Bethesda, MD 20816

Palate Pleasers II, Redeemer Women's Guild, 345 S. Kenilworth Ave., Elmhurst, IL 60126

Pegasus Presents, Pegasus of Germantown, Inc., P.O. Box 382113, Germantown, TN 38138

Pioneers of Alaska Cookbook, Pioneers of Alaska Auxiliary #4, Box 101547, Anchorage, AK 99510

Port's Galley, Port Council of Port of Portland, P.O. Box 3529, Portland, OR 97208

Quiltie Ladies Scrapbook, Variable Star Quilters, 16 Harbor Pl., Souderton, PA 18964

A Rainbow of Recipes, Education Department/Regional Treatment Center, Box 157, Fergus Falls, MN 56537

Rebel Recipes, Department of Home Economics, Meek Hall, University of Mississippi, University, MS 38677

Recipes & Recollections from Terrace Hill, Terrace Hill Society, 2300 Grand Ave., Des Moines, IA 50312

Recipes and Remembrances, Upsala Area Historical Society, Box 35, Upsala, MN 56384

Recipes to Cherish, Women's Missionary and Service Commission, 1552 S. High St., Harrisonburg, VA 22801

Rosemalers' Recipes, Vesterheim-Norwegian American Museum, 520 W. Water St., Decorah, IA 52101

RSVP: Fortress Monroe, Officers' & Civilians' Wives' Club, Box 114, Fort Monroe, VA 23651

RSVP: Recipes Shared Very Proudly, First Church of Christ, 689 Hopmeadow St., Simsbury, CT 06092

St. George Women's Auxiliary Cookbook, St. George Women's Auxiliary, 94 9th St., Oakland, CA 94607

A Samford Celebration Cookbook, Samford University Auxiliary, S.U. Box 2302, Birmingham, AL 35229

Scoops from the Bay, Cape Cod Academy, Osterville, MA 02655

The Scott & White Collection, Scott and White Memorial Hospital Auxiliary, 2401 S. 31st St., Temple, TX 76508

Seasoned with Sun, Junior League of El Paso, Inc., 520 Thunderbird, El Paso, TX 79912

Secret Recipes II, 4450th Tactical Group, Nellis Air Force Base, Las Vegas, NV 89115

Shamrock Specialties, Trinity High School Foundation, 4011 Shelbyville Rd., Louisville, KY 40207

Sharing Recipes, St. John's Women of the Evangelical Lutheran Church in America, 2477 W. Washington, Springfield, IL 62702

Something Entertaining to Cook, Southeastern Theatre Conference, Inc., 506 Stirling St., UNC-G, Greensboro, NC 27412

South Dakota Centennial Cookbook, South Dakota Historical Society, 900 Governors Dr., Pierre, SD 57501

Southern California Style, Assistance League® of Anaheim, P.O. Box 4073, Anaheim, CA 92803

Spokane Cooks!© Northwest, Spokane Community Centers Foundation, E. 2500 Sprague, Spokane, WA 99202

Stanford University Medical Center Auxiliary Cookbook, Stanford University Medical Center Auxiliary, 300 Pasteur Dr., Palo Alto, CA 94305

State Hospital Cooks, Patient/Staff Advocacy Committee, Vermont State Hospital, 103 S. Main St., Waterbury, VT 05676

Stirring Performances, Junior League of Winston-Salem, Inc., 909 S. Main St., Winston-Salem, NC 27101

Symphony of Tastes, Anchorage Youth Symphony, P.O. Box 240541, Anchorage, AK 99524

A Taste of Generations, Granger Homestead Society, Inc., Women's Council, 295 N. Main St., Canandaigua, NY 14424

A Taste of Hope, Camarillo Chapter of City of Hope, 42010 Village 42, Camarillo, CA 93012

A Taste of Memories from the Old "Bush," Italian-American Women's Mutual Aid Society, 1421 Wyldewood Dr., Madison, WI 53704

A Taste of San Francisco, San Francisco Symphony, Davies Symphony Hall, San Francisco, CA 94102

Terry Home Presents Food & Fun from Celebrities & Us, Terry Home, Inc., 15315 Elm St. E., Sumner, WA 98390

Texas Hill Country Wine & Food Festival: A Cookbook, Texas Hill Country Wine and Food Festival, 8310 Capital of Texas Hwy. N., Ste. 400, Austin, TX 78731

This Side of the River Cookbook, Hatfield Book Club, 28 Pleasant View Dr., Hatfield, MA 01038

Three Rivers Cookbook, Volume III, Child Health Association of Sewickley, 1108 Ohio River Blvd., Sewickley, PA 15143

Thymes Remembered, Junior League of Tallahassee, Inc., 259-B John Knox Rd., Tallahassee, FL 32303

Twickenham Tables, Twickenham Historic Preservation District Association, Inc., 300 Gales Ave., Huntsville, AL 35801

Two and Company, St. Thomas' Church, Garrison Forest, 232 St. Thomas Ln., Owings Mills, MD 21117

Very Innovative Parties, Loma Linda University School of Dentistry Auxiliary, P.O. Box 382, Loma Linda, CA 92354

The Village Gourmet, Bedford Historical Society, 30 S. Park St., P.O. Box 46282, Bedford, OH 44146

Visions of Sugarplums, Parents' Association, Charlotte Country Day School, 1440 Carmel Rd., Charlotte, NC 28226

Weathervane Theatre Cookbook, Weathervane Theatre, P.O. Box 127, Whitefield, NH 03598

What's Cooking?, Sisterhood of Temple Shalom, 215 S. Hillside Ave., Succasunna, NJ 07876

What's Cooking in Chagrin Falls, Chagrin Falls Parent Teacher Organization, 45 Heather Ct., Chagrin Falls, OH 44022

What's Cooking in Philadelphia, Rotary Club of Philadelphia, 1422 Chestnut St., Ste. 402, Philadelphia, PA 19102

Wild about Texas, Cypress-Woodlands Junior Forum, P.O. Box 90020, Dept. 242, Houston, TX 77290

Wilderness Ranger Cookbook, San Juan National Forest Association, 70l Camino del Rio, Durango, CO 81301

With Great Gusto, Junior League of Youngstown, 323 Wick Ave., Youngstown, OH 44503

Woman to Woman Cookbook, Zonta Club of the Black Hills, P.O. Box 8163, Rapid City, SD 57709

World Heritage of Cooking, Friends of the World Heritage Museum, 484 Lincoln Hall, 702 S. Wright St., Urbana, IL 61801

You Can't be Too Rich or Too Thin, Southampton Hospital, 240 Meeting House Ln., Southampton, NY 11968

Index